C-1056   CAREER EXAMINATION SERIES

This is your
PASSBOOK for...

Elevator Mechanic

Test Preparation Study Guide
Questions & Answers

NATIONAL LEARNING CORPORATION®

COPYRIGHT NOTICE

This book is SOLELY intended for, is sold ONLY to, and its use is RESTRICTED to individual, bona fide applicants or candidates who qualify by virtue of having seriously filed applications for appropriate license, certificate, professional and/or promotional advancement, higher school matriculation, scholarship, or other legitimate requirements of education and/or governmental authorities.

This book is NOT intended for use, class instruction, tutoring, training, duplication, copying, reprinting, excerption, or adaptation, etc., by:

1) Other publishers
2) Proprietors and/or Instructors of "Coaching" and/or Preparatory Courses
3) Personnel and/or Training Divisions of commercial, industrial, and governmental organizations
4) Schools, colleges, or universities and/or their departments and staffs, including teachers and other personnel
5) Testing Agencies or Bureaus
6) Study groups which seek by the purchase of a single volume to copy and/or duplicate and/or adapt this material for use by the group as a whole without having purchased individual volumes for each of the members of the group
7) Et al.

Such persons would be in violation of appropriate Federal and State statutes.

PROVISION OF LICENSING AGREEMENTS – Recognized educational, commercial, industrial, and governmental institutions and organizations, and others legitimately engaged in educational pursuits, including training, testing, and measurement activities, may address request for a licensing agreement to the copyright owners, who will determine whether, and under what conditions, including fees and charges, the materials in this book may be used them. In other words, a licensing facility exists for the legitimate use of the material in this book on other than an individual basis. However, it is asseverated and affirmed here that the material in this book CANNOT be used without the receipt of the express permission of such a licensing agreement from the Publishers. Inquiries re licensing should be addressed to the company, attention rights and permissions department.

All rights reserved, including the right of reproduction in whole or in part, in any form or by any means, electronic or mechanical, including photocopying, recording, or by any information storage and retrieval system, without permission in writing from the Publisher.

Copyright © 2024 by
National Learning Corporation

212 Michael Drive, Syosset, NY 11791
(516) 921-8888 • www.passbooks.com
E-mail: info@passbooks.com

PUBLISHED IN THE UNITED STATES OF AMERICA

PASSBOOK® SERIES

THE *PASSBOOK® SERIES* has been created to prepare applicants and candidates for the ultimate academic battlefield – the examination room.

At some time in our lives, each and every one of us may be required to take an examination – for validation, matriculation, admission, qualification, registration, certification, or licensure.

Based on the assumption that every applicant or candidate has met the basic formal educational standards, has taken the required number of courses, and read the necessary texts, the *PASSBOOK® SERIES* furnishes the one special preparation which may assure passing with confidence, instead of failing with insecurity. Examination questions – together with answers – are furnished as the basic vehicle for study so that the mysteries of the examination and its compounding difficulties may be eliminated or diminished by a sure method.

This book is meant to help you pass your examination provided that you qualify and are serious in your objective.

The entire field is reviewed through the huge store of content information which is succinctly presented through a provocative and challenging approach – the question-and-answer method.

A climate of success is established by furnishing the correct answers at the end of each test.

You soon learn to recognize types of questions, forms of questions, and patterns of questioning. You may even begin to anticipate expected outcomes.

You perceive that many questions are repeated or adapted so that you can gain acute insights, which may enable you to score many sure points.

You learn how to confront new questions, or types of questions, and to attack them confidently and work out the correct answers.

You note objectives and emphases, and recognize pitfalls and dangers, so that you may make positive educational adjustments.

Moreover, you are kept fully informed in relation to new concepts, methods, practices, and directions in the field.

You discover that you are actually taking the examination all the time: you are preparing for the examination by "taking" an examination, not by reading extraneous and/or supererogatory textbooks.

In short, this PASSBOOK®, used directedly, should be an important factor in helping you to pass your test.

ELEVATOR MECHANIC

DUTIES AND RESPONSIBILITES
Under supervision inspects, maintains, adjusts and repairs passenger and freight elevator systems; performs related work.

EXAMPLES OF TYPICAL TASKS
Lubricates and cleans all components of hydraulic and electric elevator systems. Makes adjustments as required to contactors and controllers in the electrical and hydraulic elements of elevator systems. Inspects and checks doors, cable rails, bumpers, safeties, overloads, relays, sheaves and governors to assure continued safe operations. Re-ropes and re-wires elevator systems as required. Checks out troubles in all types of elevator and escalator systems. Makes necessary adjustments and/or repairs to all elevator mechanical and electrical components and their control systems. Inspects, maintains, adjusts and repairs escalators, platform lifts, conveyors and dumbwaiters.

TESTS
The test may include questions on operating principles of hydraulic and electric elevator systems and control systems; electrical theory, electrical machinery, applied electronics, wiring systems, electrical instruments and diagrams; troubleshooting, adjustments, inspection, maintenance and repair of hydraulic and electric elevator systems including mechanical components and electrical components, measurements; safety; proper use of tools; basic mathematics; reading comprehension; shop techniques commonly used in affecting overhaul and repair of elevator components; and other related areas, including: wire rope, clearance and space limits, electrical, testing, engineering and inspection, safety devices, controls, operating limitations, drive mechanisms, fire service, maintenance and repairs, escalators and dumbwaiters, emergency power, accessibility equipment, elevator renovation, conveyors, and welding.

HOW TO TAKE A TEST

I. YOU MUST PASS AN EXAMINATION

A. *WHAT EVERY CANDIDATE SHOULD KNOW*

Examination applicants often ask us for help in preparing for the written test. What can I study in advance? What kinds of questions will be asked? How will the test be given? How will the papers be graded?

As an applicant for a civil service examination, you may be wondering about some of these things. Our purpose here is to suggest effective methods of advance study and to describe civil service examinations.

Your chances for success on this examination can be increased if you know how to prepare. Those "pre-examination jitters" can be reduced if you know what to expect. You can even experience an adventure in good citizenship if you know why civil service exams are given.

B. *WHY ARE CIVIL SERVICE EXAMINATIONS GIVEN?*

Civil service examinations are important to you in two ways. As a citizen, you want public jobs filled by employees who know how to do their work. As a job seeker, you want a fair chance to compete for that job on an equal footing with other candidates. The best-known means of accomplishing this two-fold goal is the competitive examination.

Exams are widely publicized throughout the nation. They may be administered for jobs in federal, state, city, municipal, town or village governments or agencies.

Any citizen may apply, with some limitations, such as the age or residence of applicants. Your experience and education may be reviewed to see whether you meet the requirements for the particular examination. When these requirements exist, they are reasonable and applied consistently to all applicants. Thus, a competitive examination may cause you some uneasiness now, but it is your privilege and safeguard.

C. *HOW ARE CIVIL SERVICE EXAMS DEVELOPED?*

Examinations are carefully written by trained technicians who are specialists in the field known as "psychological measurement," in consultation with recognized authorities in the field of work that the test will cover. These experts recommend the subject matter areas or skills to be tested; only those knowledges or skills important to your success on the job are included. The most reliable books and source materials available are used as references. Together, the experts and technicians judge the difficulty level of the questions.

Test technicians know how to phrase questions so that the problem is clearly stated. Their ethics do not permit "trick" or "catch" questions. Questions may have been tried out on sample groups, or subjected to statistical analysis, to determine their usefulness.

Written tests are often used in combination with performance tests, ratings of training and experience, and oral interviews. All of these measures combine to form the best-known means of finding the right person for the right job.

II. HOW TO PASS THE WRITTEN TEST

A. NATURE OF THE EXAMINATION

To prepare intelligently for civil service examinations, you should know how they differ from school examinations you have taken. In school you were assigned certain definite pages to read or subjects to cover. The examination questions were quite detailed and usually emphasized memory. Civil service exams, on the other hand, try to discover your present ability to perform the duties of a position, plus your potentiality to learn these duties. In other words, a civil service exam attempts to predict how successful you will be. Questions cover such a broad area that they cannot be as minute and detailed as school exam questions.

In the public service similar kinds of work, or positions, are grouped together in one "class." This process is known as *position-classification*. All the positions in a class are paid according to the salary range for that class. One class title covers all of these positions, and they are all tested by the same examination.

B. FOUR BASIC STEPS

1) Study the announcement

How, then, can you know what subjects to study? Our best answer is: "Learn as much as possible about the class of positions for which you've applied." The exam will test the knowledge, skills and abilities needed to do the work.

Your most valuable source of information about the position you want is the official exam announcement. This announcement lists the training and experience qualifications. Check these standards and apply only if you come reasonably close to meeting them.

The brief description of the position in the examination announcement offers some clues to the subjects which will be tested. Think about the job itself. Review the duties in your mind. Can you perform them, or are there some in which you are rusty? Fill in the blank spots in your preparation.

Many jurisdictions preview the written test in the exam announcement by including a section called "Knowledge and Abilities Required," "Scope of the Examination," or some similar heading. Here you will find out specifically what fields will be tested.

2) Review your own background

Once you learn in general what the position is all about, and what you need to know to do the work, ask yourself which subjects you already know fairly well and which need improvement. You may wonder whether to concentrate on improving your strong areas or on building some background in your fields of weakness. When the announcement has specified "some knowledge" or "considerable knowledge," or has used adjectives like "beginning principles of…" or "advanced … methods," you can get a clue as to the number and difficulty of questions to be asked in any given field. More questions, and hence broader coverage, would be included for those subjects which are more important in the work. Now weigh your strengths and weaknesses against the job requirements and prepare accordingly.

3) Determine the level of the position

Another way to tell how intensively you should prepare is to understand the level of the job for which you are applying. Is it the entering level? In other words, is this the position in which beginners in a field of work are hired? Or is it an intermediate or advanced level? Sometimes this is indicated by such words as "Junior" or "Senior" in the class title. Other jurisdictions use Roman numerals to designate the level – Clerk I, Clerk II, for example. The word "Supervisor" sometimes appears in the title. If the level is not indicated by the title, check the description of duties. Will you be working under very close supervision, or will you have responsibility for independent decisions in this work?

4) Choose appropriate study materials

Now that you know the subjects to be examined and the relative amount of each subject to be covered, you can choose suitable study materials. For beginning level jobs, or even advanced ones, if you have a pronounced weakness in some aspect of your training, read a modern, standard textbook in that field. Be sure it is up to date and has general coverage. Such books are normally available at your library, and the librarian will be glad to help you locate one. For entry-level positions, questions of appropriate difficulty are chosen – neither highly advanced questions, nor those too simple. Such questions require careful thought but not advanced training.

If the position for which you are applying is technical or advanced, you will read more advanced, specialized material. If you are already familiar with the basic principles of your field, elementary textbooks would waste your time. Concentrate on advanced textbooks and technical periodicals. Think through the concepts and review difficult problems in your field.

These are all general sources. You can get more ideas on your own initiative, following these leads. For example, training manuals and publications of the government agency which employs workers in your field can be useful, particularly for technical and professional positions. A letter or visit to the government department involved may result in more specific study suggestions, and certainly will provide you with a more definite idea of the exact nature of the position you are seeking.

III. KINDS OF TESTS

Tests are used for purposes other than measuring knowledge and ability to perform specified duties. For some positions, it is equally important to test ability to make adjustments to new situations or to profit from training. In others, basic mental abilities not dependent on information are essential. Questions which test these things may not appear as pertinent to the duties of the position as those which test for knowledge and information. Yet they are often highly important parts of a fair examination. For very general questions, it is almost impossible to help you direct your study efforts. What we can do is to point out some of the more common of these general abilities needed in public service positions and describe some typical questions.

1) General information

Broad, general information has been found useful for predicting job success in some kinds of work. This is tested in a variety of ways, from vocabulary lists to questions about current events. Basic background in some field of work, such as sociology or economics, may be sampled in a group of questions. Often these are principles which have become familiar to most persons through exposure rather than through formal training. It is difficult to advise you how to study for these questions; being alert to the world around you is our best suggestion.

2) Verbal ability

An example of an ability needed in many positions is verbal or language ability. Verbal ability is, in brief, the ability to use and understand words. Vocabulary and grammar tests are typical measures of this ability. Reading comprehension or paragraph interpretation questions are common in many kinds of civil service tests. You are given a paragraph of written material and asked to find its central meaning.

3) Numerical ability

Number skills can be tested by the familiar arithmetic problem, by checking paired lists of numbers to see which are alike and which are different, or by interpreting charts and graphs. In the latter test, a graph may be printed in the test booklet which you are asked to use as the basis for answering questions.

4) Observation

A popular test for law-enforcement positions is the observation test. A picture is shown to you for several minutes, then taken away. Questions about the picture test your ability to observe both details and larger elements.

5) Following directions

In many positions in the public service, the employee must be able to carry out written instructions dependably and accurately. You may be given a chart with several columns, each column listing a variety of information. The questions require you to carry out directions involving the information given in the chart.

6) Skills and aptitudes

Performance tests effectively measure some manual skills and aptitudes. When the skill is one in which you are trained, such as typing or shorthand, you can practice. These tests are often very much like those given in business school or high school courses. For many of the other skills and aptitudes, however, no short-time preparation can be made. Skills and abilities natural to you or that you have developed throughout your lifetime are being tested.

Many of the general questions just described provide all the data needed to answer the questions and ask you to use your reasoning ability to find the answers. Your best preparation for these tests, as well as for tests of facts and ideas, is to be at your physical and mental best. You, no doubt, have your own methods of getting into an exam-taking mood and keeping "in shape." The next section lists some ideas on this subject.

IV. KINDS OF QUESTIONS

Only rarely is the "essay" question, which you answer in narrative form, used in civil service tests. Civil service tests are usually of the short-answer type. Full instructions for answering these questions will be given to you at the examination. But in case this is your first experience with short-answer questions and separate answer sheets, here is what you need to know:

1) Multiple-choice Questions

Most popular of the short-answer questions is the "multiple choice" or "best answer" question. It can be used, for example, to test for factual knowledge, ability to solve problems or judgment in meeting situations found at work.

A multiple-choice question is normally one of three types—
- It can begin with an incomplete statement followed by several possible endings. You are to find the one ending which *best* completes the statement, although some of the others may not be entirely wrong.
- It can also be a complete statement in the form of a question which is answered by choosing one of the statements listed.

- It can be in the form of a problem – again you select the best answer.

Here is an example of a multiple-choice question with a discussion which should give you some clues as to the method for choosing the right answer:

When an employee has a complaint about his assignment, the action which will *best* help him overcome his difficulty is to
   A. discuss his difficulty with his coworkers
   B. take the problem to the head of the organization
   C. take the problem to the person who gave him the assignment
   D. say nothing to anyone about his complaint

In answering this question, you should study each of the choices to find which is best. Consider choice "A" – Certainly an employee may discuss his complaint with fellow employees, but no change or improvement can result, and the complaint remains unresolved. Choice "B" is a poor choice since the head of the organization probably does not know what assignment you have been given, and taking your problem to him is known as "going over the head" of the supervisor. The supervisor, or person who made the assignment, is the person who can clarify it or correct any injustice. Choice "C" is, therefore, correct. To say nothing, as in choice "D," is unwise. Supervisors have and interest in knowing the problems employees are facing, and the employee is seeking a solution to his problem.

2) True/False Questions

The "true/false" or "right/wrong" form of question is sometimes used. Here a complete statement is given. Your job is to decide whether the statement is right or wrong.

SAMPLE: A roaming cell-phone call to a nearby city costs less than a non-roaming call to a distant city.

This statement is wrong, or false, since roaming calls are more expensive.
This is not a complete list of all possible question forms, although most of the others are variations of these common types. You will always get complete directions for answering questions. Be sure you understand *how* to mark your answers – ask questions until you do.

V. RECORDING YOUR ANSWERS

Computer terminals are used more and more today for many different kinds of exams.
For an examination with very few applicants, you may be told to record your answers in the test booklet itself. Separate answer sheets are much more common. If this separate answer sheet is to be scored by machine – and this is often the case – it is highly important that you mark your answers correctly in order to get credit.
An electronic scoring machine is often used in civil service offices because of the speed with which papers can be scored. Machine-scored answer sheets must be marked with a pencil, which will be given to you. This pencil has a high graphite content which responds to the electronic scoring machine. As a matter of fact, stray dots may register as answers, so do not let your pencil rest on the answer sheet while you are pondering the correct answer. Also, if your pencil lead breaks or is otherwise defective, ask for another.

Since the answer sheet will be dropped in a slot in the scoring machine, be careful not to bend the corners or get the paper crumpled.

The answer sheet normally has five vertical columns of numbers, with 30 numbers to a column. These numbers correspond to the question numbers in your test booklet. After each number, going across the page are four or five pairs of dotted lines. These short dotted lines have small letters or numbers above them. The first two pairs may also have a "T" or "F" above the letters. This indicates that the first two pairs only are to be used if the questions are of the true-false type. If the questions are multiple choice, disregard the "T" and "F" and pay attention only to the small letters or numbers.

Answer your questions in the manner of the sample that follows:

32. The largest city in the United States is
    A. Washington, D.C.
    B. New York City
    C. Chicago
    D. Detroit
    E. San Francisco

1) Choose the answer you think is best. (New York City is the largest, so "B" is correct.)
2) Find the row of dotted lines numbered the same as the question you are answering. (Find row number 32)
3) Find the pair of dotted lines corresponding to the answer. (Find the pair of lines under the mark "B.")
4) Make a solid black mark between the dotted lines.

VI. BEFORE THE TEST

Common sense will help you find procedures to follow to get ready for an examination. Too many of us, however, overlook these sensible measures. Indeed, nervousness and fatigue have been found to be the most serious reasons why applicants fail to do their best on civil service tests. Here is a list of reminders:

- Begin your preparation early – Don't wait until the last minute to go scurrying around for books and materials or to find out what the position is all about.
- Prepare continuously – An hour a night for a week is better than an all-night cram session. This has been definitely established. What is more, a night a week for a month will return better dividends than crowding your study into a shorter period of time.
- Locate the place of the exam – You have been sent a notice telling you when and where to report for the examination. If the location is in a different town or otherwise unfamiliar to you, it would be well to inquire the best route and learn something about the building.
- Relax the night before the test – Allow your mind to rest. Do not study at all that night. Plan some mild recreation or diversion; then go to bed early and get a good night's sleep.
- Get up early enough to make a leisurely trip to the place for the test – This way unforeseen events, traffic snarls, unfamiliar buildings, etc. will not upset you.
- Dress comfortably – A written test is not a fashion show. You will be known by number and not by name, so wear something comfortable.

- Leave excess paraphernalia at home – Shopping bags and odd bundles will get in your way. You need bring only the items mentioned in the official notice you received; usually everything you need is provided. Do not bring reference books to the exam. They will only confuse those last minutes and be taken away from you when in the test room.
- Arrive somewhat ahead of time – If because of transportation schedules you must get there very early, bring a newspaper or magazine to take your mind off yourself while waiting.
- Locate the examination room – When you have found the proper room, you will be directed to the seat or part of the room where you will sit. Sometimes you are given a sheet of instructions to read while you are waiting. Do not fill out any forms until you are told to do so; just read them and be prepared.
- Relax and prepare to listen to the instructions
- If you have any physical problem that may keep you from doing your best, be sure to tell the test administrator. If you are sick or in poor health, you really cannot do your best on the exam. You can come back and take the test some other time.

VII. AT THE TEST

The day of the test is here and you have the test booklet in your hand. The temptation to get going is very strong. Caution! There is more to success than knowing the right answers. You must know how to identify your papers and understand variations in the type of short-answer question used in this particular examination. Follow these suggestions for maximum results from your efforts:

1) Cooperate with the monitor

The test administrator has a duty to create a situation in which you can be as much at ease as possible. He will give instructions, tell you when to begin, check to see that you are marking your answer sheet correctly, and so on. He is not there to guard you, although he will see that your competitors do not take unfair advantage. He wants to help you do your best.

2) Listen to all instructions

Don't jump the gun! Wait until you understand all directions. In most civil service tests you get more time than you need to answer the questions. So don't be in a hurry. Read each word of instructions until you clearly understand the meaning. Study the examples, listen to all announcements and follow directions. Ask questions if you do not understand what to do.

3) Identify your papers

Civil service exams are usually identified by number only. You will be assigned a number; you must not put your name on your test papers. Be sure to copy your number correctly. Since more than one exam may be given, copy your exact examination title.

4) Plan your time

Unless you are told that a test is a "speed" or "rate of work" test, speed itself is usually not important. Time enough to answer all the questions will be provided, but this does not mean that you have all day. An overall time limit has been set. Divide the total time (in minutes) by the number of questions to determine the approximate time you have for each question.

5) Do not linger over difficult questions

If you come across a difficult question, mark it with a paper clip (useful to have along) and come back to it when you have been through the booklet. One caution if you do this – be sure to skip a number on your answer sheet as well. Check often to be sure that you have not lost your place and that you are marking in the row numbered the same as the question you are answering.

6) Read the questions

Be sure you know what the question asks! Many capable people are unsuccessful because they failed to *read* the questions correctly.

7) Answer all questions

Unless you have been instructed that a penalty will be deducted for incorrect answers, it is better to guess than to omit a question.

8) Speed tests

It is often better NOT to guess on speed tests. It has been found that on timed tests people are tempted to spend the last few seconds before time is called in marking answers at random – without even reading them – in the hope of picking up a few extra points. To discourage this practice, the instructions may warn you that your score will be "corrected" for guessing. That is, a penalty will be applied. The incorrect answers will be deducted from the correct ones, or some other penalty formula will be used.

9) Review your answers

If you finish before time is called, go back to the questions you guessed or omitted to give them further thought. Review other answers if you have time.

10) Return your test materials

If you are ready to leave before others have finished or time is called, take ALL your materials to the monitor and leave quietly. Never take any test material with you. The monitor can discover whose papers are not complete, and taking a test booklet may be grounds for disqualification.

VIII. EXAMINATION TECHNIQUES

1) Read the general instructions carefully. These are usually printed on the first page of the exam booklet. As a rule, these instructions refer to the timing of the examination; the fact that you should not start work until the signal and must stop work at a signal, etc. If there are any *special* instructions, such as a choice of questions to be answered, make sure that you note this instruction carefully.

2) When you are ready to start work on the examination, that is as soon as the signal has been given, read the instructions to each question booklet, underline any key words or phrases, such as *least, best, outline, describe* and the like. In this way you will tend to answer as requested rather than discover on reviewing your paper that you *listed without describing*, that you selected the *worst* choice rather than the *best* choice, etc.

3) If the examination is of the objective or multiple-choice type – that is, each question will also give a series of possible answers: A, B, C or D, and you are called upon to select the best answer and write the letter next to that answer on your answer paper – it is advisable to start answering each question in turn. There may be anywhere from 50 to 100 such questions in the three or four hours allotted and you can see how much time would be taken if you read through all the questions before beginning to answer any. Furthermore, if you come across a question or group of questions which you know would be difficult to answer, it would undoubtedly affect your handling of all the other questions.

4) If the examination is of the essay type and contains but a few questions, it is a moot point as to whether you should read all the questions before starting to answer any one. Of course, if you are given a choice – say five out of seven and the like – then it is essential to read all the questions so you can eliminate the two that are most difficult. If, however, you are asked to answer all the questions, there may be danger in trying to answer the easiest one first because you may find that you will spend too much time on it. The best technique is to answer the first question, then proceed to the second, etc.

5) Time your answers. Before the exam begins, write down the time it started, then add the time allowed for the examination and write down the time it must be completed, then divide the time available somewhat as follows:
   - If 3-1/2 hours are allowed, that would be 210 minutes. If you have 80 objective-type questions, that would be an average of 2-1/2 minutes per question. Allow yourself no more than 2 minutes per question, or a total of 160 minutes, which will permit about 50 minutes to review.
   - If for the time allotment of 210 minutes there are 7 essay questions to answer, that would average about 30 minutes a question. Give yourself only 25 minutes per question so that you have about 35 minutes to review.

6) The most important instruction is to *read each question* and make sure you know what is wanted. The second most important instruction is to *time yourself properly* so that you answer every question. The third most important instruction is to *answer every question*. Guess if you have to but include something for each question. Remember that you will receive no credit for a blank and will probably receive some credit if you write something in answer to an essay question. If you guess a letter – say "B" for a multiple-choice question – you may have guessed right. If you leave a blank as an answer to a multiple-choice question, the examiners may respect your feelings but it will not add a point to your score. Some exams may penalize you for wrong answers, so in such cases *only*, you may not want to guess unless you have some basis for your answer.

7) Suggestions
   a. Objective-type questions
      1. Examine the question booklet for proper sequence of pages and questions
      2. Read all instructions carefully
      3. Skip any question which seems too difficult; return to it after all other questions have been answered
      4. Apportion your time properly; do not spend too much time on any single question or group of questions

5. Note and underline key words – *all, most, fewest, least, best, worst, same, opposite,* etc.
6. Pay particular attention to negatives
7. Note unusual option, e.g., unduly long, short, complex, different or similar in content to the body of the question
8. Observe the use of "hedging" words – *probably, may, most likely,* etc.
9. Make sure that your answer is put next to the same number as the question
10. Do not second-guess unless you have good reason to believe the second answer is definitely more correct
11. Cross out original answer if you decide another answer is more accurate; do not erase until you are ready to hand your paper in
12. Answer all questions; guess unless instructed otherwise
13. Leave time for review

  b. Essay questions
   1. Read each question carefully
   2. Determine exactly what is wanted. Underline key words or phrases.
   3. Decide on outline or paragraph answer
   4. Include many different points and elements unless asked to develop any one or two points or elements
   5. Show impartiality by giving pros and cons unless directed to select one side only
   6. Make and write down any assumptions you find necessary to answer the questions
   7. Watch your English, grammar, punctuation and choice of words
   8. Time your answers; don't crowd material

8) Answering the essay question

Most essay questions can be answered by framing the specific response around several key words or ideas. Here are a few such key words or ideas:

M's: manpower, materials, methods, money, management
P's: purpose, program, policy, plan, procedure, practice, problems, pitfalls, personnel, public relations

  a. Six basic steps in handling problems:
   1. Preliminary plan and background development
   2. Collect information, data and facts
   3. Analyze and interpret information, data and facts
   4. Analyze and develop solutions as well as make recommendations
   5. Prepare report and sell recommendations
   6. Install recommendations and follow up effectiveness

  b. Pitfalls to avoid
   1. *Taking things for granted* – A statement of the situation does not necessarily imply that each of the elements is necessarily true; for example, a complaint may be invalid and biased so that all that can be taken for granted is that a complaint has been registered

2. *Considering only one side of a situation* – Wherever possible, indicate several alternatives and then point out the reasons you selected the best one
3. *Failing to indicate follow up* – Whenever your answer indicates action on your part, make certain that you will take proper follow-up action to see how successful your recommendations, procedures or actions turn out to be
4. *Taking too long in answering any single question* – Remember to time your answers properly

IX. AFTER THE TEST

Scoring procedures differ in detail among civil service jurisdictions although the general principles are the same. Whether the papers are hand-scored or graded by machine we have described, they are nearly always graded by number. That is, the person who marks the paper knows only the number – never the name – of the applicant. Not until all the papers have been graded will they be matched with names. If other tests, such as training and experience or oral interview ratings have been given, scores will be combined. Different parts of the examination usually have different weights. For example, the written test might count 60 percent of the final grade, and a rating of training and experience 40 percent. In many jurisdictions, veterans will have a certain number of points added to their grades.

After the final grade has been determined, the names are placed in grade order and an eligible list is established. There are various methods for resolving ties between those who get the same final grade – probably the most common is to place first the name of the person whose application was received first. Job offers are made from the eligible list in the order the names appear on it. You will be notified of your grade and your rank as soon as all these computations have been made. This will be done as rapidly as possible.

People who are found to meet the requirements in the announcement are called "eligibles." Their names are put on a list of eligible candidates. An eligible's chances of getting a job depend on how high he stands on this list and how fast agencies are filling jobs from the list.

When a job is to be filled from a list of eligibles, the agency asks for the names of people on the list of eligibles for that job. When the civil service commission receives this request, it sends to the agency the names of the three people highest on this list. Or, if the job to be filled has specialized requirements, the office sends the agency the names of the top three persons who meet these requirements from the general list.

The appointing officer makes a choice from among the three people whose names were sent to him. If the selected person accepts the appointment, the names of the others are put back on the list to be considered for future openings.

That is the rule in hiring from all kinds of eligible lists, whether they are for typist, carpenter, chemist, or something else. For every vacancy, the appointing officer has his choice of any one of the top three eligibles on the list. This explains why the person whose name is on top of the list sometimes does not get an appointment when some of the persons lower on the list do. If the appointing officer chooses the second or third eligible, the No. 1 eligible does not get a job at once, but stays on the list until he is appointed or the list is terminated.

X. HOW TO PASS THE INTERVIEW TEST

The examination for which you applied requires an oral interview test. You have already taken the written test and you are now being called for the interview test – the final part of the formal examination.

You may think that it is not possible to prepare for an interview test and that there are no procedures to follow during an interview. Our purpose is to point out some things you can do in advance that will help you and some good rules to follow and pitfalls to avoid while you are being interviewed.

What is an interview supposed to test?

The written examination is designed to test the technical knowledge and competence of the candidate; the oral is designed to evaluate intangible qualities, not readily measured otherwise, and to establish a list showing the relative fitness of each candidate – as measured against his competitors – for the position sought. Scoring is not on the basis of "right" and "wrong," but on a sliding scale of values ranging from "not passable" to "outstanding." As a matter of fact, it is possible to achieve a relatively low score without a single "incorrect" answer because of evident weakness in the qualities being measured.

Occasionally, an examination may consist entirely of an oral test – either an individual or a group oral. In such cases, information is sought concerning the technical knowledges and abilities of the candidate, since there has been no written examination for this purpose. More commonly, however, an oral test is used to supplement a written examination.

Who conducts interviews?

The composition of oral boards varies among different jurisdictions. In nearly all, a representative of the personnel department serves as chairman. One of the members of the board may be a representative of the department in which the candidate would work. In some cases, "outside experts" are used, and, frequently, a businessman or some other representative of the general public is asked to serve. Labor and management or other special groups may be represented. The aim is to secure the services of experts in the appropriate field.

However the board is composed, it is a good idea (and not at all improper or unethical) to ascertain in advance of the interview who the members are and what groups they represent. When you are introduced to them, you will have some idea of their backgrounds and interests, and at least you will not stutter and stammer over their names.

What should be done before the interview?

While knowledge about the board members is useful and takes some of the surprise element out of the interview, there is other preparation which is more substantive. It *is* possible to prepare for an oral interview – in several ways:

1) Keep a copy of your application and review it carefully before the interview

This may be the only document before the oral board, and the starting point of the interview. Know what education and experience you have listed there, and the sequence and dates of all of it. Sometimes the board will ask you to review the highlights of your experience for them; you should not have to hem and haw doing it.

2) Study the class specification and the examination announcement

Usually, the oral board has one or both of these to guide them. The qualities, characteristics or knowledges required by the position sought are stated in these documents. They offer valuable clues as to the nature of the oral interview. For example, if the job involves supervisory responsibilities, the announcement will usually indicate that knowledge of modern supervisory methods and the qualifications of the candidate as a supervisor will be tested. If so, you can expect such questions, frequently in the form of a hypothetical situation which you are expected to solve. NEVER go into an oral without knowledge of the duties and responsibilities of the job you seek.

3) Think through each qualification required

Try to visualize the kind of questions you would ask if you were a board member. How well could you answer them? Try especially to appraise your own knowledge and background in each area, *measured against the job sought*, and identify any areas in which you are weak. Be critical and realistic – do not flatter yourself.

4) Do some general reading in areas in which you feel you may be weak

For example, if the job involves supervision and your past experience has NOT, some general reading in supervisory methods and practices, particularly in the field of human relations, might be useful. Do NOT study agency procedures or detailed manuals. The oral board will be testing your understanding and capacity, not your memory.

5) Get a good night's sleep and watch your general health and mental attitude

You will want a clear head at the interview. Take care of a cold or any other minor ailment, and of course, no hangovers.

What should be done on the day of the interview?

Now comes the day of the interview itself. Give yourself plenty of time to get there. Plan to arrive somewhat ahead of the scheduled time, particularly if your appointment is in the fore part of the day. If a previous candidate fails to appear, the board might be ready for you a bit early. By early afternoon an oral board is almost invariably behind schedule if there are many candidates, and you may have to wait. Take along a book or magazine to read, or your application to review, but leave any extraneous material in the waiting room when you go in for your interview. In any event, relax and compose yourself.

The matter of dress is important. The board is forming impressions about you – from your experience, your manners, your attitude, and your appearance. Give your personal appearance careful attention. Dress your best, but not your flashiest. Choose conservative, appropriate clothing, and be sure it is immaculate. This is a business interview, and your appearance should indicate that you regard it as such. Besides, being well groomed and properly dressed will help boost your confidence.

Sooner or later, someone will call your name and escort you into the interview room. *This is it.* From here on you are on your own. It is too late for any more preparation. But remember, you asked for this opportunity to prove your fitness, and you are here because your request was granted.

What happens when you go in?

The usual sequence of events will be as follows: The clerk (who is often the board stenographer) will introduce you to the chairman of the oral board, who will introduce you to the other members of the board. Acknowledge the introductions before you sit down. Do not be surprised if you find a microphone facing you or a stenotypist sitting by. Oral interviews are usually recorded in the event of an appeal or other review.

Usually the chairman of the board will open the interview by reviewing the highlights of your education and work experience from your application – primarily for the benefit of the other members of the board, as well as to get the material into the record. Do not interrupt or comment unless there is an error or significant misinterpretation; if that is the case, do not hesitate. But do not quibble about insignificant matters. Also, he will usually ask you some question about your education, experience or your present job – partly to get you to start talking and to establish the interviewing "rapport." He may start the actual questioning, or turn it over to one of the other members. Frequently, each member undertakes the questioning on a particular area, one in which he is perhaps most competent, so you can expect each member to participate in the examination. Because time is limited, you may also expect some rather abrupt switches in the direction the questioning takes, so do not be upset by it. Normally, a board member will not pursue a single line of questioning unless he discovers a particular strength or weakness.

After each member has participated, the chairman will usually ask whether any member has any further questions, then will ask you if you have anything you wish to add. Unless you are expecting this question, it may floor you. Worse, it may start you off on an extended, extemporaneous speech. The board is not usually seeking more information. The question is principally to offer you a last opportunity to present further qualifications or to indicate that you have nothing to add. So, if you feel that a significant qualification or characteristic has been overlooked, it is proper to point it out in a sentence or so. Do not compliment the board on the thoroughness of their examination – they have been sketchy, and you know it. If you wish, merely say, "No thank you, I have nothing further to add." This is a point where you can "talk yourself out" of a good impression or fail to present an important bit of information. Remember, *you close the interview yourself.*

The chairman will then say, "That is all, Mr. _____, thank you." Do not be startled; the interview is over, and quicker than you think. Thank him, gather your belongings and take your leave. Save your sigh of relief for the other side of the door.

How to put your best foot forward

Throughout this entire process, you may feel that the board individually and collectively is trying to pierce your defenses, seek out your hidden weaknesses and embarrass and confuse you. Actually, this is not true. They are obliged to make an appraisal of your qualifications for the job you are seeking, and they want to see you in your best light. Remember, they must interview all candidates and a non-cooperative candidate may become a failure in spite of their best efforts to bring out his qualifications. Here are 15 suggestions that will help you:

1) Be natural – Keep your attitude confident, not cocky

If you are not confident that you can do the job, do not expect the board to be. Do not apologize for your weaknesses, try to bring out your strong points. The board is interested in a positive, not negative, presentation. Cockiness will antagonize any board member and make him wonder if you are covering up a weakness by a false show of strength.

2) Get comfortable, but don't lounge or sprawl

Sit erectly but not stiffly. A careless posture may lead the board to conclude that you are careless in other things, or at least that you are not impressed by the importance of the occasion. Either conclusion is natural, even if incorrect. Do not fuss with your clothing, a pencil or an ashtray. Your hands may occasionally be useful to emphasize a point; do not let them become a point of distraction.

3) Do not wisecrack or make small talk

This is a serious situation, and your attitude should show that you consider it as such. Further, the time of the board is limited – they do not want to waste it, and neither should you.

4) Do not exaggerate your experience or abilities
   In the first place, from information in the application or other interviews and sources, the board may know more about you than you think. Secondly, you probably will not get away with it. An experienced board is rather adept at spotting such a situation, so do not take the chance.

5) If you know a board member, do not make a point of it, yet do not hide it
   Certainly you are not fooling him, and probably not the other members of the board. Do not try to take advantage of your acquaintanceship – it will probably do you little good.

6) Do not dominate the interview
   Let the board do that. They will give you the clues – do not assume that you have to do all the talking. Realize that the board has a number of questions to ask you, and do not try to take up all the interview time by showing off your extensive knowledge of the answer to the first one.

7) Be attentive
   You only have 20 minutes or so, and you should keep your attention at its sharpest throughout. When a member is addressing a problem or question to you, give him your undivided attention. Address your reply principally to him, but do not exclude the other board members.

8) Do not interrupt
   A board member may be stating a problem for you to analyze. He will ask you a question when the time comes. Let him state the problem, and wait for the question.

9) Make sure you understand the question
   Do not try to answer until you are sure what the question is. If it is not clear, restate it in your own words or ask the board member to clarify it for you. However, do not haggle about minor elements.

10) Reply promptly but not hastily
   A common entry on oral board rating sheets is "candidate responded readily," or "candidate hesitated in replies." Respond as promptly and quickly as you can, but do not jump to a hasty, ill-considered answer.

11) Do not be peremptory in your answers
   A brief answer is proper – but do not fire your answer back. That is a losing game from your point of view. The board member can probably ask questions much faster than you can answer them.

12) Do not try to create the answer you think the board member wants
   He is interested in what kind of mind you have and how it works – not in playing games. Furthermore, he can usually spot this practice and will actually grade you down on it.

13) Do not switch sides in your reply merely to agree with a board member
   Frequently, a member will take a contrary position merely to draw you out and to see if you are willing and able to defend your point of view. Do not start a debate, yet do not surrender a good position. If a position is worth taking, it is worth defending.

14) Do not be afraid to admit an error in judgment if you are shown to be wrong

The board knows that you are forced to reply without any opportunity for careful consideration. Your answer may be demonstrably wrong. If so, admit it and get on with the interview.

15) Do not dwell at length on your present job

The opening question may relate to your present assignment. Answer the question but do not go into an extended discussion. You are being examined for a *new* job, not your present one. As a matter of fact, try to phrase ALL your answers in terms of the job for which you are being examined.

Basis of Rating

Probably you will forget most of these "do's" and "don'ts" when you walk into the oral interview room. Even remembering them all will not ensure you a passing grade. Perhaps you did not have the qualifications in the first place. But remembering them will help you to put your best foot forward, without treading on the toes of the board members.

Rumor and popular opinion to the contrary notwithstanding, an oral board wants you to make the best appearance possible. They know you are under pressure – but they also want to see how you respond to it as a guide to what your reaction would be under the pressures of the job you seek. They will be influenced by the degree of poise you display, the personal traits you show and the manner in which you respond.

ABOUT THIS BOOK

This book contains tests divided into Examination Sections. Go through each test, answering every question in the margin. We have also attached a sample answer sheet at the back of the book that can be removed and used. At the end of each test look at the answer key and check your answers. On the ones you got wrong, look at the right answer choice and learn. Do not fill in the answers first. Do not memorize the questions and answers, but understand the answer and principles involved. On your test, the questions will likely be different from the samples. Questions are changed and new ones added. If you understand these past questions you should have success with any changes that arise. Tests may consist of several types of questions. We have additional books on each subject should more study be advisable or necessary for you. Finally, the more you study, the better prepared you will be. This book is intended to be the last thing you study before you walk into the examination room. Prior study of relevant texts is also recommended. NLC publishes some of these in our Fundamental Series. Knowledge and good sense are important factors in passing your exam. Good luck also helps. So now study this Passbook, absorb the material contained within and take that knowledge into the examination. Then do your best to pass that exam.

EXAMINATION SECTION

ELEVATOR MECHANICS

EXAMINATION SECTION
TEST 1

DIRECTIONS: Each question, or incomplete statement is followed by several suggested answers or completions. Select the one that *BEST* answers the question or completes the statement. *PRINT THE LETTER OF THE CORRECT ANSWER IN THE SPACE AT THE RIGHT.*

Questions 1-16.

DIRECTIONS: Questions 1 to 16 refer to the tools shown on page 2. (The numbers in the answer refer to the numbers beneath the tools. Tools are *NOT* drawn to scale.)

1. A 1" x 1" x 1/8" angle iron should be cut by using tool number   1.____
   A. A, 7   B. B, 12   C. 23   D. 42

2. To peen an iron rivet, you should use tool number   2.____
   A. 4   B. 7   C. 21   D. 43

3. The "star drill" is tool number   3.____
   A. 5.   B. 10   C. 20   D. 22

4. To make holes in sheet metal for sheet metal screws, you should use tool number   4.____
   A. 6   B. 10   C. 36   D. D, 46

5. To cut through a 3/8" diameter wire rope, you should use tool number   5.____
   A. 12   B. 23   C. 42   D. 54

6. To remove cutting burrs from the inside of a steel pipe, you should use tool number   6.____
   A. 5   B. 11   C. 14   D. 20

7. The depth of a bored hole may be measured *most accurately* with tool number   7.____
   A. 8   B. 16   C. 26   D. 41

8. If the marking on the blade of tool number 7 reads: "12-32," the 32 refers to the   8.____
   A. length   B. thickness
   C. weight   D. no. of teeth per inch

9. If tool number 6 bears the mark "5," it should be used to drill holes having a diameter of   9.____
   A. 5/32"   B. 5/16"   C. 5/8"   D. 5"

10. To determine *most quickly* the number of threads per inch on a bolt, you should use tool number   10.____
    A. 8   B. 16   C. 26   D. 50

1

11. Wood screws, located in positions where the headroom does not permit the use of an ordinary screwdriver, may be removed by using tool number   11.____

    A. 17   B. 28   C. 35   D. 46

12. To remove a broken-off piece of 1/2" diameter pipe from a fitting, you should use tool number   12.____

    A. 5   B. 11   C. 20   D. D, 36

13. The outside diameter of a bushing may be measured *most accurately* with tool number   13.____

    A. 8   B. 26   C. 33   D. 43

14. To rethread a stud hole in the casting of an elevator motor, you should use tool number   14.____

    A. 5   B. 20   C. 22   D. 36

TOOLS

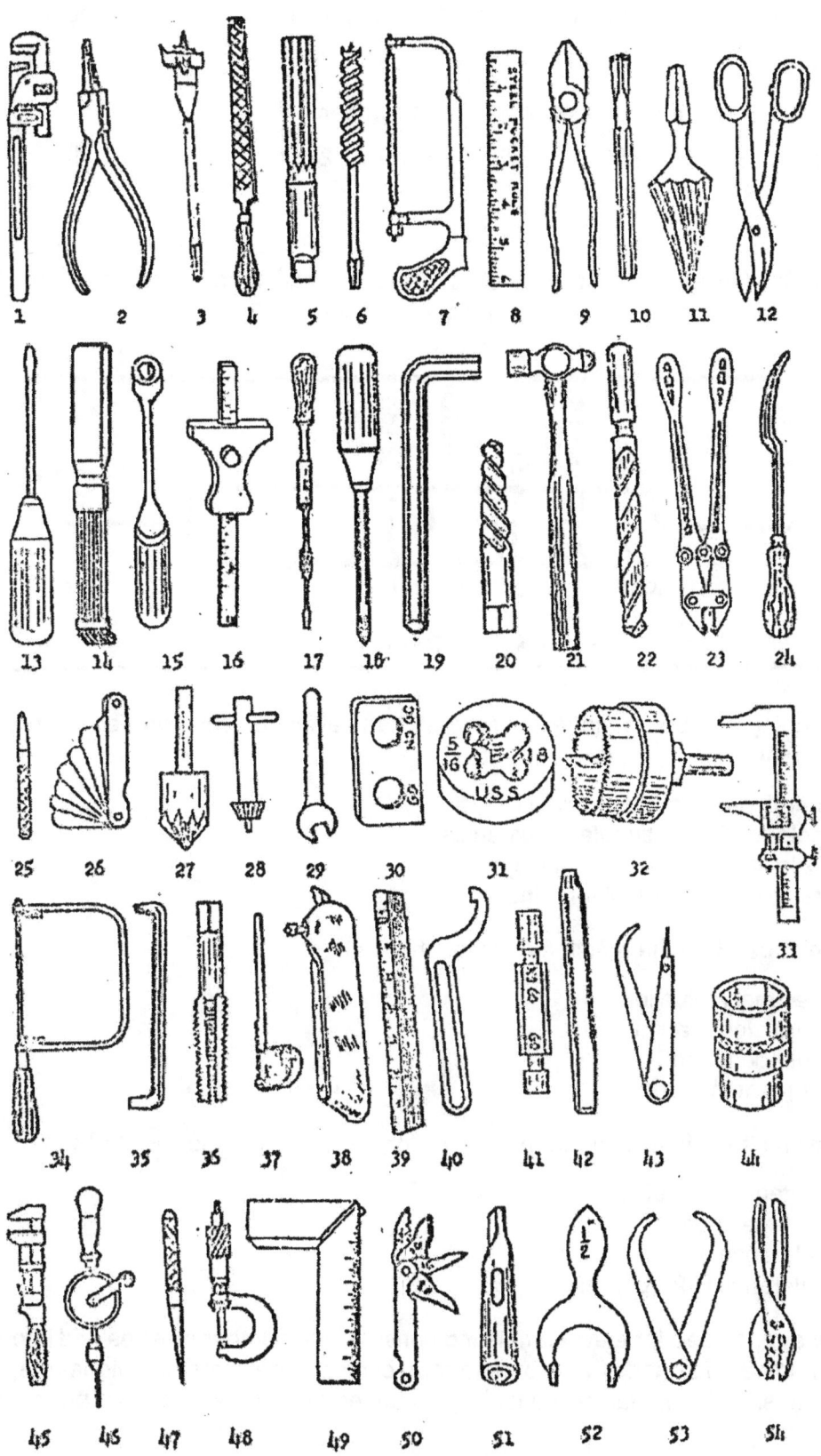

15. To enlarge *slightly* a bored hole in a steel plate, you should use tool number 15._____
    A. 5   B. 11   C. 20   D. D, 36

16. The term "16-oz." should be applied to tool number 16._____
    A. 1   B. 12   C. 21   D. 42

Questions 17-19.

DIRECTIONS: Questions 17 to 19 refer to the carbon resistor sketched below. Refer to this sketch when answering these questions.

[Carbon Resistor sketch: Band Number 1 (Green), 2 (Red), 3 (Yellow), 4 (Gold)]

17. Color coding is used on the resistor rather than having its rating printed on it MAINLY because the 17._____

    A. printing would fade in time
    B. color coding is simple to remember
    C. color coding prevents mix-ups
    D. resistor is too small for printing

18. Band number 3 on the resistor indicates the 18._____

    A. decimal multiplier
    B. third significant figure
    C. voltage rating
    D. percent tolerance

19. If band number 4 is missing from the resistor, it means that the resistor"s 19._____

    A. voltage is doubled
    B. voltage is zero
    C. tolerance is zero
    D. tolerance is 20 percent

20. The wire rope used for elevator hoisting consists of a number of wires laid into a strand, and a number of strands laid around a rope center. If the wires are laid left-handed into the strands, and the strands are laid right-handed around the rope center, the rope is called a 20._____

- A. right-lay, regular-lay rope
- B. left-lay, regular-lay rope
- C. right-lay, Lang-lay rope
- D. left-lay, Lang-lay rope

21. A *megger* should be used for the direct measurement of

   A. current   B. power   C. voltage   D. resistance

22. It is considered *bad* practice to use water to put out electrical fires MAINLY because the water may

   - A. short-circuit the wires
   - B. damage the insulation
   - C. rust delicate equipment
   - D. cause a serious electrical shock

23. Of the following, the method that should NOT be used to remove a length of hoist rope from its delivery reel is:

   - A. Take off the rope from the top side while the reel is resting on its side
   - B. Fix the free end and then roll the reel along the floor
   - C. Mount the reel on a shaft and trunnions and then rotate the reel
   - D. Mount the reel on a turntable and then rotate the turntable

24. The area of a circle, whose diameter is 24 inches, is, most nearly,

   - A. 0.84 square foot
   - B. 1.67 square feet
   - C. 3.14 square feet
   - D. 18.84 square feet

25. If an elevator mechanic opens the strands of a piece of manila rope and finds saw-dust material inside the rope, he should know that this means that the rope

   - A. is relatively new
   - B. has been damaged and should be discarded
   - C. has dried out and must be re-oiled before use
   - D. is to be used only for lights loads until the sawdust works itself out

26. Elevator mechanics are cautioned not to leave tools on scaffolding. The MOST important reason for this rule is to

   - A. avoid a safety hazard
   - B. prevent damage to the tools
   - C. prevent theft of the tools
   - D. prevent mix-ups in the mechanics' tools

Questions 27-40.

DIRECTIONS: Questions 27 to 40 are based on the sketch of a gearless elevator shown on page 6.

27. The *governor* is indicated by number 27._____
    A. 2   B. 7   C. 8   D. 16

28. The *motor generator* is indicated by number 28._____
    A. 1   B. 4   C. 7   D. 9

29. The *floor selector* is indicated by number 29._____
    A. 1   B. 2   C. 11   D. 16

30. The *hoistway limit switch* is indicated by number 30._____
    A. 8   B. 9   C. 10   D. 12

31. The *cable equalizer* is indicated by number 31._____
    A. 8   B. 9   C. 14   D. 26

32. The *brakes* are indicated by number 32._____
    A. 2   B. 5   C. 9   D. 22

33. The *buffers* are indicated by number 33._____
    A. 3   B. 9   C. 24   D. 25

34. The *compensating rope sheave* is indicated by number 34._____
    A. 8   B. 9   C. 25   D. 26

35. The *deflector sheave* is indicated by number 35._____
    A. 8   B. 9   C. 25   D. 26

36. The *door engines* are indicated by number 36._____
    A. 11   B. 12   C. 15   D. 16

37. The *guide shoes* are indicated by number 37._____
    A. 11   B. 12   C. 16   D. 20

38. The *music box* is indicated by number 38._____
    A. 3   B. 7   C. 11   D. 16

39. The *releasing carrier* is indicated by number 39._____
    A. 14   B. 16   C. 22   D. 27

40. The *rail grip shoes* are indicated by number 40._____
    A. 5   B. 17   C. 25   D. 26

7 (#1)

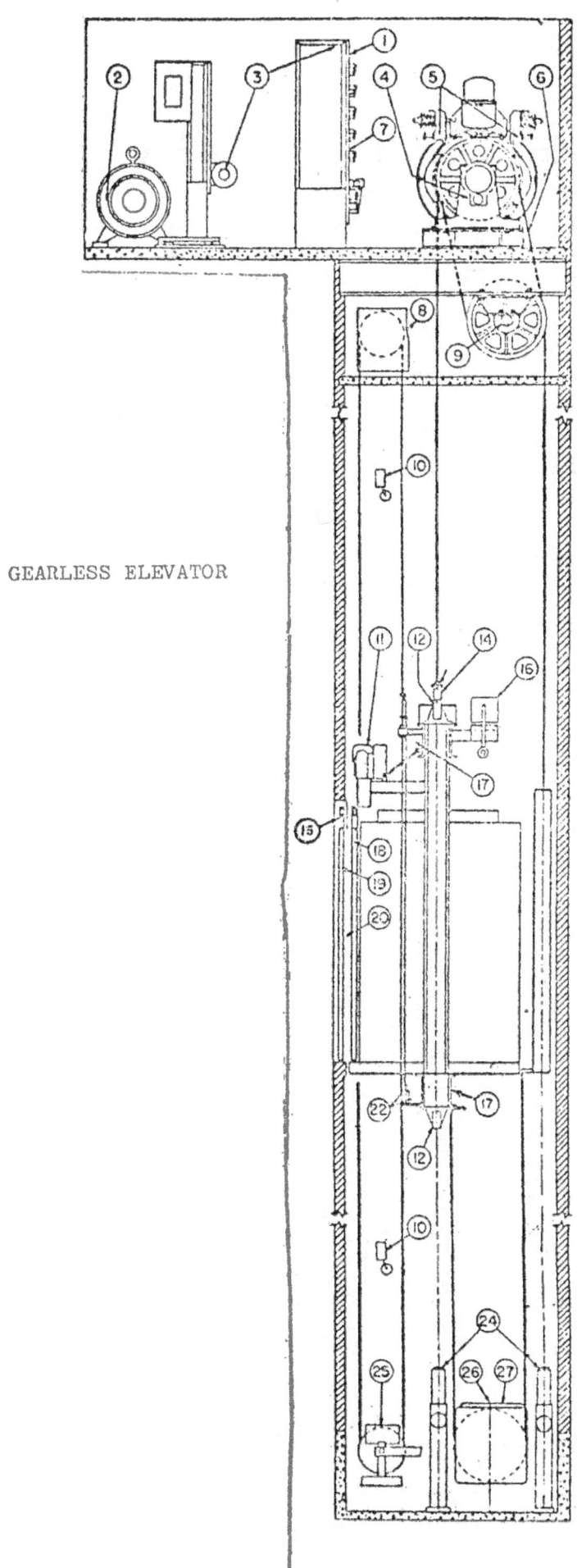

GEARLESS ELEVATOR

KEY (CORRECT ANSWER)

1. A	11. C	21. D	31. C
2. C	12. C	22. D	32. B
3. B	13. C	23. A	33. C
4. D	14. D	24. C	34. D
5. B	15. A	25. B	35. B
6. B	16. C	26. A	36. A
7. B	17. D	27. C	37. B
8. D	18. A	28. A	38. D
9. B	19. D	29. A	39. C
10. D	20. A	30. C	40. B

TEST 2

Questions 1-5.

DIRECTIONS: For Questions 1 to 5, the item referred to is shown to the right of the question.

1. The sketch shows a method of preventing a manila rope from unraveling. This is called
   A. splicing
   B. seizing
   C. mousing
   D. whipping

   1._____

2. The placing of a rope yarn on a hook to prevent the chain from being accidentally detached, as shown in the sketch, is called
   A. mousing
   B. whipping
   C. splicing
   D. seizing

   2._____

3. The knot shown is called a
   A. timber hitch
   B. clove hitch
   C. bowline
   D. becket

   3._____

4. The rigging device shown is a
   A. screw clamp
   B. shackle
   C. clevis
   D. thimble

   4._____

5. The wire-rope clip shown is a
   A. Crosby
   B. Loughlin
   C. Fist-grip
   D. C-clamp

   5._____

6. It is considered *good* practice to release the pressure from a hose containing compressed air before uncoupling the hose connection because this avoids

   A. damage to the air tool
   B. damage to the air compressor
   C. wasting compressed air
   D. possible personal injury

   6._____

7. Of the following electrical circuit components, the *one* which may give you an electrical shock even after the electrical power is turned off is a(n)

   A. charged capacitor
   B. resistor
   C. interlock
   D. relay

   7._____

Questions 8-14.

DIRECTIONS: For Questions 8 to 14, the item referred to is shown to the right of the question.

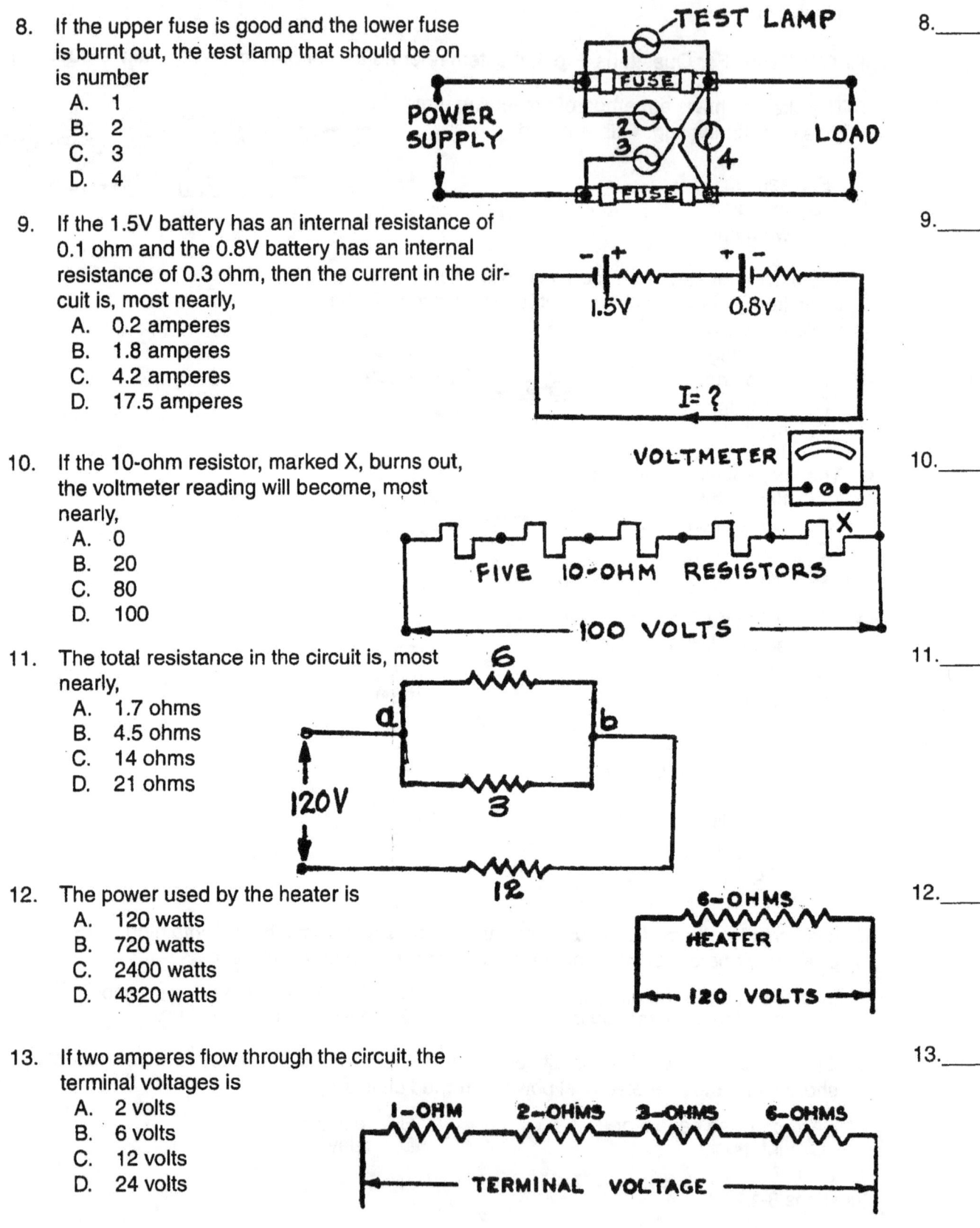

8. If the upper fuse is good and the lower fuse is burnt out, the test lamp that should be on is number
   A. 1
   B. 2
   C. 3
   D. 4

9. If the 1.5V battery has an internal resistance of 0.1 ohm and the 0.8V battery has an internal resistance of 0.3 ohm, then the current in the circuit is, most nearly,
   A. 0.2 amperes
   B. 1.8 amperes
   C. 4.2 amperes
   D. 17.5 amperes

10. If the 10-ohm resistor, marked X, burns out, the voltmeter reading will become, most nearly,
    A. 0
    B. 20
    C. 80
    D. 100

11. The total resistance in the circuit is, most nearly,
    A. 1.7 ohms
    B. 4.5 ohms
    C. 14 ohms
    D. 21 ohms

12. The power used by the heater is
    A. 120 watts
    B. 720 watts
    C. 2400 watts
    D. 4320 watts

13. If two amperes flow through the circuit, the terminal voltages is
    A. 2 volts
    B. 6 volts
    C. 12 volts
    D. 24 volts

3 (#2)

14. If the two voltmeters are identical, and the battery voltage is 120 volts, then the readings of the voltmeters should be
   A. 60 volts on each meter
   B. 120 volts on each meter
   C. 120 volts on meter #1, 240 volts on meter #2
   D. 120 volts on meter #1, zero volts on meter #2

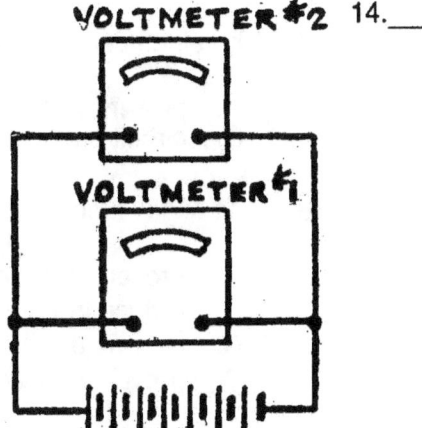

14.____

Questions 15-25.

DIRECTIONS: Questions 15 to 25 refer to the ELEVATOR WIRING DIAGRAM shown below. Refer to this diagram when answering these questions.

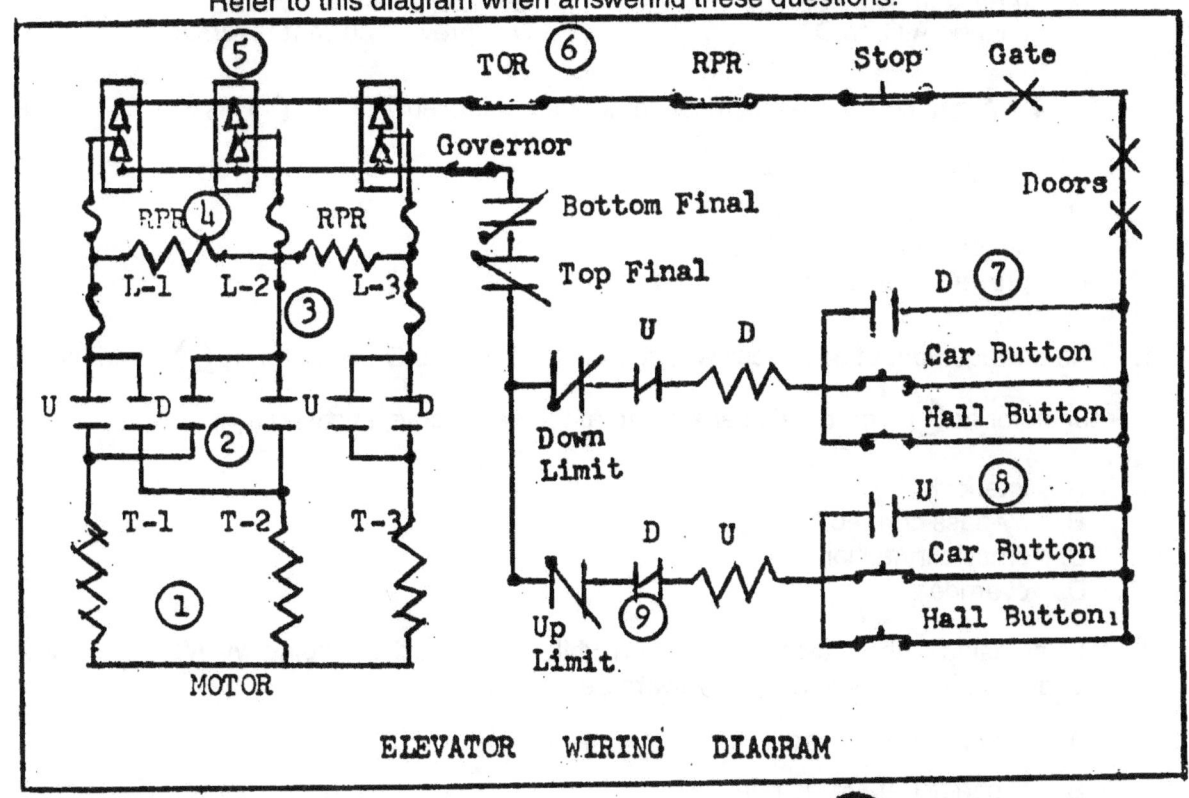

15. The electrical symbol motor's ∧∧∧ at ① indicates the motor's

   A. field windings
   B. electrical interlocks
   C. starting coil
   D. relay

15.____

16. The MAIN function of the wiring of L-l and L-2 through the U and D contactors at ② is to

   A. prevent overloading oiH;he motor
   B. permit reversing the motor
   C. prevent sharing the load between T-l, T-2
   D. permit different voltages to be applied

16.____

11

4 (#2)

17. The electrical symbols L-l, L-2 and L-3 at ③ indicate the

    A. power supply
    B. motor current
    C. circuit breakers
    D. line resistance

18. The *MAIN* function of the electrical component, labelled RPR at ④ is to

    A. prevent voltage changes in the circuit
    B. reduce the amount of current through the motor
    C. reverse the phases of the motor as the direction changes
    D. prevent elevator operation in case of reversa of the power supply phase

19. The *MAIN* function of the rectifiers at ⑤ is to

    A. reduce the voltage
    B. increase the current
    C. change A.C. to D.C.
    D. prevent current reversal

20. The *MAIN* function of the electrical component, labelled TOR at ⑥ is to

    A. prevent overspeeding
    B. cut in at terminal floor
    C. cut out at excessive torque
    D. prevent overheating

21. The arrangement of this circuit which prevents both the D contactor at ⑦ and the U contactor at ⑧ from being energized at the same time, is called a(n)

    A. interlock
    B. by-pass connection
    C. cross connection
    D. override

22. The pressing of the top-floor hall button while the car is descending will *NOT* prevent the elevator car from continuing downward because the

    A. down limit is closed
    B. D contact at ⑨ is opened
    C. down limit is opened
    D. D contact at ⑨ is closed

23. If the elevator car overspeeds, the safety device that should operate *first* is the

    A. Governor   B. Top final   C. Up limit   D. Stop

24. The *MAIN* function of the "Up Limit" and the "Down Limit" switch is to

    A. prevent the elevator car from hitting either pit or overhead

B. stop the elevator car nearly level with the landing
C. prevent the counterweight from hitting either at the top or bottom
D. keep the car speed within limits on the up and down trips

25. The "Bottom Final" and the "Top Final" switches are *usually* operated by

    A. the tiller rope
    B. the selector tape
    C. cams
    D. coils

26. It is considered *good* practice to lubricate elevator machinery

    A. during slack periods
    B. whenever it is needed
    C. at regularly scheduled times
    D. after a shut-down

27. Of the following, the *one* that should be used to dress a motor commutator is

    A. emery cloth
    B. sandpaper
    C. a flat file
    D. a mill file

28. A *tachometer* should be used for the direct measurement of

    A. torque
    B. power factor
    C. specific gravity
    D. r.p.m.

29. If 0.0375 is divided by 0.125, the result is

    A. 30.0   B. 3.0   C. 0.3   D. 0.03

30. It is considered *good* rigging practice to inspect chains more closely than wire rope prior to use MAINLY because chains

    A. twist more easily
    B. stretch more
    C. rust more readily
    D. have less reserve strength

31. A *hydrometer* should be used for the *direct* measurement of

    A. A torque
    B. power factor
    C. r.p.m.
    D. specific gravity

32. Of the following, elevator hoisting cables should be lubricated with

    A. a heavy grease
    B. medium-heavy oil
    C. graphite
    D. tar

33. If you were directed to check the "backlash" on an elevator hoisting motor, you should check the

    A. gears   B. bearings   C. contactors   D. brakes

34. The MAIN function of a "pole shader" on a coil is to

    A. prevent heating
    B. prevent hum
    C. reduce resistance
    D. reduce flux

Questions 35-40.

DIRECTIONS: Questions 35 to 40 refer to the elevator CALL BUTTON CIRCUIT shown below. Refer to this circuit when answering these questions.

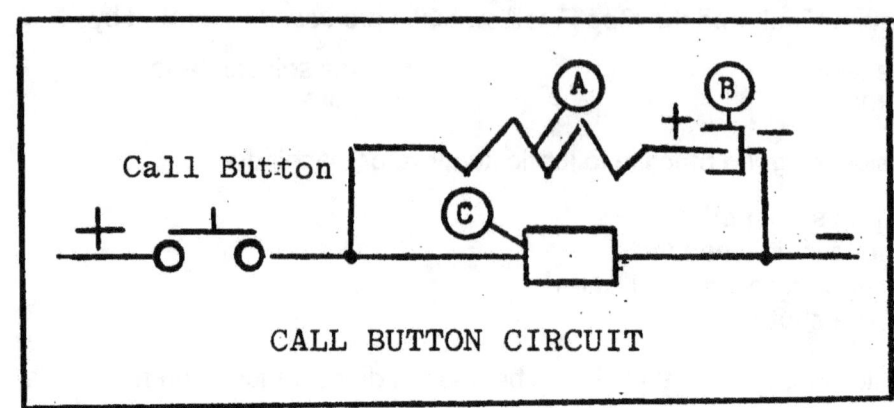

CALL BUTTON CIRCUIT

35. The electrical component shown at A is a

    A. resistor   B. coil   C. condenser   D. contactor

36. The electrical component shown at B is a

    A. resistor   B. coil   C. condenser   D. contactor

37. The electrical component shown at C is a

    A. resistor   B. coil   C. condenser   D. contactor

38. The MAIN purpose of component A is to

    A. short circuit B
    B. limit current to B
    C. reduce voltage to C
    D. increase current to C

39. The MAIN purpose of component B is to

    A. time the circuit
    B. increase the voltage
    C. decrease button resistance
    D. interrupt the circuit

40. The MAIN purpose of component C is to

    A. reduce the current
    B. increase the voltage
    C. open and close contactors
    D. reverse current polarity

KEY (CORRECT ANSWERS)

1. D	11. C	21. A	31. D
2. A	12. C	22. B	32. B
3. C	13. D	23. A	33. A
4. B	14. B	24. B	34. A
5. A	15. A	25. C	35. A
6. D	16. B	26. C	36. C
7. A	17. A	27. B	37. B
8. C	18. D	28. D	38. B
9. B	19. C	29. C	39. A
10. D	20. D	30. D	40. C

EXAMINATION SECTION
TEST 1

DIRECTIONS: Each question or incomplete statement is followed by several suggested answers or completions. Select the one that BEST answers the question or completes the statement. *PRINT THE LETTER OF THE CORRECT ANSWER IN THE SPACE AT THE RIGHT.*

1. Elevator machinery and related equipment is BEST lubricated

    A. whenever it is required
    B. after a shut-down
    C. during slack work periods
    D. at scheduled times

    1.____

2. The direction of rotation of a D.C. shunt motor can be *reversed* by reversing

    A. the line connections
    B. both the field and the armature connections
    C. either the field or the armature connections
    D. the residual field

    2.____

3. The bearings of geared type hoist motors are MOST usually of the _____ type.

    A. sleeve
    B. ball bearing
    C. ball and roller
    D. tapered roller

    3.____

4. Installation of a Type A (instantaneous) car safety is limited to cars operating at speeds, in FPM, between _____ and _____.

    A. 0; 120   B. 130; 150   C. 175; 300   D. 150; 500

    4.____

5. Of the following statements concerning the use of rubber-tired roller guides, the one which is MOST NEARLY correct is that their use would

    A. increase electric power usage
    B. help prevent hoistway fires
    C. increase maintenance costs
    D. require lubrication of the rails

    5.____

6. Of the following grades of carbon steel wire rope, the one which contains the LEAST percentage of carbon is

    A. traction
    B. improved plow
    C. plow
    D. iron

    6.____

7. In checking the neutral position of the carbon brushes in a variable voltage elevator hoist motor, a voltohmmeter is to be used as a test meter.
Of the following meter scales, the CORRECT one to use would be the _____ scale.

    A. 50-microamp
    B. 10-milliamp
    C. 10-amp
    D. 15-amp

    7.____

8. The rating of a standard cartridge fuse having a navy blue paper label is

    8.____

17

A. 250 volts, 30 amperes capacity
B. 250 volts, 15 amperes or less capacity
C. 250 volts, over 15 amperes capacity
D. 120 volts, 15 amperes capacity

9. In ordering a standard cartridge fuse, it is MOST necessary to specify the

   A. minimum length of ferrule and outside diameter of tube
   B. power factor of the connected load
   C. voltage of the circuit and the current capacity
   D. type of construction and the tolerance

10. Of the following substances, the BEST one to use to make it easier to pull wire conductors through electric conduit is

    A. powdered soapstone   B. petroleum jelly
    C. light oil   D. powdered graphite

11. A *Brinell test* is used to determine the

    A. hardness of metals
    B. strength of carbon brushes
    C. accuracy of tachometers
    D. number of broken wires in a rope

12. Of the following materials, the one which is NOT commonly used to line elevator brake shoes is

    A. asbestos   B. leather   C. wood   D. teflon

13. In a worm and gear elevator machine, metallic contact between the worm and the gear teeth is LEAST likely to occur when the oil level in the gear case is

    A. touching the bottom of the worm
    B. level with the center line of the worm-shaft
    C. level with the gear case drain plug
    D. between the bottom of the gear case and the bottom of the worm

14. The diameter of the hole of a bronze sleeve bearing is
    $+.006''$
    $2.402''-.000''$ and the diameter of the shaft for this bearing
    $+.000''$
    is $2.401''-.003''$.
    The limits of the clearance for the shaft in the bearing are MOST NEARLY _____" max; _____" min.

    A. .010; .001   B. .001; .001
    C. .007; .004   D. .006; .003

15. Of the following, the PRIMARY purpose of assigning mechanics to perform periodic inspection and testing of elevator equipment is to

    A. keep the mechanics active during slack periods
    B. provide on-the-job training for the less experienced mechanics

C. evaluate the mechanics' knowledge of the equipment
D. uncover potential equipment faults before they develop into major breakdowns

16. Of the following lubricants, the BEST one to use to lubricate elevator traction machine wire ropes is a

    A. heavy body oil mixed with graphite
    B. heavy body oil mixed with sulphur
    C. thin to medium heavy petroleum oil mixed with animal or vegetable oil
    D. very thin opaque oil mixed with a small quantity of pine tar

17. A megger tester is an instrument that is used to

    A. measure electrical insulation resistance
    B. determine the resistance of a bare copper conductor
    C. measure the rotative speed of a shaft
    D. determine the value of capacitors

18. When a mechanic is trained for a particular job, it is important that the mechanic be instructed properly. Listed below are four basic steps, in scrambled order, in training a worker:
    I. Demonstrate the actual operation to the mechanic
    II. Periodically check on the mechanic's performance
    III. Have the mechanic practice the job himself
    IV. Interest the mechanic in the job
    The CORRECT order in which these steps should be taken is

    A. II, I, III, IV
    B. III, I, IV, II
    C. II, IV, I, III
    D. IV, I, III, II

19. A suggestion is made that a machine be installed in the shop to help the mechanics on the job. You feel that the suggestion is a good one but realize that you cannot get the machine immediately, but that you may be able to obtain one at a later date.
    Of the following, the MOST effective way to handle the situation is to tell the mechanic that

    A. it is a good idea and to remind you of the suggestion at some other time
    B. you will look into the possibility and let him know if and when one can be installed
    C. the suggestion cannot be considered at the present time
    D. the shop does not require the machine and that none will be installed

20. One of the mechanics has just touched a bare electric wire carrying power and cannot let go.
    The one of the following actions that should be taken FIRST to assist the injured man is to

    A. use a dry rope or dry stick to remove the victim from the electrical source
    B. treat the mechanic for burns
    C. start artificial respiration or mouth-to-mouth breathing
    D. cut off the power, but only if it takes 5 minutes or less to find the switch

21. When lifting heavy objects without mechanical equipment, it is SAFEST to

    A. keep your back bent and knees straight

B. keep your feet as far from the object as possible
C. lift the object as fast as possible
D. use both arm and leg muscle

22. Of the following, the CHIEF cause of accidents on the job is

    A. faulty construction of elevator shafts
    B. mechanical failure of work equipment
    C. unsafe acts on the part of the workers
    D. improper work schedules

23. Assume that the men are being trained in the safe use of the ladder.
    According to accepted safety practice, if you place a 12-foot ladder against a wall, the distance between the foot of the ladder and the wall should be MOST NEARLY _____ foot(feet).

    A. 1   B. 3   C. 6   D. 9

24. Of the following types of portable fire extinguishers, the one which is the MOST suitable type for putting out *live* electrical wiring fires is a Class _____ extinguisher.

    A. A   B. B   C. C   D. D

25. Assume that you have been asked by the superintendent of a housing project to participate in a tenants' meeting regarding elevator vandalism.
    Of the following types of meetings, the one that will MOST likely have the highest tenant participation is the _____ type meeting.

    A. speaker-and-panel   B. formal conference
    C. open-discussion   D. speaker-only

KEY (CORRECT ANSWERS)

1. D		11. A	
2. C		12. D	
3. A		13. B	
4. A		14. A	
5. B		15. D	
6. D		16. C	
7. B		17. A	
8. B		18. D	
9. C		19. B	
10. A		20. A	

21. D
22. C
23. B
24. C
25. C

TEST 2

DIRECTIONS: Each question or incomplete statement is followed by several suggested answers or completions. Select the one that BEST answers the question or completes the statement. *PRINT THE LETTER OF THE CORRECT ANSWER IN THE SPACE AT THE RIGHT.*

1. The traveling crosshead or nut of a selector machine is driven vertically up and down by a

    A. flexible connection between the driving sheave and the car
    B. magnetically operated switch located on each landing
    C. steel tape attached to the car and wound on the sheaves at the top of the hoistway
    D. series of cold-cathode tubes electrically connected to a metal strip installed on the leading edge of the car door

    1._____

2. Assume that 8 mechanics have been assigned to do a job that must be finished in 5 days. At the end of 3 days, the men have completed only half the job.
   In order to complete the job on time in the remaining 2 days, the MINIMUM number of extra men that should be assigned is

    A. 2 B. 3 C. 4 D. 6

    2._____

3. Assume that the air gap between the stator and the bottom of the rotor of an A.C. motor is 0.01" less than a previously recorded clearance.
   This lessening of the air gap would MOST likely indicate that the

    A. spring tension holding the carbon brushes is excessive
    B. bearings of the motor are wearing
    C. stator laminations need to be replaced
    D. terminal voltage to the motor is too high

    3._____

4. Of the following types of wire-rope construction, the one recommended for double-wrap traction machines with sheaves under 30 inches in diameter is the

    A. 6 x 19 Warrington   B. 6 x 27 Regular
    C. 8 x 19 Seale   D. 8 x 25 Filler

    4._____

5. Upon inspecting an electrical contact in an elevator control circuit, you notice that the contact has a coating that is a dark bluish-black color.
   For this particular contact, it would be BEST to

    A. dress the contact by filing lightly with a double-cut smooth file
    B. mechanically open and close the contact periodically to break up the coating
    C. wipe the contact with a soft cloth
    D. leave the coating on the contact since it is a good conductor

    5._____

6. In a worm-gear elevator machine, the gear is GENERALLY machined from castings made of

    A. bronze   B. alloy steel   C. cast iron   D. copper

    6._____

7. An elevator supply manufacturer quotes a list price of $625 less 10 and 5 percent for ten contactors.
   The actual cost for these ten contactors is MOST NEARLY

    7._____

21

2 (#2)

A. $562 B. $554 C. $534 D. $522

8. Assume that a rectifier has been disconnected from a circuit. 8.____
Of the following meters, the one which should be used in checking the serviceability of this rectifier is a(n)

   A. ohmmeter   B. AC voltmeter
   C. ammeter   D. DC voltmeter

9. The length of a wire rope lay is APPROXIMATELY equal to _____ times the diameter of 9.____
the rope.

   A. $3\frac{1}{2}$ B. $4\frac{1}{2}$ C. $5\frac{1}{2}$ D. $6\frac{1}{2}$

10. A generator that develops the same voltage at no load and at maximum load, but with a 10.____
peak voltage in between, is called a(n) _____ compounded generator.

   A. differential   B. under   C. over   D. flat

Questions 11-17.

DIRECTIONS: Questions 11 to 17 are to be answered in accordance with the diagram shown below.

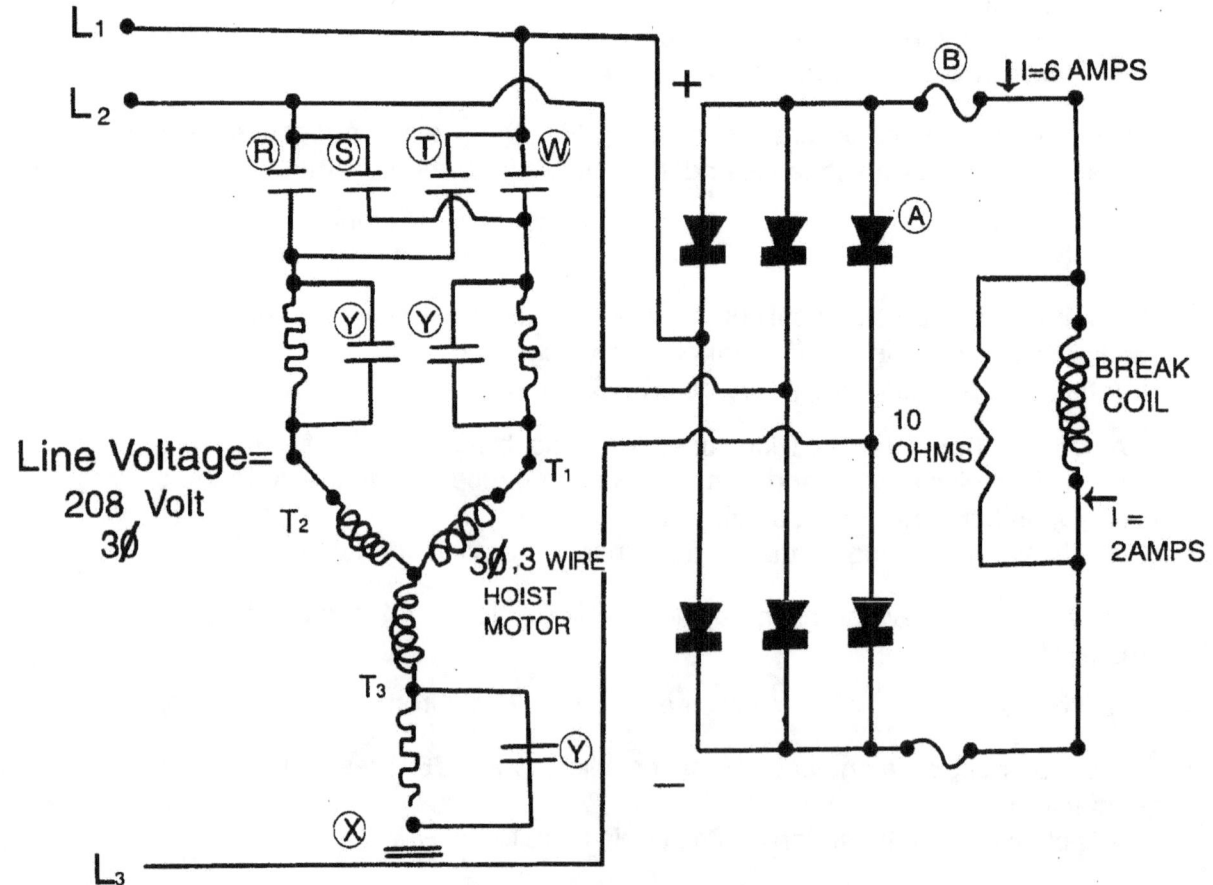

22

11. Each of the three contacts labeled Y in the above diagram are across a resistor. With respect to the operation of the hoist motor, these contacts should be

    A. closed when starting, open when running
    B. open when starting, closed when running
    C. closed when stopping, open when running
    D. open when stopping, open when running

12. Symbols such as the one labeled A in the above diagram USUALLY represent

    A. limit switches   B. detectors
    C. interlocks   D. rectifiers

13. The voltage across each of the hoist motor's three stator windings in the above diagram, when connected directly across the line, is MOST NEARLY _____ volts.

    A. 104   B. 120   C. 208   D. 416

14. Assume that the 3-phase hoist motor runs clockwise when contactors R, W, and X are closed, and contacts S and T are open.
    Of the following conditions, the one which will cause the motor to rotate in the OPPOSITE direction is

    A. open R, W, and X, close S and T
    B. open R, S, and T, close W and X
    C. close S, T, and X, open R and W
    D. close R, T, and W, open S and X

15. In the above diagram, the combined resistance of the brake coil and the 10-ohm resistor is MOST NEARLY _____ ohms.

    A. 5   B. 6 2/3   C. 10   D. 16 2/3

16. In the above diagram, the resistance of the *brake coil* is MOST NEARLY _____ ohms.

    A. zero   B. 10   C. 20   D. 30

17. In the above diagram, if the current through the fuse B is 6 amps, as shown, and the current through the brake coil is 2 amps, the voltage across the brake coil will be MOST NEARLY _____ volts.

    A. 2   B. 4
    C. 10   D. none of the above

18. Assume that you are meeting with a tenant group to explain a new, improved system of elevator maintenance for their building.
    Of the following, the LEAST effective method of maintaining the interest of this group is to

    A. concentrate only on the disadvantages of old elevator maintenance services
    B. show them how the new maintenance service will benefit them
    C. let them know what areas of the new maintenance plan you will discuss
    D. use visual aids to explain the new elevator maintenance service

19. Assume that, at a meeting with a tenant group, you are leading an open discussion on finding ways to reduce vandalism to the project's elevators.
Of the following practices, the BEST one for you to follow in leading the discussion is to

    A. make your suggestions, then give the group a chance to make theirs
    B. comment on and evaluate the contributions of members of the group to the discussion
    C. tell the group how they should operate as a discussion group
    D. encourage members of the group to speak out on the matter

20. You are asked to speak on ways to combat vandalism at a community housing project meeting.
Of the following, the BEST way to assure that the audience remembers the main points of your speech is to

    A. ask someone in the audience to read a written summary of the speech before you start speaking
    B. summarize the major points of your discussion at the end of your speech
    C. take a break during your speech and summarize the entire speech so far
    D. repeat what you have said every few paragraphs

21. The one of the following that is the MOST important characteristic of communication is that it

    A. involves just the sending of messages from one person to another
    B. transmits both information and understanding from one person to another
    C. helps the men adjust to work rules and procedures
    D. is concerned with the writing of clear, easy-to-read statements

22. The following are four important steps, in scrambled order, in the planning of a work project:
    I. Schedule the work
    II. Gather the facts
    III. Define the problem
    IV. Evaluate the facts
The CORRECT order in which these steps should be taken to do the work project properly is

    A. III, II, IV, I
    B. IV, III, II, I
    C. I, III, II, IV
    D. II, III, IV, I

23. The one of the following that is commonly considered to be the MOST serious result of a mechanic's being frequently absent is that

    A. the supervisor may become unconcerned about the employee
    B. the employee in question may worry about his being late
    C. work schedules may be disrupted
    D. re-training of the employee will be necessary

24. Of the following, the BEST way to reduce the number of rumors related to work matters among mechanics is for supervisors to

    A. have the mechanics publish a bulletin describing all rumors presently circulating so that everything is *out in the open*
    B. supply accurate information to the mechanics as soon as possible on matters that are important to them
    C. constantly change their official interpretations of work matters so that the mechanics will not have any basis for rumors
    D. informally confide in their mechanics more often

25. According to the standard procedure manual, the symbol *N*, when used to record overtime work in the elevator log book, indicates

    A. night work differential
    B. nuisance
    C. necessary approval was granted
    D. no materials used

KEY (CORRECT ANSWERS)

1.	C	11.	B
2.	C	12.	D
3.	B	13.	B
4.	C	14.	C
5.	D	15.	B
6.	A	16.	C
7.	C	17.	D
8.	A	18.	A
9.	D	19.	D
10.	D	20.	B

21. B
22. A
23. C
24. B
25. B

EXAMINATION SECTION
TEST 1

DIRECTIONS: Each question or incomplete statement is followed by several suggested answers or completions. Select the one that BEST answers the question or completes the statement. *PRINT THE LETTER OF THE CORRECT ANSWER IN THE SPACE AT THE RIGHT.*

1. Elevator car safeties are set to function 1.____

   A. in the direction determined by the installer
   B. in either the up or the down direction
   C. *only* in the down direction
   D. *only* in the up direction

2. Of the following, the BEST type of fire extinguisher to use on an electrical fire is 2.____

   A. water type stored pressure
   B. carbon dioxide
   C. soda-acid
   D. foam

3. The purpose of a rectifier is to 3.____

   A. step down 440 voltage to 220 voltage
   B. function as a starting resistance for D.C. hoist motors
   C. change alternating current to direct current
   D. stop up voltage

4. The property of a material that tends to prevent the flow of electric current through it is known as 4.____

   A. flux   B. resistance
   C. elasticity   D. excitation

5. The automatic terminal stopping devices are USUALLY located in the 5.____

   A. flexible guide clamp assembly
   B. hoistway
   C. motor brake
   D. inside of the cab

6. When using an uninsulated portable electric tool in a damp location, the hazard of an electric shock can BEST be lessened by making sure that the 6.____

   A. person using the tool is grounded
   B. tool is dry
   C. tool is grounded
   D. tool is used only with a 110-volt electric supply

7. The terminal limit switches are USUALLY operated by the 7.____

   A. cams   B. tiller rope
   C. hydraulic pressure   D. air pressure

27

8. A tool COMMONLY used to cut holes in masonry is the

   A. plane
   B. auger bit
   C. bottoming taps
   D. star drill

9. An ammeter measures

   A. watts
   B. resistance
   C. current
   D. voltage

10. A die is a tool used to cut

    A. external threads
    B. internal threads
    C. conduit
    D. broken screws

11. The BEST type of fasteners to use when mounting outlet boxes onto a concrete wall are

    A. sheet metal screws
    B. toggle bolts
    C. U-bolts
    D. expansion screw anchors

12. A VOM would be used to measure

    A. motor speed
    B. electricity
    C. brake pressure
    D. air pressure

13. The state of the charge in a lead-acid storage battery would be checked by a

    A. psychrometer
    B. interferometer
    C. calorimeter
    D. hydrometer

14. The one of the following which should be used to pull several wires at one time into a conduit is the _____ grip.

    A. basket   B. tie   C. box   D. knuckle

15. When an ammeter is used to test an electric circuit, the instrument should be connected

    A. across the line
    B. in parallel with the circuit
    C. in series with the circuit
    D. either in parallel or series with the circuit

16. The one of the following dimensions of a wire that would be measured with a micrometer is the

    A. diameter
    B. area
    C. circumference
    D. length

17. The one of the following instruments used when making a speed-load test is the

    A. tachometer
    B. potentiometer
    C. speedometer
    D. petrometer

18. When cutting non-preformed wire rope, the number of seizings that should be made on each side of the cut is

    A. three   B. four   C. five   D. six

19. BX is the term sometimes used in referring to

    A. armored cable B. lead sleeves
    C. sheet metal strips D. wire rope

20. The tool used to drive a lag screw is a(n)

    A. screwdriver B. Stillson wrench
    C. Allen wrench D. open end wrench

21. A metal washer is MOST generally used with a

    A. flat head wood screw B. carriage bolt
    C. set screw D. machine screw

22. A circuit breaker serves the same purpose as a

    A. relay B. solenoid C. fuse D. switch

23. Heat generated by dynamic braking is dissipated through

    A. rectifiers B. dashpots
    C. relays D. resistors

24. The one of the following items which can BEST be inspected from the top of the elevator car is a

    A. door operating device B. M.G. starter
    C. governor flyball weight D. brake shoe

25. Of the following, the one which is MOST frequently used to loosen a rusted bolt is

    A. graphite B. a mixture of graphite and oil
    C. linseed oil D. penetrating oil

26. A spring is sometimes used in connection with an electrical contact MAINLY to

    A. dissipate the heat arising from the contact
    B. reduce the resistance at the contact
    C. bring current to the contact
    D. act as a shunt to carry high currents

27. A broken chain test is MOST frequently performed on a(n)

    A. gearless traction machine B. overhead drum machine
    C. escalator D. basement drum machine

28. The MAIN purpose of a reverse-phase relay is to protect the

    A. hoist motor against reversal B. signal system
    C. faces of the contacts D. governor contract load

29. In general, an elevator brake should be adjusted so that its shoes _____ the brake drum.

    A. have a clearance of 0.40" from
    B. have a clearance of 0.28" from
    C. have a clearance of 0.20" from
    D. just clear

30. A 6x19 wire rope is one which

    A. has 19 strands of 6 wires each
    B. has 6 strands of 19 wires each
    C. is always a regular-lay rope
    D. is always a lang-lay rope

31. The transmission of car motion to the governor rope is performed by the

    A. rheostatic control
    B. normal terminal stop device
    C. releasing carrier
    D. generator-field control

32. When examining an elevator cable for broken wires, it is MOST important that a mechanic use a

    A. piece of chalk
    B. flashlight
    C. voltmeter
    D. shunt

33. It is BEST to lubricate elevator machinery

    A. on a regular schedule
    B. only when lubrication is needed
    C. whenever it is determined that the oil is running low
    D. when severe vibration occurs

34. An elevator mechanic generally checks for excessive *backlash* in a

    A. buffer   B. hoist   C. bearing   D. gear

35. The governor tension weight or sheave is generally located

    A. in the penthouse
    B. near the governor
    C. in the pit
    D. on the side of the car

KEY (CORRECT ANSWERS)

1.	C	11.	D	21.	D
2.	B	12.	B	22.	C
3.	C	13.	D	23.	D
4.	B	14.	A	24.	A
5.	B	15.	C	25.	D
6.	C	16.	A	26.	B
7.	A	17.	A	27.	C
8.	D	18.	A	28.	A
9.	C	19.	A	29.	D
10.	A	20.	D	30.	B
		31.	C		
		32.	B		
		33.	A		
		34.	D		
		35.	C		

TEST 2

DIRECTIONS: Each question or incomplete statement is followed by several suggested answers or completions. Select the one that BEST answers the question or completes the statement. *PRINT THE LETTER OF THE CORRECT ANSWER IN THE SPACE AT THE RIGHT.*

1. In elevator operation, the term *landing zone* means the space within a distance above or below the landing of _____ inches.   1.___

   A. 4   B. 8   C. 18   D. 40

2. Cable equalizers are installed on traction elevators in order to   2.___

   A. equalize the load on each cable
   B. prevent over-travel of the car
   C. keep all cables the same length
   D. reduce the need for manual inspection of cables

3. The one of the following that is PROPER to use to dress a motor commutator is   3.___

   A. a flat file   B. emery cloth
   C. a mill file   D. sandpaper

4. The inductor plates in an elevator installation are generally located   4.___

   A. near the worm and gear housing
   B. near the buffers
   C. in the hoistway
   D. in the machine room

5. The PROPER position of the brushes on a D.C. motor commutator is on, or close to, _____ position.   5.___

   A. the one-half   B. the neutral
   C. the one-quarter   D. 20° off the neutral

6. The MAXIMUM permitted contact arc between the ropes and sheave in a single-wrap traction machine is   6.___

   A. 180°   B. 200°   C. 230°   D. 260°

7. The one of the following that may be considered to be a miniature elevator is the   7.___

   A. safety plank   B. overhead crosshead
   C. cab enclosure   D. floor selector

8. Compared to a D.C. elevator brake of the same capacity and speed, an A.C. elevator brake is _____ the D.C. brake.   8.___

   A. the same size as   B. smoother in operation than
   C. considerably larger than   D. smaller than

9. In elevator installations, the potential switch is USUALLY found in the _____ circuit.

   A. condenser   B. lighting   C. safety   D. rectifier

10. The USUAL location of thrust bearings is on the

    A. reverse phase relays   B. governor safety jaws
    C. worm shaft   D. buffer

11. The purpose of the flux in a soldering operation is to

    A. keep the surfaces of the work clean
    B. spread the heat evenly to all parts of the work
    C. lubricate the gun tip
    D. roughen the surfaces of the work

12. Comb-plates are GENERALLY found on

    A. car overheads   B. selectors
    C. traveling cables   D. escalators

13. Ohm's Law relating current, voltage, and resistance is

    A. $E = IR$ B. $F = WD$ C. $F = MA$ D. $E = \frac{1}{R}$

14. The power lost in a field rheostat in a D.C. circuit is 125 watts with a resistance of 5 ohms.
    The current, in amperes, in the rheostat is

    A. 2.0   B. 2.5   C. 3.5   D. 5.0

15. The one of the following that is the BEST conductor of electricity is

    A. iron   B. aluminum   C. manganin   D. tin

16. The equivalent resistance, in ohms, of a circuit having three resistances, respectively 4, 5, and 10 ohms, in parallel is MOST NEARLY

    A. 4.5   B. 2.4   C. 1.8   D. 1.1

17. On elevators, the emergency release switch is used

    A. to make the door electric contacts or door interlocks inoperative
    B. to override the emergency stop switch
    C. by passengers in an emergency if the emergency stop switch is inoperative
    D. to cut off the power

18. The one of the following devices which automatically levels the elevator car at the landings is the

    A. limit switch   B. brake assembly
    C. governor   D. floor selector

19. Of the following electrical services, the one that is MOST likely to be polyphase is

    A. 2-wire, 120-volt A.C.   B. 2-wire, 115-volt B.C.
    C. 3-wire, 110/208-volt D.C.   D. 4-wire, 120/208-volt A.C.

20. When 0.750 is divided by 0.875, the result is MOST NEARLY

    A. 0.250 B. 0.312 C. 0.624 D. 0.857

21. The circumference of a 6-inch diameter circle is MOST NEARLY _____ feet.

    A. 1.57 B. 2.1 C. 2.31 D. 4.24

22. An 18" piece of cable that weighs 3 lbs. per foot has a total weight of _____ lbs.

    A. 5.5 B. 4.5 C. 3.0 D. 1.5

23. The sum of 0.135, 0.040, 0.812, and 0.961 is

    A. 1.424 B. 1.625 C. 1.843 D. 1.948

24. If an elevator carries a load of 1600 pounds uniformly distributed on a 4 feet by 5 feet floor, the weight per square foot is _____ pounds.

    A. 98 B. 80 C. 65 D. 40

25. If one cubic inch of lead weighs one-quarter of a pound, the weight of a bar of lead 1" high by 2" wide by 8" long is _____ lbs.

    A. 1.8 B. 2.5 C. 3.1 D. 4

26. A *2-to-1* roping of an elevator installation means that the rope speed is _____ the car speed.

    A. twice
    B. one-half
    C. one-quarter of
    D. one-eighth of

27. The one of the following which is NOT an indication of trouble in an electric motor or generator is that the

    A. vent holes are clogged
    B. commutator has flat spots
    C. armature is oil-soaked
    D. mica is undercut

28. Oil levels in buffers should be checked by an employee

    A. when he is available to check them
    B. at regular intervals
    C. daily
    D. only when the elevator is operating

29. Assume that the lift of an elevator is 275 feet from the bottom landing to the top landing. If the car takes 30 seconds to travel this distance in one direction, the car speed, in feet per minute, is

    A. 550 B. 450 C. 350 D. 275

30. In a rheostatic controller, speed control is achieved MAINLY through the use of

   A. capacitors
   B. resistors
   C. condensers
   D. diodes

Questions 31-35.

DIRECTIONS: Questions 31 through 35, inclusive, are to be answered in accordance with the paragraph below.

Panelboards are used to serve branch circuits to lamps, motors, elevators, or other electrical equipment. It is an *insulated* panel on which are mounted, with some degree of symmetry, various switches and circuit breakers. One *terminal* of each switch is wired to the bus bars of the panelboard, the other terminal of the switch is connected to the protective device. The bus bars of the panelboard are *energized* by a feeder which brings service to the panel from another part of the building. Panelboards are classified as flush type, service type, or by the number of wires in the feeder and branch circuit systems. Deadfront panelboards that have insulated *manually* operated main and branch breaker handles should always be used for safety reasons.

31. The word *insulated*, as used in the above paragraph, means MOST NEARLY

   A. non-conducting
   B. instrument
   C. open
   D. wall

32. The word *terminal*, as used in the above paragraph, means MOST NEARLY

   A. wire   B. connector   C. side   D. overload

33. The word *energized*, as used in the above paragraph, means MOST NEARLY

   A. enfolded
   B. enervated
   C. receded
   D. electrified

34. The word *manually*, as used in the above paragraph, means MOST NEARLY

   A. block   B. hand   C. relay   D. power

35. The number of types of classifications of panelboards is

   A. 1   B. 2   C. 3   D. 4

KEY (CORRECT ANSWERS)

1. C	11. A	21. A
2. A	12. D	22. B
3. D	13. A	23. D
4. C	14. D	24. B
5. B	15. B	25. D
6. A	16. C	26. A
7. D	17. A	27. D
8. C	18. D	28. B
9. C	19. D	29. A
10. C	20. D	30. B
	31. A	
	32. B	
	33. D	
	34. C	
	35. B	

ELEVATOR OPERATION

EXAMINATION SECTION
TEST 1

DIRECTIONS: Directly and concisely, using brief answer form, answer the following questions.

1. What is the switch called that is found on the compensating frame which operates if the compensating cables break or the frame passes the usual limit?

2. What is the type of hitch called that has a sheave in the crosshead?

3. What cooling agent is sometimes used in magnetic coil brakes?

4. To what rail are the limit switches of a high-speed elevator usually fastened?

5. What are the parts of the car frame called that is used to reinforce the joining of the cross-head and the upright stiles?

6. What type buffers are used on a high-speed elevator?

7. What is compensated for by the compensating chains?

8. On what type of elevator are rigidly fastened guide shoes used?

9. What part of a tape drive outfit is the pit?

10. What is the type of hydraulic elevator called which is raised and lowered on a vertical piston?

KEY (CORRECT ANSWERS)

1. Compensating (slack cable) (limit) (safety) switch.

2. Two-to-one (double) hitch

3. Oil

4. Main (car) rail
   Counterweight (weight) rail

5. Gussets

6. Oil

7. Cables (weight of cables)

8. Slow speed (heavy duty) (freight)

9. Tension frame (tension shave) (sheave)

10. Plunger (ram)

TEST 2

DIRECTIONS: Directly and concisely, using brief answer form, answer the following questions.

1. What actuates the limit switches mounted on the rail?
2. What is the type of elevator installation called which has the platform set diagonally to the rails?
3. What is the small control panel called that is always used with a motor generator set?
4. What piece of equipment is generally placed on an AC control board to retard the action of the switches?
5. What is the piece of electrical equipment called that is used to prevent phase reversals?
6. What type of buffers are used on a slow-speed car?
7. How many final limit switches are generally used on a high-speed elevator installation?
8. What are the chains or cables called that hang from the lower side of the counterweights?
9. What are the threaded pieces called that are put on the end of the conduit to protect wires from the sharp edges of the conduit?
10. What holds the brake shoes closed?

KEY (CORRECT ANSWERS)

1. Cam
2. Corner post
3. Starting panel
4. Resistance tubes (dash pots)
5. Reverse-phase relay (relay)
6. Spring buffers
   Rubber buffers
7. One
   Two
8. Compensating chains (ropes) (cables)
9. Bushing
10. Springs

TEST 3

DIRECTIONS: Directly and concisely, using brief answer form, answer the following Questions.

1. What is the drum called that is found under the car on which the tiller rope or cable is wound?

2. Name four materials of which gibs are usually made.

3. What piece of equipment is used to drive the selector on a high-drive elevator?

4. What tape goes through the tension frame sheave?

5. What does one call the sheave which is used to lead the hoist cables to the car or counterweight, when the hoist sheave diameter is less than the distance from the center of the car to the center of the counterweight?

6. What is commonly used to connect the floor controller to the elevator machine?

7. What are the channel irons called that form the bottom of the car frame?

8. What is the type of installation called which has the car frame straight across the center.

9. What device other than a magnet coil is used to operate an electric brake?

10. What type safety is used on the modern slow-speed elevators?

KEY (CORRECT ANSWERS)

1. Safety drum

2. Cast iron
   Fibre (composition)
   Wood (lignum vitae)
   Bronze
   Babbitt
   Leather
   Graphite
   Brass

3. Tape
   Chain
   Cable

4. Long tape (selector tape)

5. Deflector (idler) sheave

6. Chain
   Cable

7. Safety plank (safety channels)

8. Side post

9. Torque motor (motor)
   Mechanical

10. Instantaneous safety (roll safety)

TEST 4

DIRECTIONS: Directly and concisely, using brief answer form, answer the following questions.

1. What is the switch called that is found on high speed elevators which helps the limit switches to prevent overrun?

2. What is the panel called that holds the switches and wiring of an elevator?

3. What is the type of traction machine called on which the hoist rope from the car passes over the sheave and goes directly to the counterweight?

4. What is the lining of the guide shoes called which slides on the rail?

5. What percentage of the weight capacity of an elevator is added to the counterbalance besides the weight of the equipment?

6. What is used as a cushion from an AC magnetic brake?

7. What does one call the grooved wheel on the traction machine over which the hoist ropes pass?

8. How many safety plank channels are there in the usual car frame?

2 (#4)

KEY (CORRECT ANSWERS)

1. Slow-down switch (T.M. switch)

2. Controller (control Panel) (board) (box)

3. Single wrap (straight) (direct) (one-to-one) (vee traction)

4. Gibs

5. 33 to 40 percent

6. Oil
   Dash pot

7. Drive sheave (hoisting sheave) (traction sheave) (traction drum)

8. Two

TEST 5

DIRECTIONS: Directly and concisely, using brief answer form, answer the following questions.

1. What is the switch called that is found on the car controller of an AC elevator which cuts off all the power to the motor when open?

2. What is the channel irons called that form the top of the car frame?

3. What does one call the type of traction machine on which the ropes from the car pass-over the drive sheave, then the secondary, then the drive, and finally to the counterweight?

4. How many ports are there on the usual hydraulic elevator valve?

5. What two devices does the safety tiller rope connect?

6. What is the switch called that is operated by a vertical rod inside the hatch door, which must be lifted to open the door?

7. What is the large wheel called over which the hand rope of the hand power elevator passes?

2 (#5)

KEY (CORRECT ANSWERS)

1. Potential (emergency) (safety) (baby)

2. Cross-head (head beam) (cross beam) (hitch beam)

3. Two-to-one (double wrap) traction

4. Two
   Three

5. Safety (drum) and governor
   Safety (drum) and releasing carrier

6. Bar lock (interlock) (car lock)

7. Bull wheel (hand wheel) (shipper) (pull wheel)

———

EXAMINATION SECTION
TEST 1

DIRECTIONS: Answer the following questions directly, briefly, and succinctly.

1. What is used to measure the speed of the car?

2. What is the type of elevator called in which cables merely pass over the sheave?

3. In what do semi- and full-automatic gates move?

4. What is the cable called that passes over the sheave of the governor and fastens to the car safety reel?

5. What is the device called that is found on a winding drum elevator which cuts the power and stops the elevator when the car is stopped in its descent?

6. What is the cable called which counteracts the shifting of the weight of the hoisting cables from the weight of the counter weight of the elevator car?

7. What is the name of the device which prevents the normal opening of the gate or door except when the car is at the landing?

8. What is an M-G set?

KEY (CORRECT ANSWERS)

1. Tachometer
   Stopwatch

2. Traction (vee groove) (single wrap)

3. Guides (tracks) (hangers)

4. Governor cable

5. Slack cable

6. Compensating cable

7. Locking device (interlock) (safety lock) (door trip)

8. Motor generator set

TEST 2

DIRECTIONS: Answer the following questions directly, briefly, and succinctly.

1. What operates the limit switch?
2. In what way do you set a deflection sheave on a double wrap traction elevator?
3. What is the purpose of the motor on hydraulic elevators?
4. What is used on alternating current elevators to protect them?
5. What governs the number and size of the hoist cables on an elevator?
6. What is meant by 5/8 by 6 by 19 cable?
7. What is the sheave called that is used on a traction elevator to give full wrap of the cable on the traction sheave?

2 (#2)

KEY (CORRECT ANSWERS)

1. Cam

2. Set off-center (set off)

3. Operate pump (make pressure)

4. Phase-protective relay (relay)

5. Capacity (load)
   Speed

6. Six strands, 19 wires, 5/8 of an inch in diameter

7. Secondary sheave (idler) (deflector) (compensating)

———

SAFETY EXAMINATION SECTION
TEST 1

DIRECTIONS: Each question or incomplete statement is followed by several suggested answers or completions. Select the one that BEST answers the question or completes the statement. *PRINT THE LETTER OF THE CORRECT ANSWER IN THE SPACE AT THE RIGHT.*

1. Which one of the following is an INCORRECT safety guideline?

   A. All working conditions and equipment should be considered carefully before beginning an operation.
   B. Aisles should be lighted properly.
   C. Personnel should be provided with protective clothing essential to safe performance of a task.
   D. In manual lifting, the worker must keep his knees straight and lift with the arm muscles.

2. Of the following, the supply item with the GREATEST susceptibility to spontaneous heating is

   A. alcohol, ethyl   B. kerosene
   C. candles   D. turpentine

Questions 3-7.

DIRECTIONS: Questions 3 through 7 are descriptions of accidents that occurred in a warehouse. For each accident, choose the letter in front of the safety measure that is MOST likely to prevent a repetition of the accident indicated.

SAFETY MEASURE

   A. Posting warning signs
   B. Redesign of layout or facilities
   C. Repairing, improving or replacing supplies, tools or equipment
   D. Training the staff in safe practices

3. After a new all-glass door was installed at the entrance to the warehouse, one of the employees banged his head into the door causing a large lump on his forehead when he failed to realize that the door was closed.

4. While tieing up a package with manila rope, an employee got several small rope splinters in his right hand and he had to have medical treatment to remove the splinters.

5. An employee discovered a small fire in a wastepaper basket but was unable to prevent it from spreading because all the nearby fire extinguishers were inaccessible due to skids of material being stacked in front of the extinguishers.

6. When a laborer attempted to drop the tailgate of a delivery truck while the truck was being backed into the loading dock, he had his fingers crushed when the truck continued to move while he was working on lowering the tailgate.

7. An employee carrying a carton with both hands tripped over a broom which had been left lying in an aisle by another employee after the latter had swept the aisle.   7.____

8. Safety experts agree that accidents can probably BEST be prevented by   8.____

   A. developing safety consciousness among employees
   B. developing a program which publicizes major accidents
   C. penalizing employees the first time they do not follow safety procedures
   D. giving recognition to employees with accident-free records

9. The accident records of many agencies indicate that most on-the-job injuries are caused by the unsafe acts of their employees.   9.____
   Which one of the following statements pinpoints the MOST probable cause of this safety problem?

   A. Responsibility for preventing on-the-job accidents has not been delegated.
   B. Lack of proper supervision has permitted these unsafe actions to continue.
   C. No consideration has been given to eliminating environmental job hazards.
   D. Penalties for causing on-the-job accidents are not sufficiently severe.

10. Which of the following methods is LEAST essential to the success of an accident prevention program?   10.____

    A. Determining corrective measures by analyzing the causes of accidents and making recommendations to eliminate them
    B. Educating employees as to the importance of safe working conditions and methods
    C. Determining accident causes by seeking out the conditions from which each accident has developed
    D. Holding each supervisor responsible for accidents occurring during the on-the-job performance of his immediate subordinates

11. The effectiveness of a public relations program in a public agency is BEST indicated by the   11.____

    A. amount of mass media publicity favorable to the policies of the agency
    B. morale of those employees who directly serve the patrons of the agency
    C. public's understanding and support of the agency's program and policies
    D. number of complaints received by the agency from patrons using its facilities

12. Buttered bread and coffee dropped on an office floor in a terminal are   12.____

    A. minor hazards which should cause no serious injury
    B. unattractive, but not dangerous
    C. the most dangerous types of office hazards
    D. hazards which should be corrected immediately

13. A laborer was sent upstairs to get a 20-pound sack of rock salt. While going downstairs and reading the printing on the sack, he fell, and the sack of rock salt fell and broke his toe.   13.____
    Which of the following is MOST likely to have been the MOST important cause of the accident?
    The

A. stairs were beginning to become worn
B. laborer was carrying too heavy a sack of rock salt
C. rock salt was in a place that was too inaccessible
D. laborer was not careful about the way he went down the stairs

14. A COMMONLY recommended safe distance between the foot of an extension ladder and the wall against which it is placed is

    A. 3 feet for ladders less than 18 feet in height
    B. between 3 feet and 6 feet for ladders less than 18 feet in length
    C. 1/8 the length of the extended ladder
    D. 1/4 the length of the extended ladder

15. The BEST type of fire extinguisher for electrical fires is the _____ extinguisher.

    A. dry chemical   B. foam
    C. carbon monoxide   D. baking soda-acid

16. A Class A extinguisher should be used for fires in

    A. potassium, magnesium, zinc, sodium
    B. electrical wiring
    C. oil, gasoline
    D. wood, paper, and textiles

17. The one of the following which is NOT a safe practice when lifting heavy objects is:

    A. Keep the back as nearly upright as possible
    B. If the object feels too heavy, keep lifting until you get help
    C. Spread the feet apart
    D. Use the arm and leg muscles

18. In a shop, it would be MOST necessary to provide a fitted cover on the metal container for

    A. old paint brushes   B. oily rags and waste
    C. sand   D. broken glass

19. Safety shoes usually have the unique feature of

    A. extra hard heels and soles to prevent nails from piercing the shoes
    B. special leather to prevent the piercing of the shoes by falling objects
    C. a metal guard over the toes which is built into the shoes
    D. a non-slip tread on the heels and soles

20. Of the following, the MOST important factor contributing to a helper's safety on the job is for him to

    A. work slowly   B. wear gloves
    C. be alert   D. know his job well

21. If it is necessary for you to lift one end of a piece of heavy equipment with a crowbar in order to allow a maintainer to work underneath it, the BEST of the following procedures to follow is to

    A. support the handle of the bar on a box
    B. insert temporary blocks to support the piece
    C. call the supervisor to help you
    D. wear heavy gloves

22. Of the following, the MOST important reason for not letting oily rags accumulate in an open storage bin is that they

    A. may start a fire by spontaneous combustion
    B. will drip oil onto other items in the bin
    C. may cause a foul odor
    D. will make the area messy

23. Of the following, the BEST method to employ in putting out a gasoline fire is to

    A. use a bucket of water
    B. smother it with rags
    C. use a carbon dioxide extinguisher
    D. use a carbon tetrachloride extinguisher

24. When opening an emergency exit door set in the sidewalk, the door should be raised slowly to avoid

    A. a sudden rush of air from the street
    B. making unnecessary noise
    C. damage to the sidewalk
    D. injuring pedestrians

25. The BEST reason to turn off lights when cleaning lampshades on electrical fixtures is to

    A. conserve energy
    B. avoid electrical shock
    C. prevent breakage of lightbulbs
    D. prevent unnecessary eye strain

KEY (CORRECT ANSWERS)

1. D
2. D
3. A
4. D
5. B

6. D
7. D
8. A
9. B
10. D

11. C
12. D
13. D
14. D
15. A

16. D
17. B
18. B
19. C
20. C

21. B
22. A
23. C
24. D
25. B

TEST 2

DIRECTIONS: Each question or incomplete statement is followed by several suggested answers or completions. Select the one that BEST answers the question or completes the statement. *PRINT THE LETTER OF THE CORRECT ANSWER IN THE SPACE AT THE RIGHT.*

1. The MOST important reason for roping off a work area in a terminal is to   1.____
   A. protect the public
   B. protect the repair crew
   C. prevent distraction of the crew by the public
   D. prevent delays to the public

2. Shoes which have a sponge rubber sole should NOT be worn around a work area because such a sole   2.____
   A. will wear quickly
   B. is not waterproof
   C. does not keep the feet warm
   D. is easily punctured by steel objects

3. When repair work is being done on an elevated structure, canvas spreads are suspended under the working area MAINLY to   3.____
   A. reduce noise
   B. discourage crowds
   C. protect the structure
   D. protect pedestrians

4. It is poor practice to hold a piece of wood in the hands or lap when tightening a screw in the wood.   4.____
   This is for the reason that
   A. sufficient leverage cannot be obtained
   B. the screwdriver may bend
   C. the wood will probably split
   D. personal injury is likely to result

5. Steel helmets give workers the MOST protection from   5.____
   A. falling objects
   B. eye injuries
   C. fire
   D. electric shock

6. It is POOR practice to wear goggles   6.____
   A. when chipping stone
   B. when using a grinder
   C. while climbing or descending ladders
   D. when handling molten metal

7. When using a brace and bit to bore a hole completely through a partition, it is MOST important to   7.____

A. lean heavily on the brace and bit
B. maintain a steady turning speed all through the job
C. have the body in a position that will not be easily thrown off balance
D. reverse the direction of the bit at frequent intervals

8. Gloves should be used when handling 8._____

   A. lanterns B. wooden rules
   C. heavy ropes D. all small tools

Questions 9-16.

DIRECTIONS: Questions 9 through 16, inclusive, are based on the ladder safety rules given below. Read these rules fully before answering these items.

LADDER SAFETY RULES

When a ladder is placed on a slightly uneven supporting surface, use a flat piece of board or small wedge to even up the ladder feet. To secure the proper angle for resting a ladder, it should be placed so that the distance from the base of the ladder to the supporting wall is 1/4 the length of the ladder. To avoid overloading a ladder, only one person should work on a ladder at a time. Do not place a ladder in front of a door. When the top rung of a ladder rests against a pole, the ladder should be lashed securely. Clear loose stones or debris from the ground around the base of a ladder before climbing. While on a ladder, do not attempt to lean so that any part of the body, except arms or hands, extends more than 12 inches beyond the side rail. Always face the ladder when ascending or descending. When carrying ladders through buildings, watch for ceiling globes and lighting fixtures. Avoid the use of rolling ladders as scaffold supports.

9. A small wedge is used to 9._____

   A. even up the feet of a ladder resting on an uneven surface
   B. lock the wheels of a roller ladder
   C. secure the proper resting angle for a ladder
   D. secure a ladder against a pole

10. An 8 foot ladder resting against a wall should be so inclined that the distance between the base of the ladder and the wall is _____ feet. 10._____

    A. 2 B. 5 C. 7 D. 9

11. A ladder should be lashed securely when 11._____

    A. it is placed in front of a door
    B. loose stones are on the ground near the base of the ladder
    C. the top rung rests against a pole
    D. two people are working from the same ladder

12. Rolling ladders 12._____

    A. should be used for scaffold supports
    B. should not be used for scaffold supports
    C. are useful on uneven ground
    D. should be used against a pole

13. When carrying a ladder through a building, it is necessary to

    A. have two men to carry it
    B. carry the ladder vertically
    C. watch for ceiling globes
    D. face the ladder while carrying it

14. It is POOR practice to

    A. lash a ladder securely at any time
    B. clear debris from the base of a ladder before climbing
    C. even up the feet of a ladder resting on slightly uneven ground
    D. place a ladder in front of a door

15. A person on a ladder should NOT extend his head beyond the side rail by more than _____ inches.

    A. 12   B. 9   C. 7   D. 5

16. The MOST important reason for permitting only one person to work on a ladder at a time is that

    A. both could not face the ladder at one time
    B. the ladder will be overloaded
    C. time would be lost going up and down the ladder
    D. they would obstruct each other

17. Many portable electric power tools, such as electric drills, have a third conductor in the power lead which is used to connect the case of the tool to a grounded part of the electric outlet.
    The reason for this extra conductor is to

    A. have a spare wire in case one power wire should break
    B. strengthen the power lead so it cannot easily be damaged
    C. prevent the user of the tool from being shocked
    D. enable the tool to be used for long periods of time without overheating

18. Protective goggles should NOT be worn when

    A. standing on a ladder drilling a steel beam
    B. descending a ladder after completing a job
    C. chipping concrete near a third rail
    D. sharpening a cold chisel on a grinding stone

19. When the foot of an extension ladder, placed against a high wall, rests on a sidewalk or another such similar surface, it is advisable to tie a rope between the bottom rung of the ladder and a point on the wall opposite this rung.
    This is done to prevent

    A. people from walking under the ladder
    B. another worker from removing the ladder
    C. the ladder from vibrating when ascending or descending
    D. the foot of the ladder from slipping

20. In construction work, practically all accidents can be blamed on the   20.____
    A. failure of an individual to give close attention to the job assigned to him
    B. use of improper tools
    C. lack of cooperation among the men in a gang
    D. fact that an incompetent man was placed in a key position

21. If it is necessary for you to do some work with your hands under a piece of heavy equip-   21.____
    ment while a fellow worker lifts up and holds one end of it by means of a pinch bar, one
    important precaution you should take is to

    A. wear gloves
    B. watch the bar to be ready if it slips
    C. insert a temporary block to support the piece
    D. work as fast as possible

22. Employees of the transit system whose work requires them to enter upon the tracks in   22.____
    the subway are cautioned not to wear loose fitting clothing.
    The MOST important reason for this caution is that loose fitting clothing may

    A. interfere when men are using heavy tools
    B. catch on some projection of a passing train
    C. tear more easily than snug fitting clothing
    D. give insufficient protection against subway dust

23. The MOST important reason for insisting on neatness in maintenance quarters is that it   23.____
    A. keeps the men busy in slack periods
    B. prevents tools from becoming rusty
    C. makes a good impression on visitors and officials
    D. decreases the chances of accidents to employees

24. Maintenance workers whose duties require them to do certain types of work generally   24.____
    work in pairs.
    The LEAST likely of the following possible reasons for this practice is that

    A. some of the work requires two men
    B. the men can help each other in case of accident
    C. there is too much equipment for one man to carry
    D. it protects against vandalism

25. A foreman reprimands a helper for actions in violation of the rules and regulations.   25.____
    The BEST reaction of the helper in this situation is to

    A. tell the foreman that he was careful and that he did not take any chances
    B. explain that he took this action to save time
    C. keep quiet and accept the criticism
    D. demand that the foreman show him the rule he violated

KEY (CORRECT ANSWERS)

1. A
2. D
3. D
4. D
5. A

6. C
7. C
8. C
9. A
10. A

11. C
12. B
13. C
14. D
15. A

16. B
17. C
18. B
19. D
20. A

21. C
22. B
23. D
24. D
25. C

EXAMINATION SECTION
TEST 1

DIRECTIONS: Each question or incomplete statement is followed by several suggested answers or completions. Select the one that BEST answers the question or completes the statement. *PRINT THE LETTER OF THE CORRECT ANSWER IN THE SPACE AT THE RIGHT.*

1. The one of the following which is a unit of inductance is the   1._____

   A. millihenry   B. microfarad   C. kilohm   D. weber

2. Of the following, the BEST conductor of electricity is   2._____

   A. aluminum   B. copper   C. silver   D. iron

3. A voltage of 1000 microvolts is the SAME as   3._____

   A. 1,000 volts   B. 0.100 volts
   C. 0.010 volts   D. 0.001 volts

4. The function of a rectifier is SIMILAR to that of a(n)   4._____

   A. inverter   B. relay   C. commutator   D. transformer

5. A 9-ohm resistor rated at 225 watts is used in a 120-volt circuit. In order not to exceed the rating of the resistor, the MAXIMUM current, in amperes, which can flow through the circuit is   5._____

   A. 2   B. 3   C. 4   D. 5

6. The number of circular mils in a conductor 0.036 inch in diameter is   6._____

   A. 6   B. 36   C. 72   D. 1296

7. The color of the label on most commercially available 250-volt cartridge fuses of 15-amperes or less capacity is   7._____

   A. green   B. blue   C. red   D. yellow

8. Assume that a two-microfarad capacitor is connected in parallel with a three-microfarad capacitor. The resulting capacity, in microfarads, is   8._____

   A. 2/3   B. 6/5   C. 3/2   D. 5

9. The speed of the rotating magnetic field in a 12-pole 60-cycle stator is   9._____

   A. 1800 rpm   B. 1200 rpm   C. 720 rpm   D. D 600 rpm

10. The transformer connection *generally* used to convert from three-phase to two-phase by means of two transformers is the   10._____

    A. Scott or T   B. V or Open delta
    C. Wye-Delta   D. Delta-Wye

11. The conductance, in mhos, of a circuit whose resistance is one ohm is

    A. 1/10   B. 1   C. 10   D. 100

12. Assume that a 220-volt, 25 cycle, A.C., e.m.f. is impressed across a circuit consisting of a 25-ohm resistor in series with a 30-microfarad capacitor. The current in this circuit, in amperes, is, *most nearly,*

    A. 0.5   B. 0.8   C. 1.0   D. 1.5

13. An ammeter has a full scale deflection with a current of 0.010 amperes and an internal resistance of 20 ohms.
    In order for the ammeter to have a full scale deflection with a current of 10 amperes and not damage its movement, a shunt should be used having a value of

    A. 10 ohms   B. 0.2 ohms   C. 0.02 ohms   D. 0.01 ohms

14. American Wire Gage (A.W.G.) wire size numbers are set so that the resistance of wire per 1,000 ft. doubles with every increase of

    A. one gage number
    B. two gage numbers
    C. three gage numbers
    D. four gage numbers

15. In an ideal transformer for transforming or "stepping down" the voltage from 1200 volts to 120 volts, the turns ratio is

    A. 10:1   B. 12:1   C. 1:12   D. 1:10

16. When a lead-acid battery is fully charged, the negative plate consists of lead

    A. peroxide   B. sponge   C. sulfate   D. dioxide

17. Improving the commutation of a D.C. generator is MOST often done by using

    A. a rheostat in series with the equalizer
    B. an equalizer alone
    C. a compensator
    D. interpoles

18. In a wave-wound armature, the MINIMUM number of commutator brushes necessary is

    A. two times the number of poles
    B. two, regardless of the number of poles
    C. one-half times the number of poles
    D. four, regardless of the number of poles

19. A three-phase induction motor runs hot with all stator coils at the same temperature. The trouble which would cause this condition is that

    A. the motor is running single phase
    B. the motor is overloaded
    C. a part of the motor windings is inoperative
    D. the rotor bars are loose

20. Where constant speed is required, the one of the following motors that should be used is a 20._____

    A. wound-rotor motor B. series motor
    C. compound motor D. shunt motor

21. To reverse the direction of rotation of a 3-phase induction motor, 21._____

    A. the field connections should be reversed
    B. the armature connections should be reversed
    C. any two line leads should be interchanged
    D. the brushes should be shifted in the direction opposite to that of the armature rotation

22. The speed of a wound-rotor motor may be increased by 22._____

    A. *decreasing* the resistance in the secondary circuit
    B. *increasing* the resistance in the secondary circuit
    C. *decreasing* the shunt field current
    D. *increasing* the series field resistance

23. The one of the following methods which can be used to increase the slip of the rotor in a single-phase shaded-pole motor, is the 23._____

    A. reversal of the leads of the field winding
    B. addition of capacitors in series with the starting winding
    C. reduction of the impressed voltage
    D. addition of more capacitors in parallel with the starting winding

24. The direction of rotation of a single-phase A.C. repulsion motor may be reversed by 24._____

    A. interchanging the two line leads to the motor
    B. interchanging the leads to the main winding
    C. interchanging the leads to the starting winding
    D. moving the brushes to the other side of the neutral position

25. The torque developed by a D.C. series motor is 25._____

    A. *inversely proportional* to the square of the armature current
    B. *proportional* to the square of the armature current
    C. *proportional* to the armature current
    D. *inversely proportional* to the armature current

KEY (CORRECT ANSWERS)

1. A
2. C
3. D
4. C
5. D

6. D
7. B
8. D
9. D
10. A

11. B
12. C
13. C
14. C
15. A

16. B
17. D
18. B
19. B
20. D

21. C
22. A
23. C
24. D
25. B

———

TEST 2

DIRECTIONS: Each question or incomplete statement is followed by several suggested answers or completions. Select the one that BEST answers the question or completes the statement. *PRINT THE LETTER OF THE CORRECT ANSWER IN THE SPACE AT THE RIGHT.*

1. The one of the following which is MOST commonly used to clean a commutator is   1.____
    A. emery cloth
    B. graphite
    C. a smooth file
    D. fine-grit sandpaper

2. The type of motor which requires BOTH A.C. and D.C. for operation is the   2.____
    A. compound motor
    B. universal motor
    C. synchronous motor
    D. squirrel-cage motor

3. Compensators are used for starting large   3.____
    A. shunt motors
    B. series motors
    C. induction motors
    D. compound motors

4. The device MOST frequently used to correct low lagging power factor is a(n)   4.____
    A. solenoid
    B. induction regulator
    C. induction motor
    D. synchronous motor

5. Of the following motors, the one with the HIGHEST starting torque is the   5.____
    A. compound motor
    B. series motor
    C. shunt motor
    D. split phase motor

6. The approximate efficiency of a 60-cycle, 6-pole induction motor running at 1050 rpm and having a synchronous speed of 1200 rpm, is   6.____
    A. 67.0%   B. 78.5%   C. 87.5%   D. 90.0%

7. The MAIN contributing factor to motor starter failures *usually* is   7.____
    A. overloading
    B. dirt
    C. bearing trouble
    D. friction

8. The neutral or grounded conductors in branch circuit wiring must be identified by being colored   8.____
    A. black or brown
    B. black with white traces
    C. white with black traces
    D. white or natural gray

9. The SMALLEST radius for the inner edge of any field bend in a 1-inch rigid or flexible conduit when type R wire is being used, is   9.____
    A. 3 inches   B. 5 inches   C. 6 inches   D. 10 inches

10. Thermal cutouts used to protect a motor against overloads may have a current rating of not more than   10.____
    A. the starting current of the motor
    B. 125% of the full-load current rating of the motor

C. the full-load current of the motor
D. the current-carrying capacity of the branch circuit conductors

11. The MAXIMUM size of EMT permitted is

   A. 4 inches   B. 3 1/2 inches   C. 3 inches   D. 2 inches

12. The type of equipment which is defined as a set of conductors originating at the load side of the service equipment and supplying the main and/or one or more secondary distribution centers, is a

   A. sub-feeder   B. feeder   C. main   D. service cable

13. The SMALLEST size rigid conduit that may be used in wiring is

   A. 3/8 inch   B. 1/2 inch   C. 3/4 inch   D. 1 inch

14. An enclosed 600-volt cartridge fuse must be of the knife-blade contact type if its ampere rating is

   A. 20   B. 40   C. 60   D. 80

15. An insulated ground for fixed equipment should be color coded

   A. yellow
   B. green or green with a yellow stripe
   C. blue or blue with a yellow stripe
   D. black

16. Of the following, the meter that CANNOT be used to measure A.C. voltage is the

   A. electrodynamic voltmeter
   B. electrostatic voltmeter
   C. D'Arsonval voltmeter
   D. thermocouple voltmeter

17. Of the following, an instrument frequently used to measure high insulation resistance is a(n)

   A. tong-test ammeter
   B. megger
   C. ohmmeter
   D. electrostatic voltmeter

18. When using a voltmeter in testing an electric circuit, the voltmeter should be placed in

   A. *series* with the circuit
   B. *parallel* with the circuit
   C. *parallel* or in *series* with a current transformer, depending on the current
   D. *series* with the active element

19. The MINIMUM number of wattmeters necessary to measure the power in the load of a balanced 3-phase, 4-wire system, is

   A. 1   B. 2   C. 3   D. 4

20. An instrument that measures electrical energy is the

   A. current transformer
   B. watthour meter
   C. dynamometer
   D. wattmeter

21. The one of the following items which can be used to *properly* test an armature for a shorted coil is a

    A. neon light
    B. megger
    C. growler
    D. pair of series test lamps

22. The instrument that measures loads at the load terminals, averaged over specified time periods, is the

    A. coulomb meter
    B. wattmeter
    C. demand meter
    D. var-hour meter

23. A multiplier is usually used to increase the range of

    A. voltmeter
    B. watthour meter
    C. wheatstont bridge
    D. Nernst bridge

24. The instrument used to indicate the phase relation between the voltage and the current of an A.C. circuit is called a

    A. power factor meter
    B. synchroscope
    C. phase indicator
    D. var-hour meter

25. Except where busways are entering or leaving service or distribution equipment, the bottom of the busway enclosure for all horizontal busway runs should be kept at a MINIMUM height above the floor of

    A. 4 feet   B. 6 feet   C. 8 feet   D. 10 feet

KEY (CORRECT ANSWERS)

1. D		11. D	
2. C		12. B	
3. C		13. B	
4. D		14. D	
5. B		15. B	
6. C		16. C	
7. B		17. B	
8. D		18. B	
9. C		19. A	
10. B		20. B	

21. C
22. C
23. A
24. A
25. C

TEST 3

DIRECTIONS: Each question or incomplete statement is followed by several suggested answers or completions. Select the one that BEST answers the question or completes the statement. *PRINT THE LETTER OF THE CORRECT ANSWER IN THE SPACE AT THE RIGHT.*

1. The lubricant *commonly* used to make it **easier** to pull braid-covered cable into a duct is 1.___

    A. soapstone
    B. soft soap
    C. heavy grease
    D. light oil

2. Of the following, the conductor insulation which may be used in wet locations is type 2.___

    A. RH B. RHH C. RHW D. RUH

3. Assume that at a certain distribution point you notice that among several of the conductors entering the same raceway, some have a half-inch band of yellow tape, while the others do not. The conductors with the yellow tape are all 3.___

    A. grounded B. ungrounded C. A.C. D. D.C.

4. Conductors of the same length, same circular mil area and type of insulation, may be run in multiple 4.___

    A. under no circumstances
    B. if each conductor is #4 or larger
    C. if each conductor is #2 or larger
    D. if each conductor is #1/0 or larger

5. In order to keep conduits parallel where several parallel runs of conduit of varying size are installed through 45 or 90 degree bends, it is BEST to 5.___

    A. bend conduit on the job
    B. use standard factory-made elbows
    C. use flexible connectors to adjust runs
    D. bend conduit at the factory

6. The BEST way to join two lengths of conduit which cannot be turned is to 6.___

    A. use a split adapter
    B. use a conduit union ("Erickson")
    C. cut running threads on one end of one length of the conduit
    D. cut running threads on the ends of both lengths of conduit

7. When an electrical splice is wrapped with both rubber tape and friction tape, the MAIN purpose of the friction tape is to 7.___

    A. protect the rubber tape
    B. provide additional insulation
    C. build up the insulation to the required thickness
    D. increase the strength of the splice

8. Assume that explosion-proof wiring is required in a certain area. Conduits entering an enclosure in this area which contains apparatus that may produce arcs, sparks or high temperature, should be provided with

   A. a cable terminator
   B. an approved sealing compound
   C. couplings with three full threads engaged
   D. insulated bushings

   8._____

9. If installed in dry locations, wireways may be used for circuits of not more than

   A. 208 volts   B. 440 volts   C. 600 volts   D. 1100 volts

   9._____

10. An interior wiring circuit has two conductors, one white and one black. Assume that it becomes necessary to add a third conductor as a switch leg. The color of the THIRD conductor should be

    A. blue   B. red   C. green   D. natural gray

    10._____

11. Keyless lampholders rated at 1500 watts have bases which are classed as

    A. Intermediate   B. Medium   C. Mogul   D. Admedium

    11._____

12. In precast cellular concrete floor raceways, the LARGEST conductor which may be installed, except by special permission, is

    A. No. 2   B. No. 0   C. No. 00   D. No. 000

    12._____

13. The conductor insulation which may be used for fixture wire is type

    A. TF   B. TW   C. TA   D. RW

    13._____

14. Multiple fuses are permissible

    A. under no circumstances
    B. for conductors longer than 1/0
    C. for conductors larger than 2/0
    D. for conductors larger than 4/0

    14._____

15. In loosening a nut, a socket wrench with a ratchet handle should be used in preference to other types of wrenches if

    A. the nut is out of reach
    B. the turning space for the handle is limited
    C. the nut is worn
    D. greater leverage is required

    15._____

16. Solders used for electrical connections are alloys of

    A. tin and lead   B. tin and zinc
    C. lead and zinc   D. tin and copper

    16._____

17. Another name for a pipe wrench is a

    A. crescent wrench   B. torque wrench
    C. Stillson wrench   D. monkey wrench

    17._____

18. The tool used to cut raceways is a hacksaw with fine teeth, *commonly* called a

    A. crosscut saw B. keyhole saw
    C. rip saw D. tube saw

19. Lead expansion anchors are MOST commonly used to fasten conduit to a

    A. wooden partition wall B. plaster wall
    C. solid concrete wall D. gypsum wall

20. The use of "running" threads when coupling two sections of conduit is

    A. always good practice
    B. good practice only when installing enameled conduit
    C. good practice only if it is impossible to turn one of the conduits
    D. always poor practice

21. A quick-break knifeswitch is often used rather than a standard knifeswitch of the same rating because the quick-break knife switch

    A. resists burning due to arcing at the contact points
    B. is easier to install and align
    C. is simpler in construction
    D. can carry a higher current without over-heating

22. The tip of a soldering iron is made of copper because

    A. copper is a very good conductor of heat
    B. solder will not stick to other metals
    C. it is the cheapest metal available
    D. the melting point of copper is very high

23. Good practice requires that cartridge fuses be removed from their clips by using a fuse puller rather than the bare hand. The reason for using the fuse puller is that the

    A. bare hand may be burned or otherwise injured
    B. fuse is less likely to break
    C. fuse clips may be damaged when pulled
    D. use of the bare hands slows down removal of fuse and causes arcing

24. The frame of a portable electric tool should be grounded in order to

    A. reduce leakage from the winding
    B. prevent short circuits
    C. reduce the danger of overheating
    D. prevent the frame from becoming alive to ground

25. The LEAST desirable device for measuring the dimensions of an electrical equipment cabinet containing live equipment, is a

    A. wooden yardstick
    B. six-foot folding wooden ruler
    C. twelve-inch plastic ruler
    D. six-foot steel tape

KEY (CORRECT ANSWERS)

1. A
2. C
3. D
4. D
5. A

6. B
7. A
8. B
9. C
10. B

11. C
12. B
13. A
14. A
15. B

16. A
17. C
18. D
19. C
20. D

21. A
22. A
23. A
24. D
25. D

TEST 4

DIRECTIONS: Each question or incomplete statement is followed by several suggested answers or completions. Select the one that BEST answers the question or completes the statement. *PRINT THE LETTER OF THE CORRECT ANSWER IN THE SPACE AT THE RIGHT.*

1. If three equal resistance coils are connected in parallel, the resistance of this combination is equal to

    A. one-third the resistance of one coil
    B. the resistance of one coil
    C. three times the resistance of one coil
    D. nine times the resistance of one coil

    1.___

2. The voltage to neutral of a 3-phase, 4-wire system, is 120 volts. The line-to-line voltage is

    A. 208 volts   B. 220 volts   C. 230 volts   D. 240 volts

    2.___

3. Three 6-ohm resistances are connected in Y across a 3-phase circuit. If a current of 10 amperes flows through each resistance, the TOTAL power in watts drawn by this load is, *most nearly,*

    A. 600   B. 1200   C. 1800   D. 2400

    3.___

4. A conduit in an outlet box should be provided with a locknut

    A. on the outside and bushing on the inside
    B. and bushing on the inside
    C. on the inside and bushing on the outside
    D. and bushing on the inside

    4.___

5. If the current in a single-phase, 120-volt circuit is 10 amperes and a wattmeter in this circuit reads 1080 watts, the power factor is, *most nearly,*

    A. 1.11   B. .9   C. .8   D. .7

    5.___

6. It is poor practice to use a file without a handle because the

    A. file may be dropped and damaged
    B. unprotected end may mar the surface being filed
    C. user may be injured
    D. file marks will be too deep

    6.___

7. If a 60-cycle, 4-pole squirrel-cage, induction motor has a slip of 5%, its speed is, *most nearly,*

    A. 1800 rpm   B. 1795 rpm   C. 1750 rpm   D. 1710 rpm

    7.___

8. The PROPER way to reverse the direction of rotation of a 3-phase wound rotor induction motor is to

    A. reverse two leads between the rotor and the control resistances
    B. shift the brushes
    C. reverse two supply leads
    D. open one rotor lead

    8.___

9. Sulphuric acid should **always** be poured into the water when new electrolyte for a lead-acid battery is prepared. The reason for this precaution is to

   A. *avoid* splattering of the acid
   B. *avoid* explosive fumes
   C. *prevent* corrosion of the mixing vessel
   D. *prevent* clotting of the acid

10. The direction of rotation of a d.c. shunt motor can be reversed PROPERLY by

    A. reversing the two supply leads
    B. shifting the position of the brushes
    C. reversing the connections to both the armature and the field
    D. reversing the connections to the field

Questions 11-13.

DIRECTIONS: Questions 11 to 13, inclusive, refer to this excerpt from the electrical code on the subject of grounding electrodes.

Each buried plate electrode shall present not less than two square feet of surface to the exterior soil. Electrodes of plate copper shall be at least .06 inch in thickness. Electrodes of iron or steel plate shall be at least one-quarter inch in thickness. Electrodes of iron or steel pipe shall be galvanized and not less than three-quarter inch in internal diameter. Electrodes of rods of steel or iron shall be at least three-quarter inch minimum cross-section dimension... Driven electrodes of pipes or rods... shall be driven to a depth of at least eight feet regardless of the size or number of electrodes used... Each electrode used shall be separated at least six feet from any other electrode including those used for signal circuits, radio, lightning rods or any other purposes.

11. According to the above paragraph, all grounding electrodes MUST be

    A. of plate copper
    B. of iron pipe
    C. at least three-quarter inch minimum cross-section dimension
    D. separated at least six feet from any other electrode

12. According to the above paragraph, the one of the following electrodes which meets the code requirements is a(n)

    A. copper plate 12" X 18" X .06"
    B. steel plate 14" X 24" X .06"
    C. copper plate 12" X 24" X .06"
    D. iron plate 12" X 18" X .25'"

13. According to the above paragraph, the one of the following electrodes which meets the code requirements is

    A. plain iron pipe, 1" in internal diameter, driven to a depth of 10 feet
    B. galvanized iron pipe, 3/4" in internal diameter, driven to a depth of 6 feet
    C. plain steel pipe, 1" in internal diameter, driven to a depth of 7 feet
    D. galvanized steel pipe, 3/4" in internal diameter, driven to a depth of 9 feet

14. With reference to armature windings, lap windings are often called

   A. ring windings
   B. multiple windings
   C. series windings
   D. toroidal windings

15. The question refers to the diagram below.

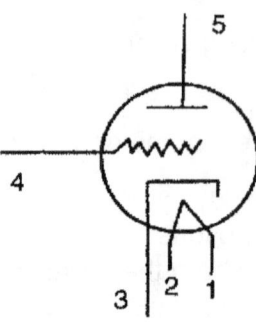

   The element numbered 4 is usually called the

   A. plate   B. grid   C. filament   D. cathode

16. To properly mount an outlet box on a concrete ceiling, it is BEST to use

   A. expansion screw anchors
   B. wooden plugs
   C. wood screws
   D. masonry nails

17. A d.c. motor takes 30 amps, at 110 volts and has an efficiency of 90%. The horsepower available at the pulley is, *approximately,*

   A. 5   B. 4   C. 3   D. 2

18. If the armature current drawn by a series motor doubles, the torque

   A. remains the same
   B. doubles
   C. becomes 4 times as great
   D. becomes 8 times as great

19. The full load current, in amperes, of a 110-volt, 10 H.P., d.c. motor having an efficiency of 80% is, *approximately,*

   A. 62   B. 85   C. 99   D. 133

Questions 20-21.

   DIRECTIONS: Questions 21 and 22 are to be answered in accordance with the diagram below.

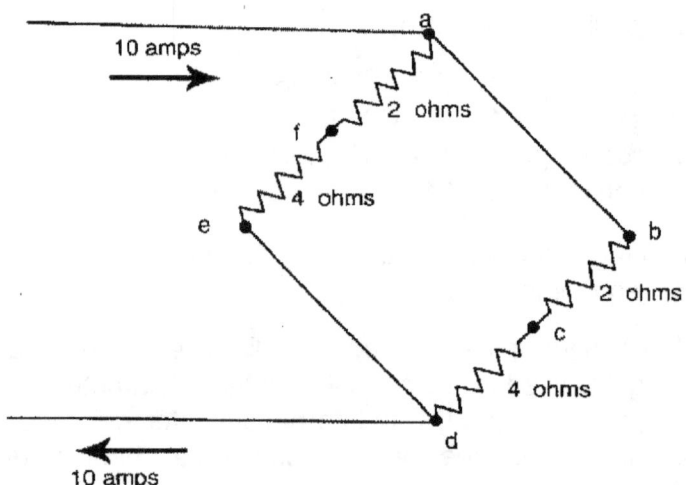

20. With reference to the above diagram, the voltage difference between points c and f is, most nearly,   20._____

   A. 40 volts   B. 20 volts   C. 10 volts   D. 0 volts

21. With reference to the above diagram, the current flowing through the resistance c d is, most nearly,   21._____

   A. 10 amperes   B. 5 amperes   C. 4 amperes   D. 2 amperes

Questions 22-25.

DIRECTIONS: Questions 22 through 25, inclusive, refer to the diagram below

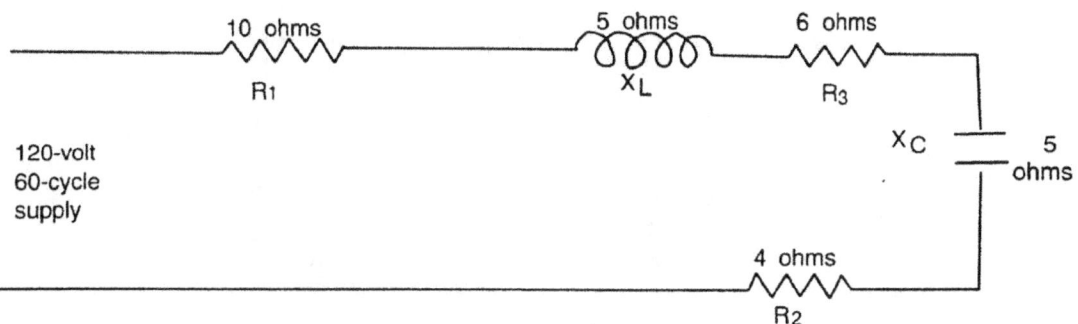

22. The value of the impedance in ohms of the above circuit is, most nearly,   22._____

   A. 60   B. 30   C. 25   D. 20

23. The current, in amperes, flowing in the above circuit is, most nearly,   23._____

   A. 2   B. 3   C. 6   D. 8

24. The potential drop, in volts, across R_3 is, most nearly,   24._____

   A. 12   B. 18   C. 36   D. 48

25. The power, in watts, consumed in the above circuit is, most nearly,   25._____

   A. 1080   B. 720   C. 180   D. 80

KEY (CORRECT ANSWERS)

1. A
2. A
3. C
4. A
5. B

6. C
7. D
8. C
9. A
10. D

11. D
12. C
13. D
14. B
15. B

16. A
17. B
18. C
19. B
20. D

21. B
22. D
23. C
24. C
25. B

TEST 5

DIRECTIONS: Each question or incomplete statement is followed by several suggested answers or completions. Select the one that BEST answers the question or completes the statement. *PRINT THE LETTER OF THE CORRECT ANSWER IN THE SPACE AT THE RIGHT.*

1. The heat dissipation, W, in a resistor having a resistance of R ohms connected across a supply of E volts, is proportional to E^2/R.
   If R is reduced to one-half of its former value and E is doubled, the heat dissipation in this resistor is *now*

   A. 8W B. 2W C. 4W D. 1/2W

   1._____

2. Solder commonly used for electrical work is composed, *most likely,* of

   A. lead and tin B. antimony and zinc
   C. lead and zinc D. silver and antimony

   2._____

3. A condenser having a capacitance of 3 microfarads is connected in parallel with a condenser having a capacitance of 2 microfarads. The combination is equal to a single condenser having a capacitance, in microfarads, of, *most nearly,*

   A. 5/6 B. 6/5 C. 5 D. 6

   3._____

4. Of the following units, the one which is a unit of inductance is the

   A. maxwell B. henry C. weber D. oersted

   4._____

5. The tool *commonly* used for bending conduit of small sizes is called a

   A. mandrel B. bending wrench C. hickey D. kinker

   5._____

6. If a cartridge fuse clip makes contact with its fuse with much less than normal spring tension, the result would MOST likely be that the

   A. fuse will immediately burn out
   B. voltage at the supply will be high
   C. voltage at the load will be high
   D. clips will become warm

   6._____

7. Of the following units, the one which is a unit of work or energy is the

   A. joule B. faraday C. coulomb D. farad

   7._____

8. The one of the following substances which is the BEST conductor of electricity is

   A. iron B. aluminum C. tin D. copper

   8._____

9. The formula for the resistance of one branch of a wye which is equivalent to a given delta is $R_a = \dfrac{A}{A+B+C}$.
   If $A = B = C = 3$, the value of R_a is, *most nearly,*

   A. 1 B. 3 C. 6 D. 9

   9._____

77

10. When a splice is soldered, flux is used to

    A. act as a binder
    B. lubricate the surfaces
    C. keep the surfaces clean
    D. prevent rapid loss of heat

11. A 2000 ft. cable which has an insulation resistance of 180 megohms is cut in half. The insulation resistance of one of the 1000-ft. lengths will be, *most nearly,*

    A. 720 megohms
    B. 360 megohms
    C. 90 megohms
    D. 45 megohms

12. The area in circular mils of a piece of bare copper wire whose diameter is 0.1" is, *most nearly,*

    A. 780
    B. 1,000
    C. 7,800
    D. 10,000

13. The resistance of a piece of copper wire is

    A. *directly* proportional to its diameter
    B. *inversely* proportional to its length
    C. *directly* proportional to the square of its diameter
    D. *inversely* proportional to its cross-sectional area

14. If an incandescent lamp is operated at a voltage which is higher than its rated voltage, the

    A. lumens output will be less than rated value
    B. current drawn will be less than rated value
    C. power consumed will be less than rated value
    D. life of the lamp will be less than rated value

15. The one of the following that is BEST suited to fight electrical fires is a

    A. CO_2 fire extinguisher
    B. soda-acid fire extinguisher
    C. foam fire extinguisher
    D. very fine spray of water

16. In order to get MAXIMUM power output from a battery, the external resistance should *equal*

    A. zero
    B. one-half of the internal resistance of the battery
    C. the internal resistance of the battery
    D. twice the internal resistance of the battery

17. A voltmeter with a scale range of 0-5 has a resistance of 500 ohms. The resistance, in ohms, of a multiplier for this instrument which will give it a range of 0 to 150 volts is, *most nearly,*

    A. 750
    B. 2,500
    C. 14,500
    D. 75,000

18. The one of the following items which is *commonly* used to increase the range of a d.c. ammeter is a

    A. ceramicon
    B. shunt
    C. current transformer
    D. bridging transformer

19. Continuity of the conductors in an electrical circuit can be determined *conveniently* in the field by means of a(n)

    A. bell and battery set
    B. Maxwell bridge
    C. Preece test
    D. ammeter

Questions 20-25.

DIRECTIONS: Questions 20 to 25, inclusive, refer to the symbols of the A.S.A. which are listed below.

20. A push button is designated by the symbol numbered

    A. 4 B. 7 C. 13 D. 15

21. A fire alarm station is designated by the symbol numbered

    A. 3 B. 6 C. 9 D. 10

22. A duplex convenience outlet is designated by the symbol numbered

    A. 1 B. 2 C. 5 D. 17

23. A battery is designated by the symbol numbered

    A. 10 B. 13 C. 16 D. 18

24. A double pole switch is designated by the symbol numbered

    A. 1 B. 2 C. 8 D. 15

25. The designation for a 3-wire circuit is numbered

    A. 3 B. 5 C. 11 D. 14

KEY (CORRECT ANSWERS)

1.	A	11.	B
2.	A	12.	D
3.	C	13.	D
4.	B	14.	D
5.	C	15.	A
6.	D	16.	C
7.	A	17.	C
8.	D	18.	B
9.	A	19.	A
10.	C	20.	B

21. C
22. B
23. C
24. C
25. D

TEST 6

DIRECTIONS: Each question or incomplete statement is followed by several suggested answers or completions. Select the one that BEST answers the question or completes the statement. *PRINT THE LETTER OF THE CORRECT ANSWER IN THE SPACE AT THE RIGHT.*

1. A good magnetic material is   1._____

   A. aluminum   B. iron   C. brass   D. carbon

2. A thermo-couple is a device for   2._____

   A. changing frequency   B. changing d.c. to a.c.
   C. measuring temperature   D. heat insulation

3. It is desired to operate a 6-volt lamp from a 120-volt a.c source. This can be done with   3._____
   the LEAST waste of power by using a

   A. series resistor   B. rectifier
   C. step-down transformer   D. rheostat

4. Rosin is a material *generally* used   4._____

   A. in batteries   B. as a dielectric
   C. as a soldering flux   D. for high voltage insulation

5. A milliampere is   5._____

   A. 1000 amperes   B. 100 amperes
   C. .01 ampere   D. .001 ampere

6. A compound motor usually has   6._____

   A. only a shunt field   B. only a series field
   C. no brushes   D. both a shunt and a series field

7. To connect a d.c. voltmeter to measure a voltage higher than the scale maximum, use a   7._____

   A. series resistance   B. shunt
   C. current transformer   D. voltage transformer

8. The voltage applied to the terminals of a storage battery to charge it CANNOT be   8._____

   A. rectified a.c.   B. straight d.c.
   C. pulsating d.c.   D. ordinary a.c.

9. When two unequal condensers are connected in parallel, the   9._____

   A. total capacity is decreased
   B. total capacity is increased
   C. result will be a short-circuit
   D. smaller one will break down

10. A megohm is   10._____

    A. 10 ohms   B. 100 ohms
    C. 1000 ohms   D. 1,000,000 ohms

11. Of the following, the poorest conductor of electricity is

   A. brass   B. lead   C. an acid solution   D. slate

12. A flashlight battery, a condenser, and a flashlight bulb are connected in series with each other. If the bulb burns brightly and steadily, then the condenser is

   A. open-circuited
   B. short-circuited
   C. good
   D. fully charged

13. A kilowatt of power will be taken from a 500-volt d.c. supply by a load of

   A. 200 amperes   B. 20 amperes   C. 2 amperes   D. 0.2 ampere

14. A commutator is used on a shunt generator in order to

   A. step-up voltage
   B. step-up current
   C. change a.c. to d.c.
   D. control generator speed

15. The number of cells connected in series in a 6-volt storage battery of the lead-acid type is

   A. 2   B. 3   C. 4   D. 5

16. A 15-ampere circuit breaker as compared to a 15-ampere plug fuse

   A. can be reclosed
   B. is cheaper
   C. is safer
   D. is smaller

17. Lengths of rigid conduit are connected together to make up a long run by means of

   A. couplings   B. bushings   C. hickeys   D. lock nuts

18. BX is *commonly* used to indicate

   A. rigid conduit without wires
   B. flexible conduit without wires
   C. insulated wires covered with flexible steel armor
   D. insulated wires covered with a non-metallic covering

19. Good practice is to cut BX with a

   A. hacksaw
   B. 3-wheel pipe cutter
   C. bolt cutter
   D. heavy pliers

20. Silver is used for relay contacts in order to

   A. improve conductivity
   B. avoid burning
   C. reduce costs
   D. avoid arcing

21. Rigid conduit is fastened on the inside of the junction box by means of

   A. a bushing
   B. a locknut
   C. a coupling
   D. set-screw clamps

22. Of the following, the material which can BEST withstand high temperature is   22.____

    A. plastic   B. enamel   C. fiber   D. mica

23. A lead-acid type of storage battery exposed to freezing weather is *most likely* to freeze   23.____
    when the

    A. battery is fully charged   B. battery is complete discharged
    C. water level is low   D. cap vent holes are plugged

24. An important reason making it poor practice to put telephone wires in the same conduit   24.____
    with a.c. power lines is that

    A. power will be lost from the a.c. line
    B. the conduit will overheat
    C. the wires may be confused
    D. the telephone circuits will be noisy

25. In a loaded power circuit, it is MOST dangerous to   25.____

    A. *close* the circuit with a circuit breaker
    B. *close* the circuit with a knife switch
    C. *open* the circuit with a knife switch
    D. *open* the circuit with a circuit breaker

KEY (CORRECT ANSWERS)

1. B	11. D
2. C	12. B
3. C	13. C
4. C	14. C
5. D	15. B
6. D	16. A
7. A	17. A
8. D	18. C
9. B	19. A
10. D	20. A

21. A
22. D
23. B
24. D
25. C

TEST 7

DIRECTIONS: Each question or incomplete statement is followed by several suggested answers or completions. Select the one that BEST answers the question or completes the statement. *PRINT THE LETTER OF THE CORRECT ANSWER IN THE SPACE AT THE RIGHT.*

1. When fastening electrical equipment to a hollow tile wall, it is good practice to use 1.____
    A. toggle bolts   B. wood screws
    C. nails   D. ordinary bolts and nuts

2. Of the following, the MOST important reason for keeping the oil in a transformer tank moisture-free is to prevent 2.____
    A. rusting   B. voltage breakdown
    C. freezing of the oil   D. overheating

3. A voltmeter is generally connected to a high potential a.c. bus through a(n) 3.____
    A. auto-transformer   B. potential transformer
    C. resistor   D. relay

4. The HIGHEST total voltage which can be measured by using two identical 0-300 volt range d.c. meters connected in series would be 4.____
    A. 150 volts   B. 300 volts   C. 450 volts   D. 600 volts

5. Transistors are MAINLY employed in electrical circuits to take the place of 5.____
    A. resistors   B. condensers   C. inductances   D. vacuum tubes

6. The MINIMUM number of 10-ohm,1-ampere resistors which would be required to give an equivalent resistance of 10 ohms capable of carrying a 2-ampere load is 6.____
    A. 2   B. 3   C. 4   D. 5

7. To increase the current measuring range of an ammeter, the equipment *commonly* employed is a 7.____
    A. series resistor   B. shunt
    C. short-circuiting switch   D. choke

8. If a 10-watt lamp and a 100-watt lamp, each rated at 120 volts, are connected in series to a 240-volt source, then the voltage *across* the 10-watt lamp will be 8.____
    A. zero   B. about 24 volts
    C. exactly 120 volts   D. much more than 120 volts

9. If the load on the secondary of a small 10 to 1 step-up transformer is 100 watts, then the power being taken by the *primary* from the power line 9.____
    A. is less than 100 watts
    B. is exactly 100 watts
    C. is more than 100 watts
    D. may be more or less than 100 watts depending on the nature of the load

10. A 1/2-ohm, a 2-ohm, a 5-ohm, and a 25-ohm resistor are connected in series to a power source. The resistor which will consume the MOST power is the

    A. 1/2-ohm   B. 2-ohm   C. 5-ohm   D. 25-ohm

11. With respect to 60-cycle current, it is CORRECT to say that one cycle takes

    A. 1/60th of a second   B. 1/30th of a second
    C. 1/60th of a minute   D. 1/30th of a minute

12. A rheostat is used in the field circuit of a shunt generator to control the

    A. generator speed   B. load
    C. generator voltage   D. power factor

13. If a condenser has a safe working voltage of 250 volts d.c. then it would be *most likely* to break down if used across a

    A. 250-volt, 60-cycle a.c. line   B. 250-volt d.c. line
    C. 240-volt battery   D. 120-volt, 25-cycle a.c. line

14. Transformer cores are generally made up of thin steel lamin-ations. The MAIN purpose of this is to

    A. reduce the transformer losses
    B. reduce the initial cost of the transformer
    C. increase the weight of the transformer
    D. prevent voltage breakdown in the transformer

15. The MAIN reason for using copper tips in soldering irons is that copper

    A. is a good heat conductor   B. is a good electrical conductor
    C. has a low melting point   D. is very soft

16. Five identical electric fans, each rated at 120-volts d.c., are connected in series with each other on a 600-volt circuit. If one fan develops an open circuit, then

    A. the remaining fans will run, but at slow speed
    B. the remaining fans will run, but at above normal speed
    C. only one fan will run
    D. none of the fans will run

17. The pressure of a carbon brush on a commutator is measured with a

    A. spring balance   B. feeler gage   C. taper gage   D. wire gage

18. A non-inductive carbon resistor consumes 50 watts when connected across a 120-volt d.c. source. If it is connected across a 120-volt a.c. source, the power consumed by the resistor will be nearest to

    A. 30 watts   B. 40 watts   C. 50 watts   D. 60 watts

19. Of the following, the combination of lamps which will draw the MOST current from a standard 120-volt branch circuit is one with

    A. three 150-watt lamps   B. one 300-watt lamp
    C. four 100-watt lamps   D. six 50-watt lamps

20. A condenser is sometimes connected across contact points which make and break a d.c. circuit in order to reduce arcing of the points. The condenser produces this effect because it 20.____

    A. discharges when the contacts open
    B. charges when the contacts open
    C. charges while the contacts are closed
    D. discharges when the contacts are closed

KEY (CORRECT ANSWERS)

1.	A	11.	A
2.	B	12.	C
3.	B	13.	A
4.	D	14.	A
5.	D	15.	A
6.	C	16.	D
7.	B	17.	A
8.	D	18.	C
9.	C	19.	A
10.	D	20.	B

EXAMINATION SECTION
TEST 1

DIRECTIONS: Each question or incomplete statement is followed by several suggested answers or completions. Select the one that *BEST* answers the question or completes the statement. *PRINT THE LETTER OF THE CORRECT ANSWER IN THE SPACE AT THE RIGHT.*

1. Of the following, the best conductor of electricity is 1.____

   A. aluminum
   B. carbon
   C. copper
   D. water

2. Good practice requires that the end of a piece of conduit be reamed after it has been cut to length. The purpose of the reaming is to 2.____

   A. prevent insulation damage when pulling in the wires
   B. finish the conduit accurately to length
   C. make the threading easier
   D. remove loose rust

3. According to the national electrical code, a run of conduit between two outlet boxes should not contain more than four quarter-bends. The most likely reason for this limitation is that more bends will 3.____

   A. result in cracking the conduit
   B. make the pulling of the wire too difficult
   C. increase the wire length unnecessarily
   D. not be possible in one standard length of conduit

4. Asbestos is commonly used as the covering of electric wires in locations where there is likely to be high 4.____

   A. voltage
   B. temperature
   C. humidity
   D. current

5. The *LEAST* likely result of a severe electric shock is 5.____

   A. unconsciousness
   B. a burn
   C. stoppage of breathing
   D. bleeding

6. Electrical helpers on the subway system are instructed in the use of fire extinguishers. The probable reason for including helpers in this instruction is that the helper 6.____

   A. cannot do the more important work
   B. may be the cause of a fire because of his inexperience
   C. may be alone when a fire starts
   D. will become interested in fire prevention

7. Transit employees are cautioned, as a safety measure, not to use water to extinguish fires involving electrical equipment. One logical reason for this caution is that the water 7.____

   A. will cause harmful steam
   B. will not extinguish a fire started by electricity

C. may transmit electrical shock to the user
D. may crack hot insulators

8. When the level of the liquid in a lead-acid storage cell is low, a maintainer should normally add

   A. alkaline solution
   B. diluted alcohol
   C. battery acid
   D. distilled water

9. Portable lamp cord is likely to have

   A. steel armor
   B. stranded wires
   C. paper insulation
   D. number 8 wire

10. The one of the following terms which could NOT correctly be used in describing a knife switch is

    A. quick-break
    B. single throw
    C. four-pole
    D. toggle

11. A transit employee is required to make a written report of any unusual occurrence promptly. The best reason for requiring such promptness is that

    A. the report will tend to be more accurate as to facts
    B. the employee will not be as likely to forget to make the report
    C. there is always a tendency to do a better job under pressure
    D. the report may be too long if made at an employee's convenience

12. With respect to common electric light bulbs, it is correct to state that the

    A. circuit voltage has no effect on the life of the bulb
    B. filament is made of carbon
    C. base has a left hand thread
    D. lower wattage bulb has the higher resistance

13. It is generally known that the voltage of the third rail on the New York City Transit System is about

    A. 3000   B. 1000   C. 600   D. 120

14. The resistance of a 1000-foot coil of a certain size copper wire is 10 ohms. If 300 feet is cut off, the resistance of the remainder of the coil is

    A. 7 ohms   B. 3 ohms   C. 0.7 ohms   D. 0.3 ohm

15. The term "15-ampere" is commonly used in Identifying

    A. an insulator
    B. a fuse
    C. a conduit
    D. an outlet box

16. When you are first appointed as a helper and are assigned to work with a maintainer, he will probably expect you to

    A. do very little work
    B. make plenty of mistakes
    C. pay close attention to instructions
    D. do all of the unpleasant work

17. When connecting the two lead wires of a test instrument to a live d.c. circuit, the best procedure is to first make the negative or ground connection and then the positive connection. The reason for this procedure is that

    A. electricity flows from positive to negative
    B. there is less danger of accidental shock
    C. the reverse procedure may blow the fuse
    D. less arcing will occur when the connection is made

17._____

Questions 18 - 24.

Questions 18 through 24 in Column I are materials each of which is commonly used for one of the electrical equipment parts listed in Column II. For each material in Column I, select the most closely associated part from Column II. *PRINT,* in the correspondingly numbered item space at the right, the letter given beside your selected part.

COLUMN I (materials)	COLUMN II (electrical equipment parts)	
18. steel	A. acid storage battery plates	18._____
19. lead	B. transformer cores	19._____
20. mica	C. d.c. motor brushes	20._____
21. porcelain	D. insulating tape	21._____
22. rubber	E. cartridge fuse cases	22._____
23. copper	H. commutator insulation	23._____
24. carbon	J. strain insulators	24._____
	K. knife-switch blades	

25. To make a good soldered connection between two stranded wires, it is *LEAST* important to

    A. twist the wires together before soldering
    B. use enough heat to make the solder flow freely
    C. clean the wires carefully
    D. apply solder to each strand before twisting the two wires together

25._____

26. When a step-up transformer is used, it increases the

    A. voltage   B. current
    C. power   D. frequency

26._____

27. Lock nuts are frequently used in making electrical connections on terminal boards. The purpose of such lock nuts is to

    A. make tighter connections with less effort
    B. make it difficult to tamper with the connections
    C. avoid stripping the threads
    D. keep the connections from loosening through vibration

27._____

28. If a fellow worker has stopped breathing after an electric shock, the best first-aid treatment is

    A. massage his chest
    B. a hot drink
    C. an application of cold compresses
    D. artificial respiration

28._____

29. According to a recent safety report, an outstanding cause of accidents to workers is the improper use of tools. The most helpful conclusion that you can draw from this statement is that

    A. most tools are dangerous to use
    B. most tools are difficult to use properly
    C. many accidents from tools occur because of poor working habits
    D. many accidents from tools are unavoidable

29._____

Questions 30 - 39.

Questions 30 through 39 refer to the use of tools shown on the next page. Read the item, and for the operation given, select the proper tool to be used from those shown. *PRINT,* in the correspondingly numbered item space at the right, the letter given below your selected tool.

30. Tightening a coupling on a piece of one-inch conduit.   30._____

31. Drilling a hole in a concrete wall for a lead anchor.   31._____

32. Bending a piece of 3/4-inch conduit.   32._____

33. Tightening a wire on the terminal of a standard electric light socket.   33._____

34. Cutting off a piece of 4/0 insulated copper cable.   34._____

35. Measuring the length of a proposed long conduit run.   35._____

36. Tightening a small nut on a terminal board.   36._____

37. Removing the burrs from the end of a piece of conduit after cutting.   37._____

38. Removing the flat rubber gasket stuck to the cover of a watertight pull box.   38._____

39. Knocking the head off a bolt that is rusted in place.   39._____

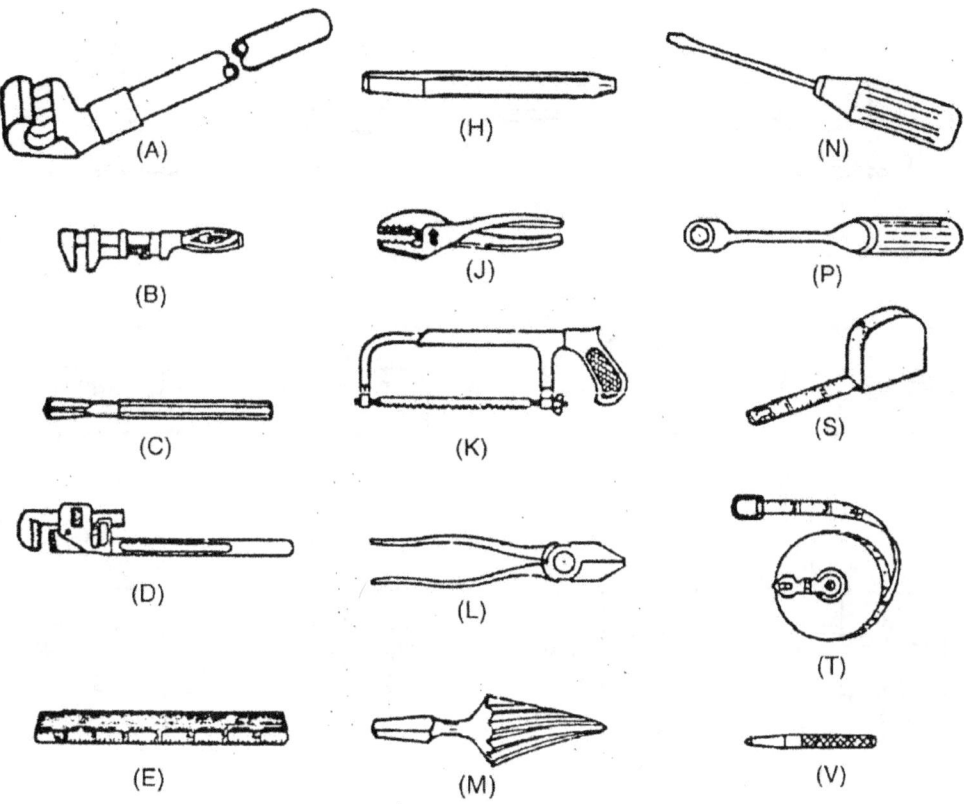

Questions 40 - 45.

Questions 40 through 45 show common electrical jobs. Each item shows four methods (A), (B), (C), and (D) of doing the particular job. Only *ONE* of the four methods is entirely *CORRECT* in accordance with good practice. For each item, examine the four sketches and select the sketch showing the correct method. *PRINT*, in the correspondingly numbered item space at the right, the letter given below your selected sketch.

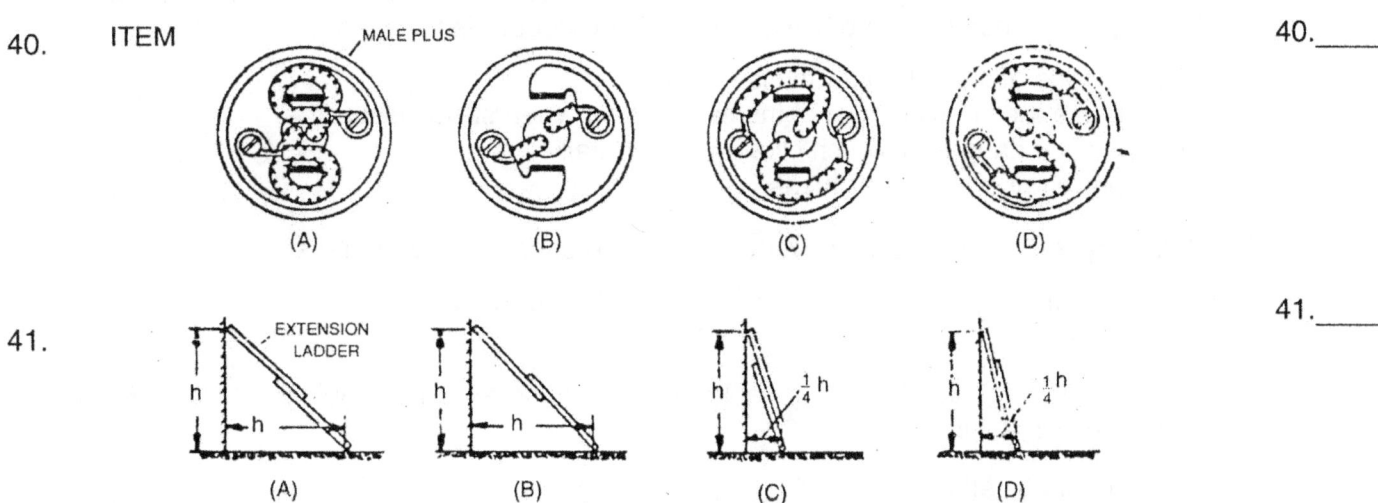

40. _____

41. _____

42.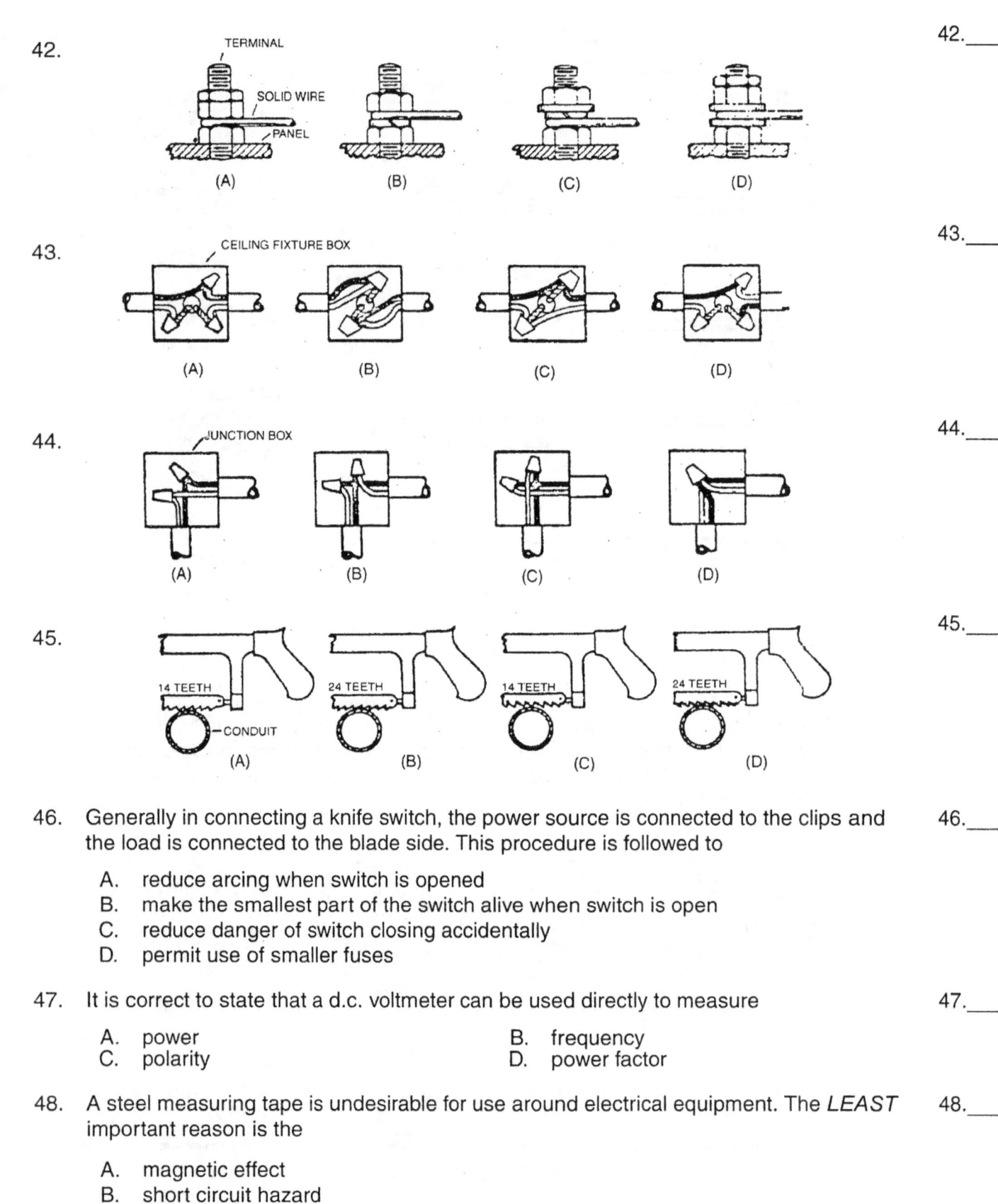

43.

44.

45.

46. Generally in connecting a knife switch, the power source is connected to the clips and the load is connected to the blade side. This procedure is followed to

   A. reduce arcing when switch is opened
   B. make the smallest part of the switch alive when switch is open
   C. reduce danger of switch closing accidentally
   D. permit use of smaller fuses

47. It is correct to state that a d.c. voltmeter can be used directly to measure

   A. power   B. frequency
   C. polarity   D. power factor

48. A steel measuring tape is undesirable for use around electrical equipment. The LEAST important reason is the

   A. magnetic effect
   B. short circuit hazard
   C. shock hazard
   D. danger of entanglement in rotating machines

49. If you had to telephone for an ambulance because of an accident, the most important information for you to give the person who answered the telephone would be the

    A. exact time of the accident
    B. place where the ambulance is needed
    C. cause of the accident
    D. names and addresses of those injured

50. The book of rules and regulations states that employees must give notice in person or by telephone of their intention to be absent from work at least two hours before they are scheduled to report for duty. The most logical reason for having this rule is that

    A. it allows time to check the employee's excuse
    B. it has a nuisance value in limiting absences
    C. the employee's time record can be corrected in advance
    D. a substitute can be provided

KEY (CORRECT ANSWERS)

1. C	11. A	21. J	31. C	41. C
2. A	12. D	22. D	32. A	42. D
3. B	13. C	23. K	33. N	43. C
4. B	14. A	24. C	34. K	44. A
5. D	15. B	25. D	35. T	45. B
6. C	16. C	26. A	36. P	46. B
7. C	17. B	27. D	37. M	47. C
8. D	18. B	28. D	38. N	48. A
9. B	19. A	29. C	39. H	49. B
10. D	20. H	30. D	40. D	50. D

TEST 2

DIRECTIONS: Each question or incomplete statement is followed by several suggested answers or completions. Select the one that BEST answers the question or completes the statement. *PRINT THE LETTER OF THE CORRECT ANSWER IN THE SPACE AT THE RIGHT.*

Questions 1-7.

Questions 1 through 7 are based on the fuse information given below. Read this information carefully before answering these items.

FUSE INFORMATION

Badly bent or distorted fuse clips cannot be permitted. Sometimes the distortion or bending is so slight that it escapes notice, yet it may be the cause for fuse failures through the heat that is developed by the poor contact. Occasionally the proper spring tension of the fuse clips has been destroyed by overheating from loose wire connections to the clips. Proper contact surfaces must be maintained to avoid faulty operation of the fuse. Maintenance men should remove oxides that form on the copper and brass contacts, check the clip pressure, and make sure that contact surfaces are not deformed or bent in any way. When removing oxides, use a well-worn file and remove only the oxide film. Do not use sandpaper or emery cloth as hard particles may come off and become embedded in the contact surfaces. All wire connections to the fuse holders should be carefully inspected to see that they are tight.

1. Fuse failure because of poor clip contact or loose connections is due to the resulting 1.____

   A. excessive voltage
   B. increased current
   C. lowered resistance
   D. heating effect

2. Oxides should be removed from fuse contacts by using 2.____

   A. a dull file
   B. emery cloth
   C. fine sandpaper
   D. a sharp file

3. One result of loose wire connections at the terminal of a fuse clip is stated in the above paragraph to be 3.____

   A. loss of tension in the wire
   B. welding of the fuse to the clip
   C. distortion of the clip
   D. loss of tension of the clip

4. Simple reasoning will show that the oxide film referred to is undesirable chiefly because it 4.____

   A. looks dull
   B. makes removal of the fuse difficult
   C. weakens the clips
   D. introduces undesirable resistance

5. Fuse clips that are bent very slightly 5.____

   A. should be replaced with new clips
   B. should be carefully filed

94

C. may result in blowing of the fuse
D. may prevent the fuse from blowing

6. Prom the fuse information paragraph it would be reasonable to conclude that fuse clips   6.____

   A. are difficult to maintain
   B. must be given proper maintenance
   C. require more attention than other electrical equipment
   D. are unreliable

7. A safe practical way of checking the tightness of the wire connection to the fuse clips of a   7.____
   live 120-volt lighting circuit is to

   A. feel the connection with your hand to see if it is warm
   B. try tightening with an insulated screwdriver or socket wrench
   C. see if the circuit works
   D. measure the resistance with an ohmmeter

Questions 8 - 11.

Questions 8 through 11 in Column I below are wiring diagrams of the various positions of a 4-position switch each of which is shown in simplified form by one of the circuit diagrams in Column II below. For each wiring diagram in Column I, select the simplified circuit diagram from Column II. *PRINT,* in the correspondingly numbered item space at the right, the letter given beside your selected circuit diagram.

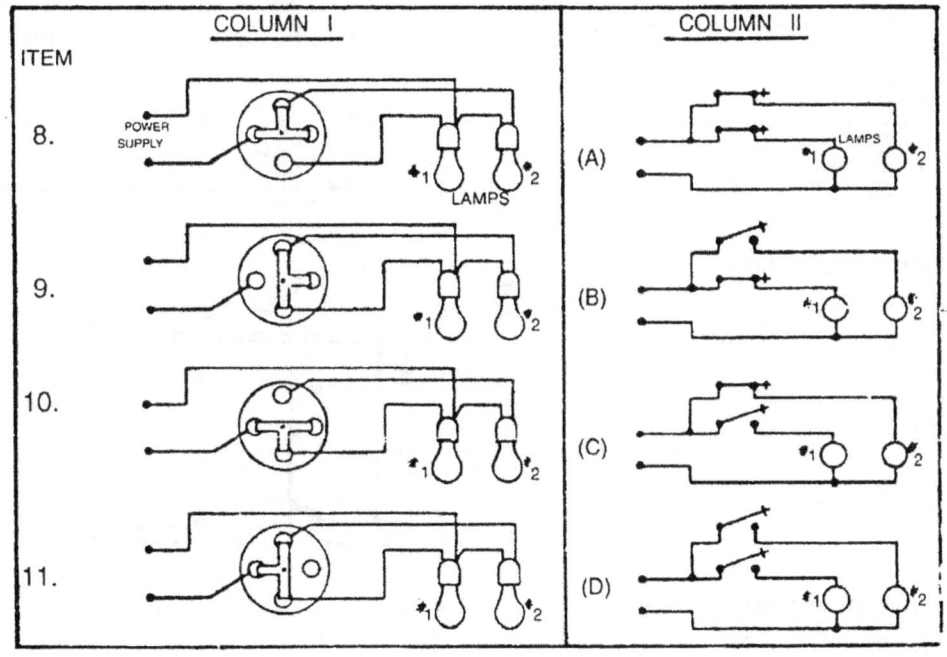

Questions 12 - 16.
Questions 12 through 16 in Column I are supply voltages each of which can be obtained by one of the dry cell battery connections in Column II. For each voltage in Column I, select the proper battery connections from Column II. PRINT, in the correspondingly numbered item space at the right, the letter given below your selected battery connections.

COLUMN I
(supply voltages)

COLUMN II
(battery connections)
Note: Each dry cell - 1 1/2 volts.

12. 1 1/2 volts

13. 3 volts

14. 4 1/2 volts

15. 6 volts

16. 9 volts

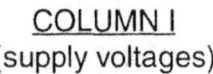
(A)

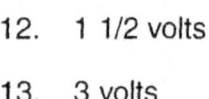
(B)

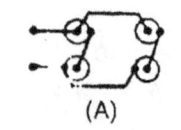
(C)

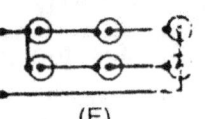
(E)

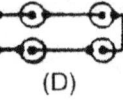
(D)

12.___
13.___
14.___
15.___
16.___

17. The sketch shows the ends of 4 bare copper wires full size with diameters as given. From left to right, the #14 wire is

A. first
C. third
B. second
D. fourth

17.___

18. Regardless of the battery voltage, it is clear by inspection that the highest current is in the
   A. 1-ohm resistor
   B. 2-ohm resistor
   C. 3-ohm resistor
   D. 4-ohm resistor

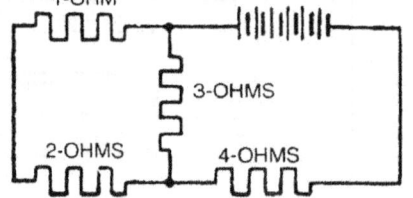

18.___

19. On the transformer, the dimension marked X is
   A. 29 1/2"
   B. 27"
   C. 25 1/2"
   D. 21 1/2"

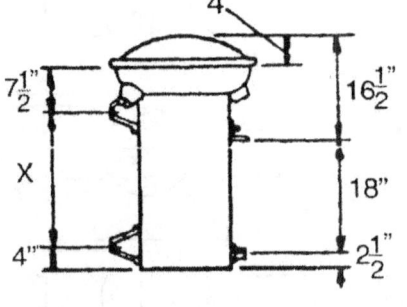

19.___

20. The reading of the voltmeter in the accompanying sketch will be
   A. 0 volts
   B. 80 volts
   C. 120 volts
   D. 240 volts

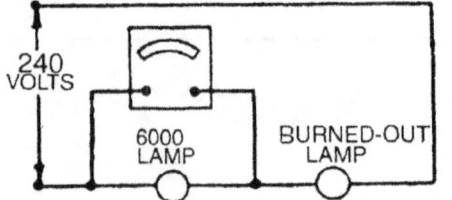

20.___

21. The total resistance in ohms between points X and Y is
    A. 0.30
    B. 3.33
    C. 15
    D. 30

    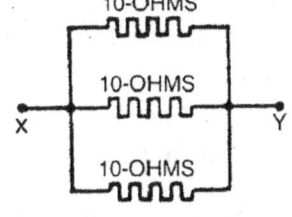

    21.____

22. The resistance box shown can be set to any value of resistance up to 10,000 ohms. The reading shown is
    A. 3875
    B. 5738
    C. 5783
    D. 8375

    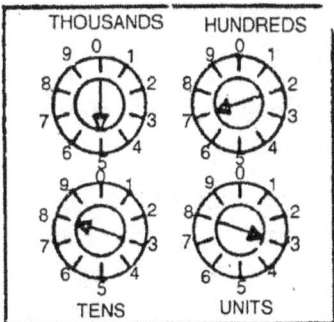

    22.____

23. If switch "S" is closed, the ammeter readings will change as follows
    A. both will increase
    B. #1 only will increase
    C. both will decrease
    D. #2 only will increase

    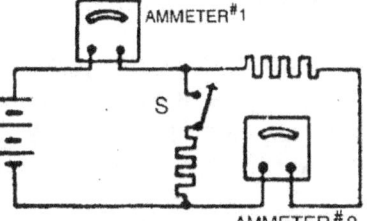

    23.____

24. The reading on the meter scale shown is
    A. 56
    B. 52
    C. 51
    D. 46

    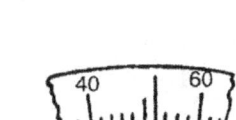

    24.____

25. The voltage "X" is
    A. 25
    B. 20
    C. 15
    D. 5

    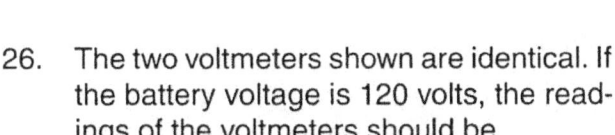

    25.____

26. The two voltmeters shown are identical. If the battery voltage is 120 volts, the readings of the voltmeters should be
    A. 120 volts on each meter
    B. 60 volts on each meter
    C. 120 volts on meter #1 and 240 volts on #2
    D. 120 volts on meter #1 and zero on #2

    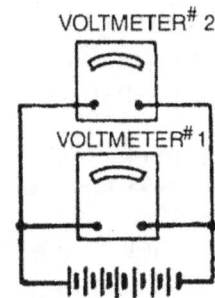

    26.____

27. Standard tables are available showing the safe carrying capacity of copper wire of various sizes to avoid damage to insulation from overheating. The allowable current given is dependent on the

   A. voltage
   B. length of wire
   C. type of current (a.c. or d.c.)
   D. room temperature

28. A test lamp using an ordinary lamp bulb can NOT be used to test for

   A. live circuits
   B. overloads
   C. grounds
   D. blown fuses

29. Consumers are warned never to use a coin instead of a spare fuse. The reason for this warning is that

   A. the protection of the fuse will be lost
   B. additional resistance will be placed in the circuit
   C. mutilating coins is illegal
   D. shock hazard is increased

30. Maintainers are cautioned not to smoke or permit open flames in a storage battery room. The probable reason for this caution is that

   A. the liquid in the battery is inflammable
   B. the terminals are greased
   C. batteries give off an explosive gas when charging
   D. fire extinguishers are not permitted in battery rooms

31. Safety on the job is best assured by

   A. working very slowly
   B. following every rule
   C. never working alone
   D. keeping alert

32. If you think you have found an improvement for a piece of standard equipment used in your department, the most sensible course for you to follow would be to

   A. examine it critically before making the suggestion
   B. try to sell it to an outside company
   C. forget it because you will probably get no credit
   D. get a definite promise of reward from the management before disclosing it

33. As a helper you will be assigned to a maintainer under the general supervision of a foreman. If you do not understand the operation of some special equipment on which you work, your best procedure would be to

   A. ask the foreman since he is more competent
   B. study up at home
   C. forget the matter until you are more experienced
   D. ask the maintainer first

34. A proper use for an electrician's knife is to

   A. cut small wires
   B. mark the point where a conduit is to be cut
   C. pry out a small cartridge fuse
   D. skin wires

35. Specifying a machine screw as an 8-32 screw fixes the

    A. material
    B. type of head
    C. diameter
    D. length

36. It is good practice to connect the ground wire for a building electrical system to a

    A. gas pipe
    B. cold water pipe
    C. vent pipe
    D. steam pipe

37. When removing the insulation from a wire before making a splice, care should be taken to avoid nicking the wire mainly because the

    A. current carrying capacity will be reduced
    B. resistance will be increased
    C. wire is more likely to break
    D. tinning on the wire will be injured

38. The term "ampere-hours" is associated with

    A. motors
    B. transformers
    C. electromagnets
    D. storage batteries

39. It is generally true that most accidents to employees result because of

    A. too heavy work schedules
    B. poor light
    C. carelessness
    D. complicated equipment

40. It is NOT correct to state that

    A. current flowing through a resistor causes heat
    B. rectifiers change d.c. to a.c.
    C. the conduit of an electrical system should be grounded
    D. ammeters are used in series in the circuit

41. When a d.c. voltage of 1.50 volts is applied to a certain coil, the current in the coil is 6 amperes. The resistance of this coil is

    A. 1/4 ohm   B. 4 ohms   C. 7 1/2 ohms   D. 9 ohms

Questions 42 - 50.

Questions 42 through 50 in Column I (on the next page) are electrical symbols, each of which represents one of the electrical devices shown in Column II (on the next page). For each symbol shown in Column I, select the corresponding device from Column II. PRINT, in the correspondingly numbered item space at the right, the letter given below your selected device.

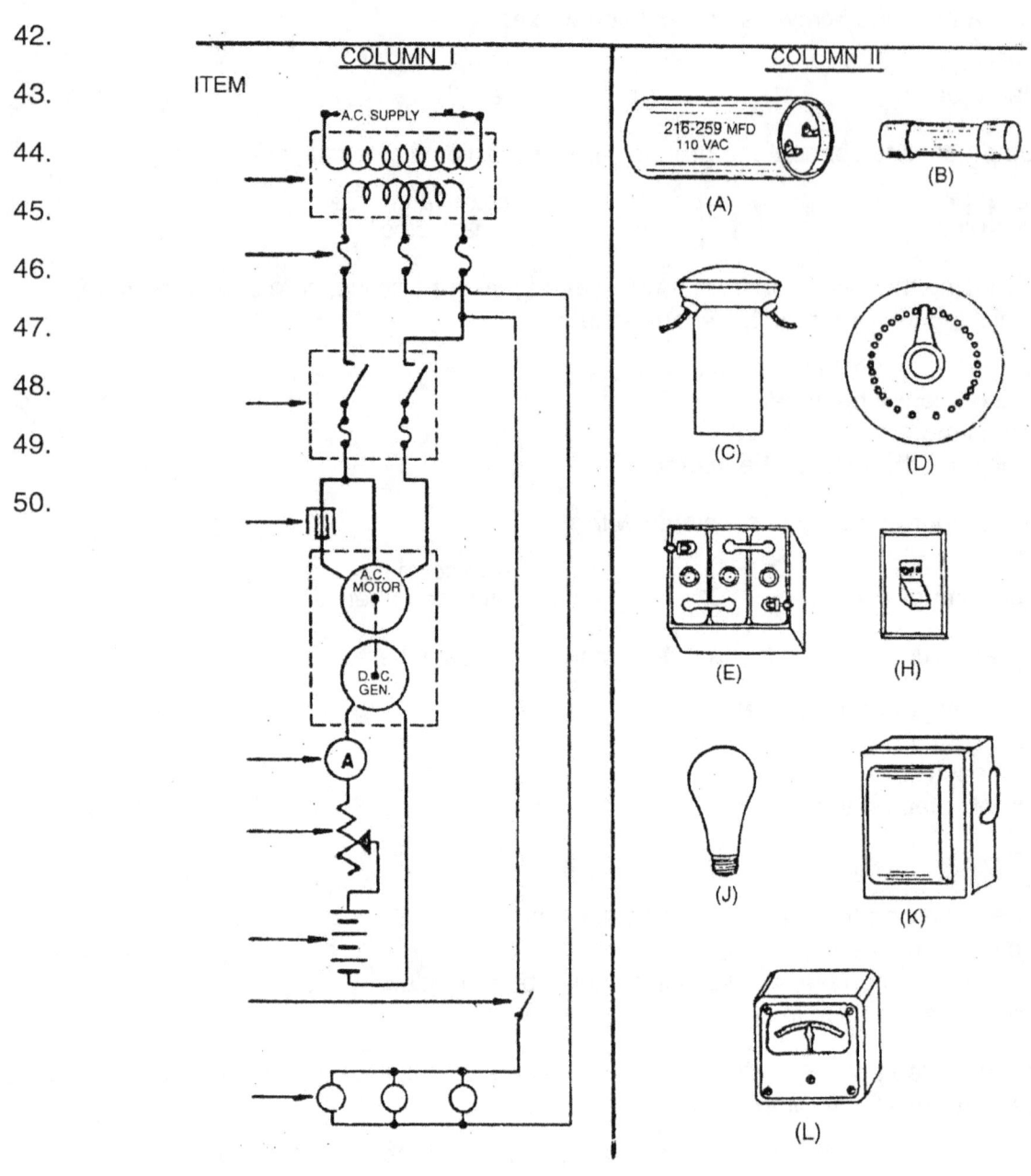

42.		42. __
43.		43. __
44.		44. __
45.		45. __
46.		46. __
47.		47. __
48.		48. __
49.		49. __
50.		50. __

KEY (CORRECT ANSWERS)

1. D	11. A	21. B	31. D	41. A
2. A	12. B	22. C	32. A	42. C
3. D	13. A	23. B	33. D	43. B
4. D	14. E	24. B	34. D	44. K
5. C	15. D	25. A	35. C	45. A
6. B	16. C	26. A	36. B	46. L
7. B	17. C	27. D	37. C	47. D
8. C	18. D	28. B	38. D	48. E
9. D	19. D	29. A	39. C	49. H
10. B	20. A	30. C	40. B	50. J

ARITHMETICAL REASONING
EXAMINATION SECTION
TEST 1

DIRECTIONS: Each question or incomplete statement is followed by several suggested answers or completions. Select the one that BEST answers the question or completes the statement. *PRINT THE LETTER OF THE CORRECT ANSWER IN THE SPACE AT THE RIGHT.*

1. A supplier quotes a list price of $172.00 less 15 and 10 percent for twelve tools. The actual cost for these twelve tools is MOST NEARLY

    A. $146   B. $132   C. $129   D. $112

2. If the diameter of a circular piece of sheet metal is 1 1/2 feet, the area, in square inches, is MOST NEARLY

    A. 1.77   B. 2.36   C. 254   D. 324

3. The sum of 5'6", 7'3", 9'3 1/2", and 3'7 1/4" is

    A. 19'8 1/2"   B. 22' 1/2"   C. 25'7 3/4"   D. 28'8 3/4"

4. If the floor area of one shop is 15' by 21'3" and the size of an adjacent shop is 18' by 30'6", then the TOTAL floor area of these two shops is _____ square feet.

    A. 1127.75   B. 867.75   C. 549.0   D. 318.75

5. The fraction which is equal to 0.875 is

    A. 7/16   B. 5/8   C. 3/4   D. 7/8

6. The sum of 1/2, 2 1/32, 4 3/16, and 1 7/8 is MOST NEARLY

    A. 9.593   B. 9.625   C. 9.687   D. 10.593

7. If the base of a right triangle is 9" and the altitude is 12", the length of the third side will be

    A. 13"   B. 14"   C. 15"   D. 16"

8. If a steel bar 1" in diameter and 12' long weighs 32 lbs., then the weight of a piece of this bar 5'9" long is MOST NEARLY _____ lbs.

    A. 15.33   B. 15.26   C. 16.33   D. 15.06

9. The diameter of a circle whose circumference is 12" is MOST NEARLY

    A. 3.82"   B. 3.72"   C. 3.62"   D. 3.52"

10. A dimension of 39/64 inches converted to decimals is MOST NEARLY

    A. .600"   B. .609"   C. .607"   D. .611"

11. A farm worker was paid a weekly wage of $415.20 for a 44-hour work week. As a result of a new labor contract, he is paid $431.40 a week for a 40-hour work week with time and one-half pay for time worked in excess of 40 hours in any work week.
    If he continues to work 44 hours weekly under the new contract, the amount by which his average hourly rate for a 44-hour work week under the new contract exceeds the hourly rate previously paid him lies between _____ and _____, inclusive.

    A. 80¢; $1.00   B. $1.00; $1.20
    C. $1.25; $1.45   D. $1.50; $1.70

12. The sum of 4 feet 3 1/4 inches, 7 feet 2 1/2 inches, and 11 feet 1/4 inch is _____ feet _____ inches.

    A. 21; 6 1/4   B. 22; 6   C. 23; 5   D. 24; 5 3/4

13. The number 0.038 is read as

    A. 38 tenths   B. 38 hundredths
    C. 38 thousandths   D. 38 ten-thousandths

14. Assume that an employee is paid at the rate of $10.86 per hour with time and a half for overtime past 40 hours in a week.
    If he works 43 hours in a week, his gross weekly pay is

    A. $434.40   B. $438.40   C. $459.18   D. $483.27

15. The sum of the following dimensions: 3'2 1/4", 8 7/8", 2'6 3/8", 2'9 3/4", and 1'0" is

    A. 16'7 1/4"   B. 10'7 1/4"   C. 10'3 1/4"   D. 9'3 1/4"

16. Two gears are meshed together and have a gear ratio of 6 to 1.
    If the small gear rotates 120 revolutions per minute, the large gear rotates at

    A. 20   B. 40   C. 60   D. 720

17. The vacuum side of a compound gage reads 14 inches of vacuum. The barometer reading is 29.76 inches of mercury. The equivalent absolute pressure of the compound gage reading, in inches of mercury, is MOST likely

    A. 15.06   B. 15.76   C. 43.06   D. 43.76

18. The fraction 5/8 expressed as a decimal is

    A. 0.125   B. 0.412   C. 0.625   D. 0.875

19. If 300 feet of a certain size pipe weighs 450 pounds, the number of pounds that 100 feet will weigh is

    A. 1,350   B. 150   C. 300   D. 250

20. As an oiler, you work for a facility that has automobiles that use, on the average, 600 quarts of one grade of lubricating oil every month.
    The number of one-gallon cans of the above oil that should be ordered each month to meet this requirement is

    A. 100   B. 125   C. 140   D. 150

21. The inside dimensions of a rectangular oil gravity tank are: height 15", width 9", length 10".
    The amount of oil in the tank, in gallons, (231 cu.in. = 1 gallon), when the oil level is 9" high, is MOST NEARLY

    A. 2.3   B. 3.5   C. 5.2   D. 5.8

22. If 30 gallons of oil cost $76.80, 45 gallons of oil at the same rate will cost

    A. $91.20   B. $115.20   C. $123.20   D. $131.20

23. If an oiler earns $18,000 in the first six months of a year and receives a 10% raise in salary for the next six months of the same year, his TOTAL earnings for the year will be

    A. $36,000   B. $37,500   C. $37,800   D. $39,600

24. If the cost of lubricating oil increases 15%, then a gallon of oil which used to cost $10.00 will now cost MOST NEARLY

    A. $10.50   B. $11.00   C. $11.50   D. $12.00

25. The sum of 7/8", 3/4", 1/2", and 3/8" is

    A. 2 1/8"   B. 2 1/4"   C. 2 3/8"   D. 2 1/2"

KEY (CORRECT ANSWERS)

1. B		11. A	
2. C		12. B	
3. C		13. C	
4. B		14. D	
5. D		15. C	
6. A		16. A	
7. C		17. B	
8. A		18. C	
9. A		19. B	
10. B		20. D	

21. B
22. B
23. C
24. C
25. D

4 (#1)

SOLUTIONS TO PROBLEMS

1. Actual cost = ($172)(.85)(.90) = $131.58 ≈ $132

2. Radius = .75', then area = (3.14)(.75)^2 ≈ 1.77 sq.ft.
   Since 1 sq.ft. = 144 sq.in., the area ≈ 254 sq.in.

3. 5'6" + 7'3" + 9'3 1/2" + 3'7 1/4" = 24'19 3/4" = 25'7 3/4"

4. Total area = (15)(21.25) + (18)(30.5) = 867.75 sq.ft.

5. .875 = 875/1000 = 7/8

6. 1 1/2 + 2 1/32 + 4 3/16 + 1 7/8 = 8 51/32 = 9 19/32 = 9.593

7. Third side = $\sqrt{9^2+12^2} = \sqrt{225} = 15"$

8. Let x = weight. Then, 12/32 = 5.75/x . Solving, x ≈ 15.33 lbs.

9. 12" = (3.14)(diameter), so diameter ≈ 3.82"

10. $\frac{39}{64}$" = .609375" ≈ .609"

11. Under his new contract, the weekly wage for 44 hours can be found by first determining his hourly rate for the first 40 hours = $431.40 ÷ 40 ≈ $10.80. Now, his time and one-half pay will = ($10.80)(1.5) = $16.20. His weekly wage for the new contract = $431.40 + (4)($16.20) = $496.20. His new hourly rate for 44 hours = $496.20 ÷ 44 ≈ $10.34. Under the old contract, his hourly rate for 44 hours was $415.20 ÷ 44 = $9.44. His hourly rate increase = $10.34 - $9.44 = $0.90. (Answer key: between $0.80 and $1.00)

12. 4'3 1/4" + 7'2 1/2" + 11' 1/4" = 22'6"

13. .038 = 38 thousandths

14. ($10.86)(40) + ($16.29)(3) = $483.27

15. 3'2 1/4" + 8 7/8" + 2'6 3/8" + 2'9 3/4" + 1'0" = 8'25 18/8" = 10'3 1/4"

16. The gear ratio is inversely proportional to the gear size. Let x = large gear's rpm. Then, 6/1 = 120/x . Solving, x = 20

17. Subtract 14 from 29.76

18. 5/8 = .625

19. Let x = number of pounds. Then, 300/450 = 100/x . Solving, x = 150

20. 600 quarts = 150 gallons, since 4 quarts = 1 gallon

21. (9")(9")(10") = 810 cu.in. Then, 810 ÷ 231 ≈ 3.5

22. Let x = unknown cost. Then, 30/$76.80 = 45/x. Solving, x = $115.20

23. $18,000 + ($18,000)(1.10) = $37,800

24. ($10.00)(1.15) = $11.50

25. 7/8" + 3/4" + 1/2" + 3/8" = 20/8" = 2 1/2"

TEST 2

DIRECTIONS: Each question or incomplete statement is followed by several suggested answers or completions. Select the one that BEST answers the question or completes the statement. *PRINT THE LETTER OF THE CORRECT ANSWER IN THE SPACE AT THE RIGHT.*

1. A sheet metal plate has been cut in the form of a right triangle with sides of 5, 12, and 13 inches.
   The area of this plate, in square inches, is

   A. 30   B. 32 1/2   C. 60   D. 78

2. If steel weighs 480 lbs. per cubic foot, the weight of an 18" x 18" x 2" steel base plate is _____ lbs.

   A. 180   B. 216   C. 427   D. 648

3. By trial, it is found that by using 2 cubic feet of sand, a 5 cubic foot batch of concrete is produced.
   Using the same proportions, the amount of sand, in cubic feet, required to produce 2 cubic yards of concrete is MOST NEARLY

   A. 7   B. 22   C. 27   D. 45

4. The total number of cubic yards of earth to be removed to make a trench 3'9" wide, 25'0" long, and 4'3" deep is MOST NEARLY

   A. 53.1   B. 35.4   C. 26.6   D. 14.8

5. A large number of 2 x 4 studs, some 10'5" long and some 6'5 1/2" long, are required for a job.
   To minimize waste, it would be PREFERABLE to order lengths of _____ feet.

   A. 16   B. 17   C. 18   D. 19

6. A 6" pipe is connected to a 4" pipe through a reducer. If 100 cubic feet of water is flowing through the 6" pipe per minute, the flow, in cubic feet, per minute through the 4" pipe is

   A. 225   B. 100   C. 66.6   D. 44.4

7. If steel weighs 0.28 pounds per cubic inch, then the weight, in pounds, of a 2" square steel bar 120" long is MOST NEARLY

   A. 115   B. 125   C. 135   D. 155

8. A three-inch diameter steel bar two feet long weighs MOST NEARLY (assume steel weighs 480 lbs./cu.ft.) _____ lbs.

   A. 48   B. 58   C. 68   D. 78

9. The area of a circular plate will be reduced by 5% if a sector removed from it has an angle of _____ degrees.

   A. 18   B. 24   C. 32   D. 60

10. If a 4 1/16 inch shaft wears six thousandths of an inch, the NEW diameter will be _____ inches.

    A. 4.0031   B. 4.0565   C. 4.0578   D. 4.0605

11. A set of mechanical plan drawings is drawn to a scale of 1/8" = 1 foot. If a length of pipe measures 15 7/16" on the drawing, the ACTUAL length of the pipe is _____ feet.

    A. 121.5   B. 122.5   C. 123.5   D. 124.5

12. An electrical drawing is drawn to a scale of 1/4" = 1'. If a length of conduit on the drawing measures 7 3/8", the actual length of the conduit, in feet, is

    A. 7.5   B. 15.5   C. 22.5   D. 29.5

13. Assume that you have assigned 6 mechanics to do a job that must be finished in 4 days. At the end of 3 days, your men have completed only two-thirds of the job. In order to complete the job on time and because the job is such that it cannot be speeded up, you should assign a MINIMUM of _____ extra men.

    A. 3   B. 4   C. 5   D. 6

14. Assume that a trench is 42" wide, 5' deep, and 100' long. If the unit price of excavating the trench is $105 per cubic yard, the cost of excavating the trench is MOST NEARLY

    A. $6,805   B. $15,330   C. $21,000   D. $63,000

15. If the scale on a shop drawing is 1/4 inch to the foot, then the length of a part which measures 2 3/8 inches long on the drawing is ACTUALLY _____ feet.

    A. 9 1/2   B. 8 1/2   C. 7 1/4   D. 4 1/4

16. It is necessary to pour a new concrete floor for a shop. If the dimensions of the concrete slab for the floor are to be 27' x 18' x 6", then the number of cubic yards of concrete that must be poured is

    A. 9   B. 16   C. 54   D. 243

17. The jaws of a vise move 1/4" for each complete turn of the handle. The number of complete turns necessary to open the jaws 2 3/4" is

    A. 9   B. 10   C. 11   D. 12

18. Assume that a jobbing shop is to submit a price for a contract involving 300 pieces of work. Assume that material costs 50 cents per piece, labor costs $7.50 an hour, and a lathe operator can complete 5 pieces in an hour.
    If overhead is 40% of material and labor costs and the profit is 10% of all costs, the submitted price for the entire job will be

    A. $630.24   B. $872.80   C. $900.00   D. $924.00

19. The following formula is used in connection with the three-wire method of measuring pitch diameters of screw threads: $G = \dfrac{0.57735}{N}$, where G = wire size and N = number of threads per inch.
According to this formula, the proper size of wire for a 1"-8NC thread is MOST NEARLY

   A. .0722"   B. .7217"   C. .0072"   D. .0074"

20. A millimeter is 1/25.4 of an inch and there are 10 millimeters to a centimeter.
If a piece of stock measures 127 centimeters long, the length of the stock, in feet and inches, would be MOST NEARLY

   A. 2'1"   B. 4'2"   C. 8'4"   D. 41'8"

21. For a certain job, you will need 25 steel bars 1 inch in diameter and 4"6" long.
If these bars weigh 3 pounds per foot of length, then the TOTAL weight for all 25 bars is _____ pounds.

   A. 13.5   B. 75.0   C. 112.5   D. 337.5

22. If steel weighs 0.30 pounds per cubic inch, then the weight of a 2 inch square steel bar 90 inches long is _____ pounds.

   A. 27   B. 54   C. 108   D. 360

23. A concrete wall is 36' long, 9' high, and 1 1/2' thick. The number of cubic yards of concrete that were needed to make this wall is

   A. 14   B. 18   C. 27   D. 36

24. If the scale on a shop drawing is 1/2 inch to the foot, then the length of a part which measures 4 1/4 inches long on the drawing has a length of APPROXIMATELY _____ feet.

   A. 2 1/8   B. 4 1/4   C. 8 1/2   D. 10 3/4

25. If the allowable load on a wooden scaffold is 60 pounds per square foot and the scaffold surface area is 3 feet by 12 feet, then the MAXIMUM total distributed load that is permitted on the scaffold is _____ pounds.

   A. 720   B. 1,800   C. 2,160   D. 2,400

KEY (CORRECT ANSWERS)

1. A
2. A
3. B
4. D
5. B

6. B
7. C
8. A
9. A
10. B

11. C
12. D
13. A
14. A
15. A

16. A
17. C
18. D
19. A
20. B

21. D
22. C
23. B
24. C
25. C

SOLUTIONS TO PROBLEMS

1. Area = (1/2)(base)(height) = (1/2)(5")(12") = 30 sq.in.

2. Volume = (18") (18") (2") = 648 cu.in. = 648/1720 cu.ft.
   Then, (480)(648/1720) = ≈ 180 lbs.

3. 2 cu.yds. = 54 cu.ft. Let x = required cubic feet of sand. Then, 2/5 = x/54. Solving, x = 21.6 (or about 22)

4. (3.75')(25')(4.25') = 398.4375 cu.ft. ≈ 14.8 cu.yds.

5. 10'5" + 6'5 1/2" = 16'10 1/2", so lengths of 17 feet are needed

6. The amount of water flowing through each pipe must be equal.

7. (2")(2")(120") = 480 cu. in. Then, (480)(.28) ≈ 135 lbs.

8. Volume = $(\pi)(.125')^2(2)$ ≈ .1 cu.ft. Then, (.1)(480) = 48 lbs.

9. (360°)(.05) - 18°

10. 4 1/16 - .006 = 4.0625 - .006 = 4.0565

11. 15 7/16" ÷ 1/8" = 247/16 . 8/1 = 123.5. Then, (123.5)(1 ft.) = 123.5 ft.

12. 7 3/8" ÷ 1/4" = 59/8 . 4/1 = 29.5 Then, (29.5)(1 ft.) = 29.5 ft.

13. (6)(4) = 24 man-days normally required. Since after 3 days only the equivalent of (2/3)(24) = 16 man-days of work has been 1 done, 8 man-days of work is still left. 16 ÷ 3 = 5 1/3, which means the crew is equivalent to only 5 1/3 men. To do the 8 man-days of work, it will require at least 8 - 5 1/3 = 2 2/3 = 3 additional men.

14. (3.5')(5')(100') = 1750 cu.ft. ≈ 64.8 cu.yds. Then, (64.8)($105) ≈ $6805

15. 2 3/8" ÷ 1/4" = 19/8 . 4/1 = 9 1/2 Then, (9 1/2)(1 ft.) = 9 1/2 feet

16. (27')(18')(1/2') = 243 cu.ft. = 9 cu.yds. (1 cu.yd. = 27 cu.ft.)

17. 2 3/4" ÷ 1/4" = 11/4 . 4/1 = 11

18. Material cost = (300)($.50) = $150. Labor cost = ($7.50)(300/5) = $450. Overhead = (.40)($150+$450) = $240. Profit = .10($150+$450+$240) = $84. Submitted price = $150 + $450 + $240 + $84 = $924

19. 6 = .57735" ÷ 8 = .0722"

20. 127 cm = 1270 mm = 1270/25.4" ≈ 50" = 4.2"

21. (25)(4.5') = 112.5' Then, (112.5X3) = 337.5 lbs.

22. (2")(2")(90") = 360 cu.in. Then, (360)(30) = 108 lbs.

23. (36')(9')(1 1/2') = 486 cu.ft. = 18 cu.yds. (1 cu.yd. = 27 cu.ft.)

24. 4 1/4" ÷ 1/2" = 17/4 . 2/1 = 8 1/2. Then, (8 1/2)(1 ft.) = 8 1/2 ft.

25. (12')(3') = 36 sq.ft. Then, (36)(60) = 2160 lbs.

TEST 3

DIRECTIONS: Each question or incomplete statement is followed by several suggested answers or completions. Select the one that BEST answers the question or completes the statement. *PRINT THE LETTER OF THE CORRECT ANSWER IN THE SPACE AT THE RIGHT.*

1. A right triangular metal sheet for a roofing job has sides of 36 inches and 4 feet. The length of the remaining side is

    A. 7 feet
    B. 6 feet
    C. 60 inches
    D. 90 inches

2. A U.S. Standard Gauge thickness is given as 0.15625. This thickness, in fractions of an inch, is MOST NEARLY _____ inches.

    A. 1/8　　B. 4/32　　C. 5/32　　D. 3/64

3. The weight per 100 of sheet metal fasteners is given as 2/3 pound. The APPROXIMATE number of fasteners in a 2-pound package is

    A. 166　　B. 200　　C. 300　　D. 266

4. The decimal equivalent of 27/32 is MOST NEARLY

    A. 0.813　　B. 0.828　　C. 0.844　　D. 0.859

5. If a scaled measurement of 1'3" on the drawing of a sheet metal layout represents an actual length of 10'0", then the drawing has been made to a scale of _____ inch to the foot.

    A. 3/4　　B. 1 1/4　　C. 1 1/2　　D. 1 3/4

6. Two and two-thirds tees can be made from one sheet of steel. If 24 tees must be made, then the number of sheets required is

    A. 6　　B. 7　　C. 8　　D. 9

7. A main duct 20 inches in diameter discharges into two branch ducts. The sum of the areas of the branches is to be equal to the area of the main duct. One branch is 12 inches in diameter. The diameter of the other branch is _____ inches.

    A. 16　　B. 12　　C. 10　　D. 8

8. If steel weighs 480 lbs. per cubic foot, the weight of 10 sheets, each 6 feet by 3 feet by 1/32 inch, is _____ lbs.

    A. 2,700　　B. 1,237　　C. 270　　D. 225

9. The area, in square inches, of a right triangle that has sides of 12 1/2, 10, and 7 1/2 inches is

    A. 18 1/4　　B. 37 1/2　　C. 75　　D. 60

10. In making a container to hold 1 gallon (231 cu.in.) and to be 6 inches in diameter at the top and 8 inches in diameter at the bottom, the height must be, in inches,

   A. 10.0   B. 8.2   C. 4.6   D. 6

11. A sheet metal worker is given a job to make a transition piece from a 8 1/2" diameter duct to an 11 1/4" diameter duct. If the length of the transition piece is 5 1/2" for each inch change in diameter, then the length of the transition piece is

   A. 14 7/8"   B. 15"   C. 15 1/8"   D. 15 1/4"

12. A duct layout is drawn to a scale of 3/8" to a foot. If the length of a run shown on the drawing scales 7 1/2", then the ACTUAL length of the run is

   A. 19'6"   B. 19'9"   C. 20'0"   D. 20'3"

13. An 18" x 24" duct is to be connected to a 24" x 24" duct by means of an eccentric transition piece (3 sides flush). If the taper is to be 1" in 4", then the length of the transition piece is

   A. 6"   B. 12"   C. 18"   D. 24"

14. Twenty-seven pairs of 3/8" diameter rods each 3'3 1/2" long are needed to support a duct.
   If the available rods are ten feet long, then the MINIMUM number of rods that will be needed to make the twenty-seven sets is

   A. 9   B. 12   C. 15   D. 18

15. A rectangular sheet metal air duct with open ends is 12 feet long and 15" x 20" in cross-section. If one square foot of the sheet metal weighs 1/2 pound, then the TOTAL weight of the duct is _____ lbs.

   A. 10   B. 17 1/2   C. 35   D. 150

16. The sum of 1/12 and 1/4 is

   A. 1/3   B. 5/12   C. 7/12   D. 3/8

17. The product of 12 and 2 1/3 is

   A. 27   B. 28   C. 29   D. 30

18. If 4 1/2 is subtracted from 7 1/5, the remainder is

   A. 3 7/10   B. 2 7/10   C. 3 3/10   D. 2 3/10

19. The number of cubic yards in 47 cubic feet is MOST NEARLY

   A. 1.70   B. 1.74   C. 1.78   D. 1.82

20. A wall 8'0" high by 12'6" long has a window opening 4'0" high by 3'6" wide. The net area of the wall (allowing for the window opening) is, in square feet,

   A. 86   B. 87   C. 88   D. 89

21. A worker's hourly rate is $11.36. 21.____
    If he works 11 1/2 hours, he should receive
    A. $129.84   B. $130.64   C. $131.48   D. $132.24

22. The number of cubic feet in 3 cubic yards is 22.____
    A. 81   B. 82   C. 83   D. 84

23. At an annual rate of $.40 per $100, what is the fire insurance premium for one year on a 23.____
    house that is insured for $80,000?
    A. $120   B. $160   C. $240   D. $320

24. A meter equals approximately 1.09 yards. 24.____
    How much longer, in yards, is a 100-meter dash than a 100-yard dash?
    A. 6   B. 8   C. 9   D. 12

25. A train leaves New York City at 8:10 A.M. and arrives in Buffalo at 4:45 P.M. on the same 25.____
    day. How long, in hours and minutes, does it take the train to make the trip?
    _____ hours, _____ minutes.
    A. 6; 22   B. 7; 16   C. 7; 28   D. 8; 35

KEY (CORRECT ANSWERS)

1. C		11. C	
2. C		12. C	
3. C		13. D	
4. C		14. D	
5. C		15. C	
6. D		16. A	
7. A		17. B	
8. D		18. B	
9. B		19. B	
10. D		20. A	

21. B
22. A
23. D
24. C
25. D

SOLUTIONS TO PROBLEMS

1. Let x = remaining side. Converting to inches, $x^2 = 36^2 + 48^2$ So, $x^2 = 3600$. Solving, x = 60 inches.

2. $.15625 = \dfrac{15{,}625}{100{,}000} = \dfrac{5}{32}$

3. 2 ÷ 2/3 = 3. Then, (3)(100) = 300 fasteners

4. 27/32 = .84375 ≈ .844

5. 1'3" ÷ 10 = 15" ÷ 10 = 1 1/2"

6. 24 ÷ 2 2/3 = 24/1.3/8 = 9

7. Area of main duct = $(\pi)(10^2) = 100\pi$. One of the branches has an area of $(\pi)(6^2) = 36\pi$. Thus, the area of the 2nd branch = $100\pi - 36\pi = 64\pi$. The 2nd branch's radius must be 8" and its diameter must be 16".

8. Volume = (1/384')(6')(3') = .046875 cu.ft. Then, 10 sheets have a volume of .46875 cu.ft. Now, (.46875)(480) = 225 lbs.

9. Note that $(7\,1/2)^2 + (10)^2 = (12\,1/2)^2$, so that this is a right triangle. Area = (1/2)(10")(7 1/2") = 37 1/2 sq.in.

10. $231 = \dfrac{h}{3}[(\pi)(3)^2 + (\pi)(4)^2 + \sqrt{(9\pi)(16\pi)}]$, where h = required height. Then,

    $231 = \dfrac{h}{3}(9\pi + 16\pi + 12\pi)$. Simplifying, $231 = 37\pi h/3$.
    Solving, h ~ 5.96" or 6"

11. 11 1/4 - 8 1/2 = 2 3/4. Then, (2 3/4)(5 1/2) = 11/4 .11/2 = 15 1/8

12. 7 1/2 " ÷ 3/8" = 15/2 .8/3 = 20 Then, (20)(1 ft.) = 20 feet

13. 24" - 18" = 6" Then, (6")(4) = 24"

14. 3'3 1/2" = 39.5". Now, (27)(2)(39.5") = 2133". 10 ft. = 120". Finally, 2133 ÷ 120 = 17.775, so 18 rods are needed.

15. Surface area = (2)(12')(1 1/4') + (2)(12')(1 2/3') = 70 sq.ft. Then, (70)(1/2 lb.) - 35 lbs.

16. 1/12 + 1/4 = 4/12 = 1/3

17. (12)(2 1/3) = 12/1 . 7/3 = 28

18. 7 1/5 - 4 1/2 = 7 2/10 - 4 5/10 = 6 12/10 - 4 5/10 = 2 7/10

19. 47 cu.ft. = 47/27 cu.yds. = 1.74 cu.yds.

20. (8')(12.5') - (4')(3.5') = 86 sq.ft.

21. ($11.36)(11.5) = $130.64

22. 1 cu.yd. = 27 cu.ft., so 3 cu.yds. = 81 cu.ft.

23. $80,000 ÷ $100 = 800. Then, (800)($.40) = $320

24. 100 meters = 109 yds. Then, 109 - 100 = 9 yds.

25. 4:45 P.M. - 8:10 A.M. = 8 hrs. 35 min.

BASIC FUNDAMENTALS OF GEARS

CONTENTS

		Page
I.	Types of Gears	1
II.	The Bevel Gear	2
III.	The Worm and Worm Wheel	3
IV.	Changing Direction with Gears	4
V.	Changing Speed	5
VI.	Magnifying Force with Gears	6
VII.	Summary	7

BASIC FUNDAMENTALS OF GEARS

Did you ever take a clock apart to see what made it tick? Of course you came out with some parts left over when you got it back together again. And they probably included a few gear wheels. Gears are used in many machines. Frequently the gears are hidden from view in a protective case filled with grease or oil, and you may not see them.

An egg beater gives you a simple demonstration of the three things that gears do. They can change the direction of motion; increase or decrease the speed of the applied motion; and magnify or reduce the force which you apply. Gears also give you a positive drive. There can be, and usually is, creep or slip in a belt drive. But gear teeth are always in mesh, and there can be no creep and slip.

Follow the directional changes in figure 1. The crank handle is turned in the direction indicated by the arrow-clockwise, when viewed from the right. The 32 teeth on the large vertical wheel A mesh with the 8 teeth on the right-hand horizontal wheel B, which rotates as indicated by the arrow. Notice that as B turns in a clockwise direction, its teeth mesh with those of wheel C and cause wheel C to revolve in the opposite direction. The rotation of the crank handle has been transmitted by gears to the beater blades, which also rotate.

Now figure out how the gears change the speed of motion. There are 32 teeth on gear A and 8 teeth on gear B. But the gears mesh, so that one complete revolution of A results in four complete revolutions of gear B. And since gears B and C have the same number of teeth, one revolution of B results in one revolution of C. Thus the blades revolve four times as fast as the crank handle.

Previously you learned that third-class levers increase speed at the expense of force. The same thing happens with this egg beater. The magnitude of the force is changed. The force required to turn the handle is greater than the force applied to the frosting by the blades. Therefore a mechanical advantage of less than one results.

1. TYPES OF GEARS

When two shafts are not lying in the same straight line, but are parallel, motion can be transmitted from one to the other by means of spur gears. This setup is shown in figure 2.

Spur gears are wheels with mating teeth cut in their surfaces so that one can turn the other without slippage. When the mating teeth are cut so that they are parallel to the axis of rotation, as shown in figure 2, the gears are called straight spur gears.

When two gears of unequal size are meshed together, the smaller of the two is usually called a pinion. By unequal size, we mean an unequal number of teeth causing one gear to be of a larger diameter than the other. The teeth, themselves, must be of the same size in order to mesh properly.

The most commonly used type are the straight spur gears, but quite often you'll run across another type of spur gear called the helical spur gear.

In helical gears the teeth are cut slantwise across the working face of the gear. One end of the tooth, therefore, lies ahead of the other. In other words, each tooth has a leading end and a trailing end. A look at these gears in figure 3A will show you how they're constructed.

In the straight spur gears the whole width of the teeth comes in contact at the same time. But with helical (spiral) gears contact between two teeth starts first at the leading ends and moves progressively across the gear faces until the trailing ends are in contact. This kind of meshing action keeps the gears in constant contact with one another. Therefore, less lost motion and

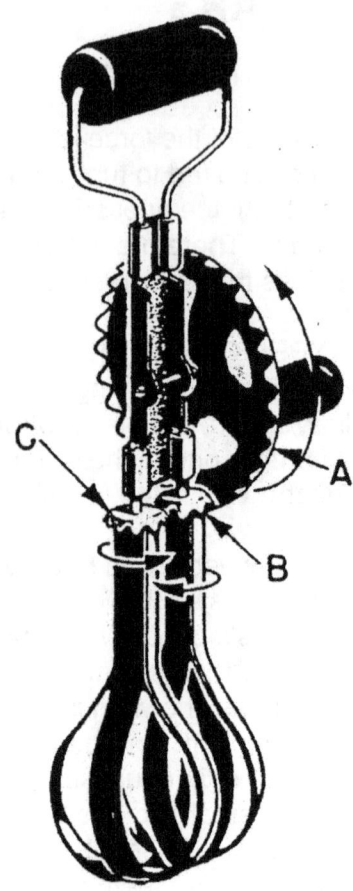

Figure 1.—A simple gear arrangement.

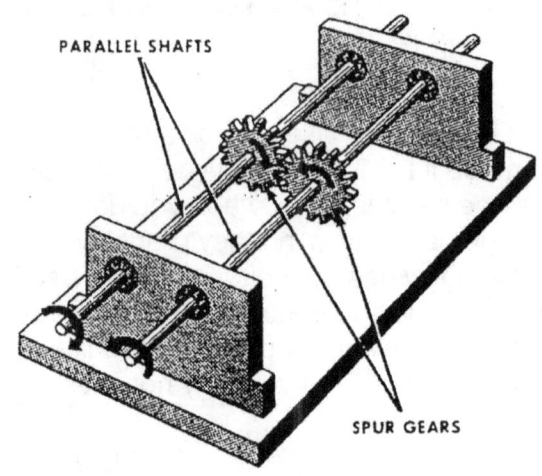

Figure 2.—Spur gears coupling two parallel shafts.

smoother, quieter action is possible. One disadvantage of this helical spur gear is the tendency of each gear to thrust or push axially on its shaft. It is necessary to put a special thrust bearing at the end of the shaft to counteract this thrust.

Thrust bearings are not needed if herringbone gears like those shown in figure 4 are used. Since the teeth on each half of the gear are cut in opposite directions, each half of the gear develops a thrust which counterbalances that of the other half. You'll find herringbone gears used mostly on heavy machinery.

Figure 3 also shows you three other gear arrangements in common use.

The internal gear in figure 3B has teeth on the inside of a ring, pointing inward toward the axis of rotation. An internal gear is always meshed with an external gear, or pinion, whose center is offset from the center of the internal gear. Either the internal or pinion gear can be the driver gear, and the gear ratio is calculated the same as for other gears-by counting teeth.

Often only a portion of a gear is needed where the motion of the pinion is limited. In this case the sector gear (fig. 3C) is used to save space and material. The rack and pinion in figure 3D are both spur gears. The rack may be considered as a piece cut from a gear with an extremely large radius. The rack-and-pinion arrangement is useful in changing rotary motion into linear motion.

II. THE BEVEL GEAR.-So far most of the gears you've learned about transmit motion between parallel shafts. But when shafts are not parallel (at an angle), another type of gear is used-the bevel gear. This type of gear can connect shafts lying at any given angle because they can be beveled to suit the angle.

Figure 5A shows a special case of the bevel gear-the miter gear. A pair of miter gears is used to connect shafts having a 90 angle, which means the gear faces are beveled at a 45° angle.

You can see in figure 5B how bevel gears are designed to join shafts at any angle. Gears cut at any angle other than 45 are called just plain bevel gears.

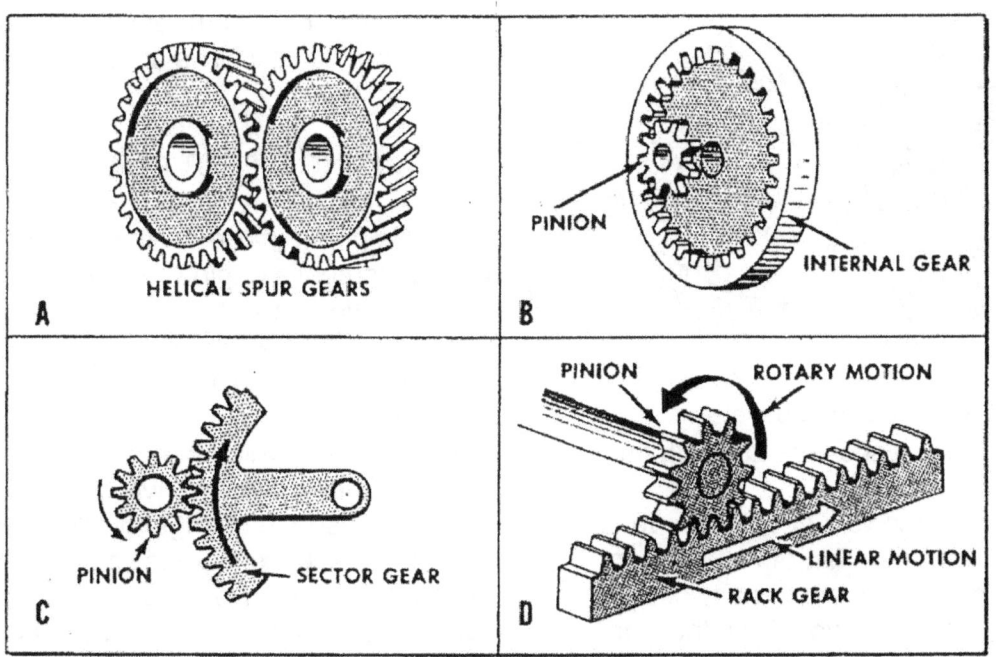

Figure 3.—Gear types.

The gears shown in figure 5 are called straight bevel gears, because the whole width of each tooth comes in contact with the mating tooth at the same time. However, you'll also run across spiral bevel gears with teeth cut so as to have advanced and trailing ends. Figure 6 shows you what spiral bevel gears look like. They have the same advantages as other spiral (helical) gearsless lost motion and smoother, quieter operation.

III. THE WORM AND WORM WHEEL.-Worm and worm-wheel combinations, like those in figure 7, have many uses and advantages. But it's better to understand their operating theory before learning of their uses and advantages.

Figure 7A shows the action of a single-thread worm. For each revolution of the worm, the worm wheel turns one tooth.

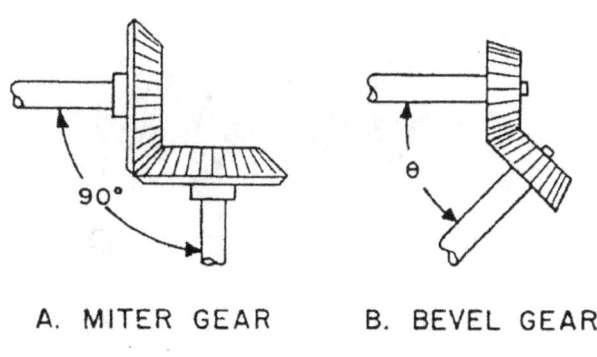

A. MITER GEAR   B. BEVEL GEAR

Figure 5.—Bevel gears.

Figure 4.—Herringbone gear.

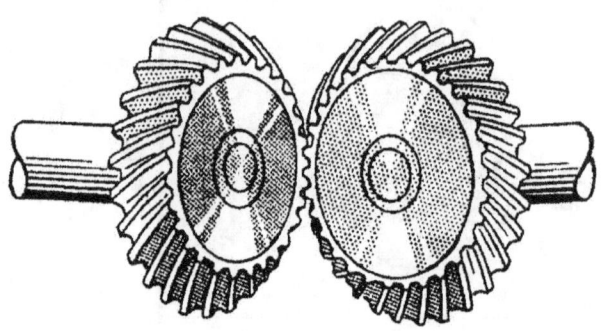

Figure 6 —Spiral bevel gears.

Thus if the worm wheel has 25 teeth the gear ratio is 25:1.

Figure 7B shows a double-thread worm. For each revolution of the worm in this case, the worm wheel turns two teeth. That makes the gear ratio 25:2 if the worm wheel has 25 teeth.

Likewise, a triple-threaded worm would turn the worm wheel three teeth per revolution of the worm.

A worm gear is really a combination of a screw and a spur gear. Tremendous mechanical advantages can be obtained with this arrangement. Worm drives can also be designed so that only the worm is the driver—the spur cannot drive the worm. On a hoist, for example, you can raise or lower the load by pulling on the chain which turns the worm. But if you let go of the chain, the load cannot drive the spur gear and let the load drop to the deck. This is a non-reversing worm drive.

IV. CHANGING DIRECTION WITH GEARS

No doubt you know that the crankshaft in an automobile engine can turn in only one direction. If you want the car to go backwards, the effect of the engine's rotation must be reversed. This is done by a reversing gear in the transmission, not by reversing the direction in which the crankshaft turns.

A study of figure 8 will show you how gears are used to change the direction of motion. This is a schematic diagram of the sight mounts on a Navy gun. If you crank the range-adjusting handle A in a clockwise direction the gear B directly above it is made to rotate in a counterclockwise direction. This motion causes the two pinions C and D on the shaft to turn in the same direction as gear B against the teeth cut in the bottom of the table. The table is tipped in the direction indicated by the arrow.

As you turn the deflection-adjusting handle E in a clockwise direction the gear F directly above it turns in the opposite direction. Since the two bevel gears G and H are fixed on the shaft with F, they also turn.

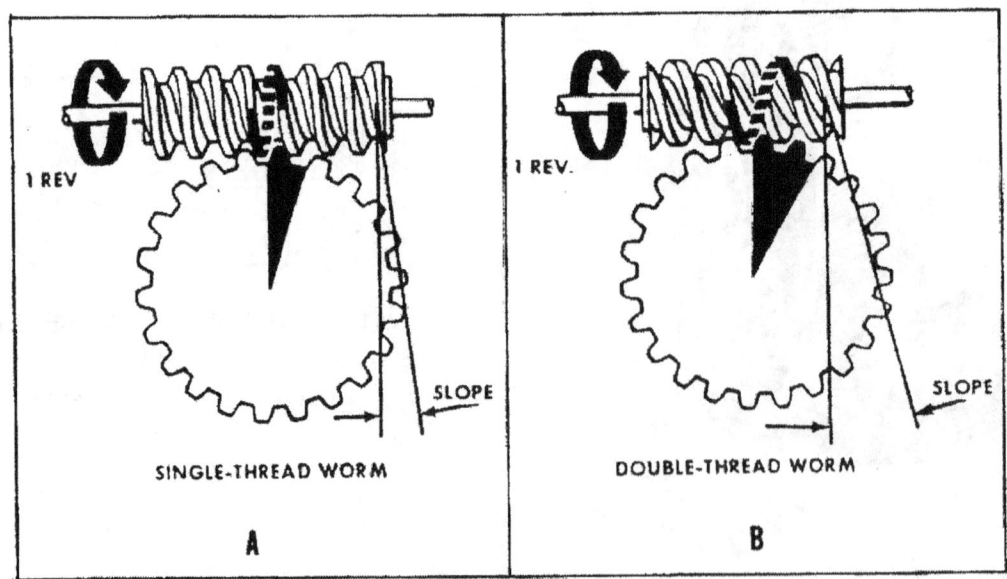

Figure 7.—Worm gears.

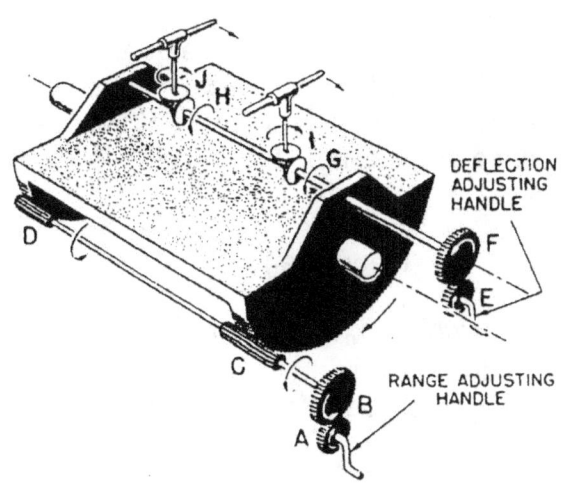

Figure 8.—Gears change direction of applied motion.

These bevel gears, meshing with the horizontal bevel gears I and J, cause I and J to swing the front ends of the telescopes to the right. Thus with a simple system of gears, it is possible to keep the two telescopes pointed at a moving target. In this and many other practical applications, gears serve one purpose—to change the direction of motion.

V. CHANGING SPEED

As you've already seen in the eggbeater, gears can be used to change the speed of motion. Another example of this use of gears is found in your clock or watch. The mainspring slowly unwinds and causes the hour hand to make one revolution in 12 hours. Through a series—or train—of gears, the minute hand makes one revolution each hour, while the second hand goes around once per minute.

Figure 6-9 will help you to understand how speed changes are made possible. Wheel A has 10 teeth which mesh with the 40 teeth on wheel B. Wheel A will have to rotate four times to cause B to make one revolution. Wheel C is rigidly fixed on the same shaft with B. Thus C makes the same number of revolutions as B. However, C has 20 teeth, and meshes with wheel D which has only 10 teeth. Hence, wheel D turns twice as fast as wheel C.

Now, if you turn A at a speed of four revolutions per second, B will be rotated at one revolution per second. Wheel C also moves at one revolution per second, and causes D to turn at two revolutions per second. You get out two revolutions per second after having put in four revolutions per second. Thus the overall speed reduction is 2/4 or 1/2, which means that you got half the speed out of the last driven wheel that you put into the first driver wheel.

You can solve any gear speed-reduction problem with this formula

$$S_2 = S_1 \times \frac{T_1}{T_2}$$

where

S_1 = speed of first shaft in train
S_2 = speed of last shaft in train
T_1 = product of teeth on all drivers
T_2 = product of teeth on all driven gears

Now use the formula on the gear train of figure 6-8.

$$S_2 = S_1 \times \frac{T_1}{T_2} = 4 \times \frac{10 \times 20}{40 \times 10} =$$

$$\frac{800}{400} = 2 \, revs. \, per \, sec.$$

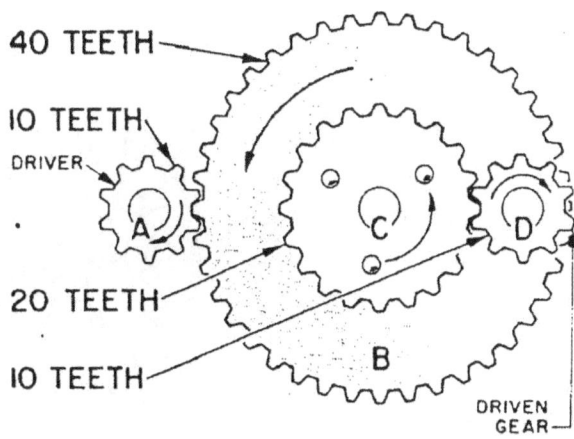

Figure 9.—Gears can change speed of applied motion.

Almost any increase or decrease in speed can be obtained by choosing the correct gears for the job. For example, the turbines on a ship have to turn at high speeds-say 5800 rpm-if they are going to be efficient. But the propellers, or screws, must turn rather slowly say 195 rpm-to push the ship ahead with maximum efficiency. So, a set of reduction gears is placed between the turbines and the propeller shaft.

When two external gears mesh, they rotate in opposite directions. Often you'll want to avoid this. Put a third gear, called an idler, between the driver and the driven gear. But don't let this extra gear confuse you on speeds. Just neglect the idler entirely. It doesn't change the gear ratio at all, and the formula still applies. The idler merely makes the driver and its driven gear turn in the same direction. Figure 10 will show you how this works.

VI. MAGNIFYING FORCE WITH GEARS

Gear trains are used to increase the mechanical advantage. In fact, wherever there is a speed reduction, the effect of the effort you apply is multiplied. Look at the cable winch in figure 11. The crank arm is 30 inches long, and the drum on which the cable is wound has a 15-inch radius. The small pinion gear has 10 teeth, which mesh with the 60 teeth on the internal spur gear. You will find it easier to figure the mechanical advantage of this machine if you think of it as two machines.

First, figure out what the gear and pinion do for you. The theoretical mechanical advantage of any arrangement of two meshed gears can be found by the following formula

$$M.A. \text{ (theoretical)} = \frac{T_o}{T_a}$$

In which, T_o = number of teeth on driven gear;
T_a = number of teeth on drive gear.
In this case, $T_o = 60$ and $T_a = 10$. Then,

$$M.A. \text{ (theoretical)} = \frac{T_o}{T_a} = \frac{60}{10} = 6$$

Now, for the other part of the machine, which is a simple wheel-and-axle arrangement consisting of the crank arm and the drum. The theoretical mechanical advantage of this can be found by dividing the distance the effort moves $2\pi R$ in making one complete revolution, by the distance the cable is drawn up in one revolution of the drum - $2\pi r$.

$$M.A. \text{ (theoretical)} = \frac{2\pi R}{2\pi r} = \frac{R}{r} = \frac{30}{15} = 2$$

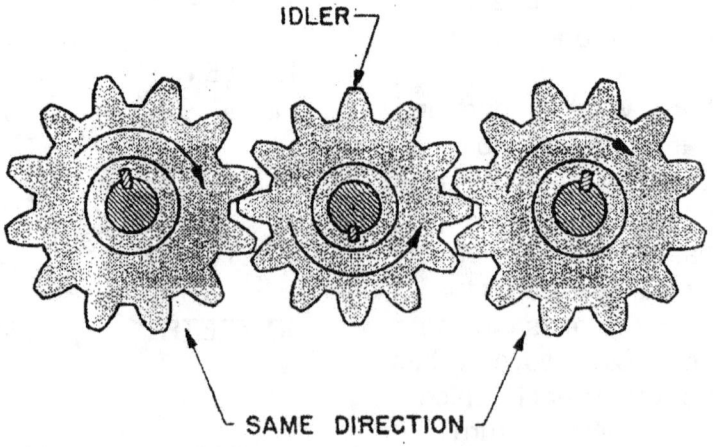

Figure 10.—An idler gear.

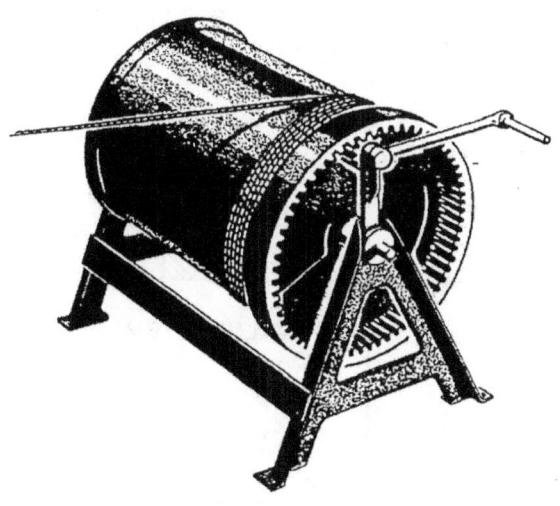

Figure 11.—This magnifies your effort.

You know that the total, or overall, theoretical mechanical advantage of a compound machine is equal to the product of the mechanical advantages of the several simple machines that make it up. In this case you considered the winch as being two machines—one having an M. A. of 6, and the other an M. A. of 2. Therefore, the over-all theoretical mechanical advantage of the winch is 6 x 2, or 12. Since friction is always present, the actual mechanical advantage may be only 7 or 8. Even so, by applying a force of 100 pounds on the handle, you could lift a load of 700 or 800 pounds.

You use gears to produce circular motion. But you often want to change rotary motion into up-and-down or linear motion. You can use cams to do this. For example—

The cam shaft in figure 12 is turned by the gear. A cam is keyed to the shaft and turns with it. The cam has an irregular shape which is designed to move the valve stem up and down, giving the valve a straight-line motion as the cam shaft rotates.

When the cam shaft rotates, the high point-lobe-of the cam raises the valve to its open position. As the shaft continues to rotate, the high point of the cam is passed and the valve is lowered to closed position.

A set of cams, two to a cylinder, driven by timing gears from the crankshaft operate the exhaust and intake valves on the gasoline automobile engine as shown in figure 13. Cams are widely used in machine tools and other devices to make rotating gears and shafts do up-and-down work.

VII. SUMMARY

These are the important points you should keep in mind about gears-

- Gears can do a job for you by changing the direction, speed, or size of the force which you apply.
- When two external gears mesh, they always turn in opposite directions. You can make them turn in the same direction by placing an idler gear between the two.
- The product of the number of teeth on each of the driver gears, divided by the product of the number of teeth on each of the driven gears, gives you the speed ratio of any gear train.
- The theoretical mechanical advantage of any gear train is the product of the number of teeth on the driven gear wheels, divided by the product of the number of teeth on the driver gears.
- The overall theoretical mechanical advantage of a compound machine is equal to the product of the theoretical mechanical advantages of all the simple machines which make it up.
- Cams are used to change rotary motion into linear motion.

One of the gear systems you'll get to see frequently aboard ship is that on the anchor winch. Figure 14 shows you one type in which you can readily see how the wheels go 'round. The driving gear A is turned by the winch engine or motor. This gear has 22 teeth, which mesh with the 88 teeth on the large wheel B. Thus, you know that the large wheel makes one revolution for every four revolutions of the driving gear A. You get a 4-to-l theoretical mechanical advantage out of that pair. Secured to the same shaft with B is the small spur gear C, covered up here. The gear C has 30 teeth which mesh with the 90

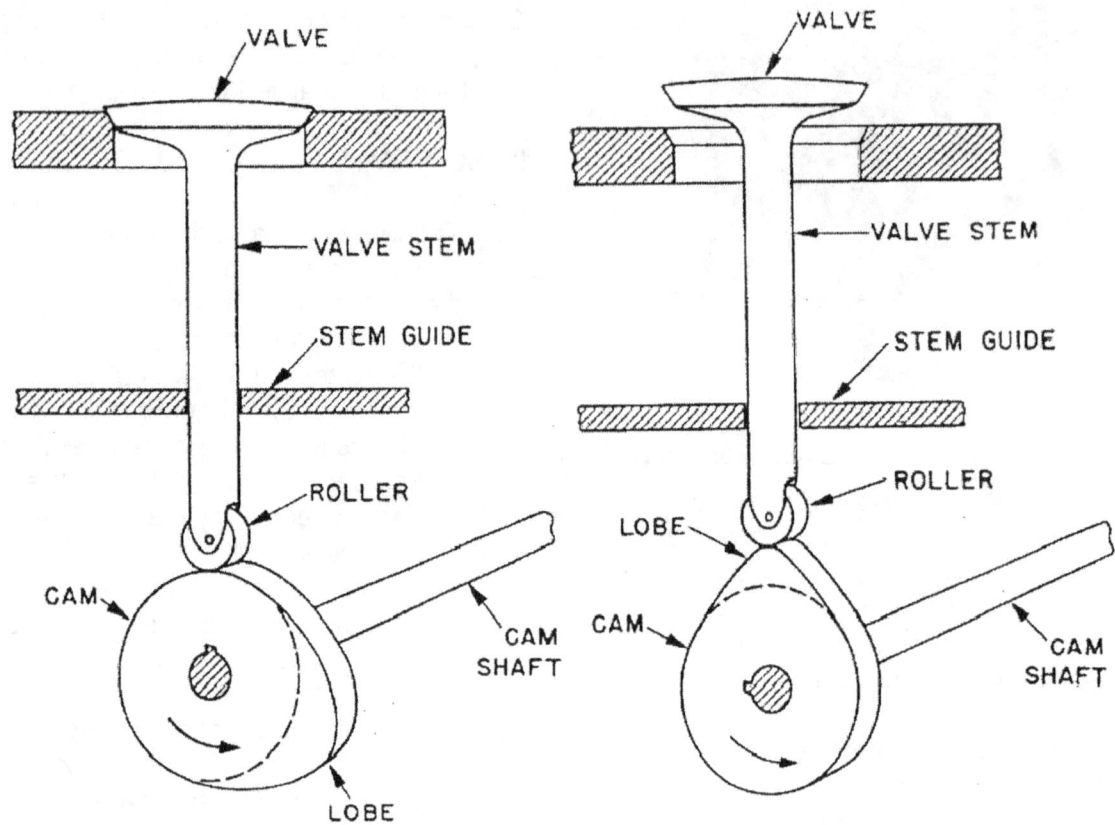

Figure 12.—Cam-driven valve.

teeth on the large gear D, also covered up. The advantage from C to D is 3 to 1.

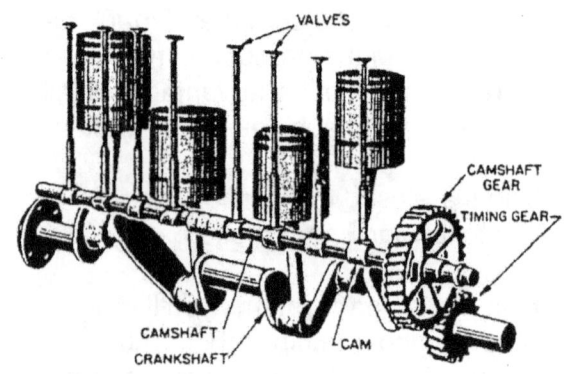

Figure 13.—Automobile valve gear.

The sprocket wheel to the far left, on the same shaft with D, is called a wildcat. The anchor chain is drawn up over this. Every second link is caught and held by the protruding teeth of the wildcat. The overall mechanical advantage of the winch is 4 x 3, or 12 to 1.

Figure 15 shows you an application of the rack and pinion as a steering mechanism. Turning the ship's wheel turns the small pinion A. This pinion causes the internal spur gear to turn. Notice that there is a large mechanical advantage in the arrangement.

Now you see that center pinion P turns. It meshes with the two vertical racks. When the wheel is turned full to the right, one rack moves downward and the other moves upward to the positions of the racks. Attached to the bottom of the racks are two hydraulic pistons which control the steering of the ship. You'll get some information on this hydraulic system in a later chapter.

Figure 14.—An anchor winch.

Figure 15.—A steering mechanism.

ELECTRIC MOTOR AND GENERATOR REPAIR

CONTENTS

	Page
I. TROUBLESHOOTING DATA FOR GENERATORS AND MOTORS	1
Section I. DC Generators	1
1. Failure to Build up Voltage	1
2. Output Voltage too Low	1
3. Output Voltage too High	1
4. Armature Overheats	1
5. Field Coils Overheat	2
6. Sparking at Brushes	2
Section II. DC Motors	2
7. Failure to Start	2
8. Stops After Running a Short Time	2
9. Attempts to Start, but Overload Relays Trip Out	2
10. Runs too Slow	3
11. Runs too Fast Under Load	3
12. Sparking at Brushes	3
13. Overheating	3
Section III. AC Generators	3
14. Noisy Operation	3
15. Overheating	3
16. No Output Voltage	3
17. Output Voltage Unsteady	4
18. Output Voltage too High	4
19. Frequency Incorrect or Fluctuating	4
20. Voltage Hunting	4
21. Stator Overheats in Spots	4
22. Field Overheating	4
23. Alternator Produces Shock When Touched	4
Section IV. AC Induction Motors	4
24. Failure to Start	4
25. Noisy Operation	4
26. Overheating	5
Section V. AC Wound Rotor Motors	5
27. Runs Slow with External Resistance Cutout	5
Section VI. AC Synchronous Motors	5
28. Failure to Start	5
29. Runs Slow	5
30. Failure to Pull into Step	5
31. No Field Excitation	5
32. Pulls Out of Step, or Trips Breakers	6
33. Hunting	6
34. Stator Overheats in Spots	6
35. Field Overheats	6
36. Overheating	6
Section VII. AC Repulsion Induction Motors	6
37. Failure to Start	6
38. Runs Slow	7
39. Overheating	7
40. Noisy Operation	7
41. Motor Produces Shock when Touched	7

continued ....

ELECTRIC MOTOR AND GENERATOR REPAIR (cont'd)

CONTENTS

	Page
Section VIII. AC Split-Phase, Capacitor-Start, and Transformer-Capacitor Motors	7
42. Failure to Start	7
43. Overheating	7
44. Noisy Operation	8
II. TROUBLESHOOTING DATA FOR DC AND AC CONTROLLERS	9
Section I. DC Controllers	9
45. Failure to Close	9
46. Failure to Open	9
47. Sluggish Operation	9
48. Erratic Operation (Unwanted openings and closures, and failure of overload protection)	9
49. Overheating of Coils	10
50. Contacts Welded Together	10
51. Overheating of Contacts	10
52. Excessive Arcing of Contacts	10
53. Pitting or Corroding of Contacts	11
Section II. AC Controllers	11
54. Failure to Close	11
55. Failure to Open	11
56. Sluggish Operation	11
57. Erratic Operation (Unwanted openings and closures, and failure of overload protection)	12
58. Overheating of Coils	12
59. Contacts Welded Together	12
60. Overheating or Contacts	12
61. Arcing at Contacts	13
62. Pitting or Corroding of Contacts	13
63. Noisy Operation (Hum or Chatter)	13
64. Vibration After Repairs	13

ELECTRIC MOTOR AND GENERATOR REPAIR

I. TROUBLESHOOTING DATA FOR GENERATORS AND MOTORS

Section I. DC GENERATORS

1. Failure to Build up Voltage

Probable cause	Remedy
Voltmeter not operating	Check output voltage with separate voltmeter. Replace voltmeter.
Open field resistor	Repair or replace resistor.
Open field circuit	Check coils for open and loose connections. Replace the defective coil or coils. Tighten or solder loose connections.
Absence of residual magnetism in a self-excited generator.	Flash the field.
Dirty commutator	Clean or dress commutator.
High mica	Undercut mica.
Brushes not making proper contact	Free, if binding in holders. Replace and reseat if worn.
Newly seated brushes not contacting sufficient area on the commutator.	Run in by reducing load and use a brush-seating stone.
Armature shorted internally, or to ground	Remove, test, and repair or replace.
Grounded or shorted field coil	Test, and repair or replace.
Shorted filtering capacitor	Replace.
Open filter choke	Replace.
Open ammeter shunt	Replace ammeter and shunt.
Broken brush shunts or pigtails	Replace brushes.

2. Output Voltage too Low

Probable cause	Remedy
Prime mover speed too low	Check speed with tachometer. Adjust governor on prime mover.
Brushes not seated properly	Run in with partial load, use brush-seating stone.
Commutator is dirty or film is too heavy	Clean, or if film is too heavy, replace brushes with a complete set of proper grade.
Field resistor not properly adjusted	Adjust field strength. Tighten all connections. Make shim adjustment.
Reversed field coil or armature connection	Check and connect properly.

3. Output Voltage Too High

Probable cause	Remedy
Prime mover speed too high	Check speed with tachometer. Adjust governor on prime mover.
Faulty voltage regulator	Adjust or replace.

4. Armature Overheats

Probable cause	Remedy
Overloaded	Check meter readings against nameplate ratings. Reduce load.
Excessive brush pressure	Adjust pressure or replace tension springs.
Couplings not alined	Aline units properly

Probable cause	Remedy
End bells improperly positioned	Assemble correctly
Bent shaft	Straighten or replace
Armature coil shorted	Repair or replace armature
Armature rubbing or striking poles	Check for bent shaft, loose or worn bearings. Straighten and realine shaft. Replace bearings, tighten pole pieces, or replace armature.
Clogged air passages (poor ventilation)	Clean equipment
Repeated changes in load of great magnitude. (Improper design for the application).	Generator should be used with a steady load application.
Unequal brush tension	Equalize brush tension
Broken shunts or pigtails	Replace brushes
Open in field rheostat	Repair or replace rheostat

5. Field Coils Overheat

Probable cause	Remedy
Shorted or grounded coils	Repair or replace
Clogged air passages (poor ventilation)	Clean equipment. Remove obstructions.
Overload (compound generator)	Check meter reading against nameplate rating. Reduce load.

6. Sparking at Brushes

Probable cause	Remedy
Overload	Check meter readings against nameplate ratings. Reduce load.
Brushes off neutral plane	Adjust brush rigging.
Dirty brushes and commutator	Clean brushes and commutator.
High mica	Undercut mica.
Rough or eccentric commutator	Resurface commutator.
Open circuit in the armature	Repair or replace armature.
Grounded, open- or short-circuited field winding	Repair or replace defective coil or coils.
Insufficient brush pressure	Adjust or replace tension springs.
Brushes sticking in the holders	Clean holders. Sand brushes.

Section II. DC MOTORS

7. Failure to Start

Probable cause	Remedy
Open circuit in the control	Check for open. Replace open resistor or fuse.
Low supply voltage	Check with voltmeter and apply proper voltage.
Frozen bearing	Replace bearing and recondition shaft.
Overload	Reduce load or use larger motor.
Excessive friction	Check for air gap, bent shaft, loose or worn bearings, misalined end bells. Straighten shaft, replace bearings, tighten pole pieces, aline end bells.

8. Stops After Running a Short Time

Probable cause	Remedy
Failure of supply voltage	Apply proper voltage, replace fuses, or reset overload relay.
Overload	Check meter readings against nameplate ratings. Reduce load.
Ambient temperature too high	Ventilate space to reduce ambient temperature.
Overload relays set too low for application	Adjust relays for the application.

9. Attempts to Start, But Overload Relays Trip Out

Probable cause	Remedy
Motor field weak or non-existent	Check field circuit. Repair or replace defective field coils. Tighten all connections.
Overload	Check meter readings against nameplate ratings. Replace motor with one suitable to the application.
Relays adjusted too low for the application	Adjust relays for the application.

10. Runs too Slow

Probable cause	Remedy
Line voltage low	Apply proper voltage.
Bushes ahead of neutral plane	Adjust brush rigging.
Overload	Check meter reading against nameplate readings. Reduce load.

11. Runs too Fast under Load

Probable cause	Remedy
Weak field	Check field circuit. Replace open coils or open starter resistors.
Line voltage too high	Reduce line voltage.
Brushes off adjustment with neutral plane	Adjust brush rigging.

12. Sparking at Brushes

Probable cause	Remedy
Same as dc generator (par. 6)	Same as dc generator (par. 6).

13. Overheating

Probable cause	Remedy
Same as dc generator (par. 4 and 5)	Same as dc generator (par. 4 and 5).

Section III. AC GENERATORS

14. Noisy Operation

Probable cause	Remedy
Unbalanced load	Balance load.
Coupling loose or misalined	Reline coupling and tighten.
Improper air gap	Check for bent shaft, loose or worn bearings. Straighten and realine shaft. Replace bearings.
Loose laminations	Tighten bolts. Dip in varnish and bake.

15. Overheating

Probable cause	Remedy
Overloaded	Check meter readings against nameplate ratings. Reduce load.
Unbalanced load	Balance load.
Open load-line fuse	Replace fuse.
Restricted ventilation	Clean, and remove obstructions to ventilation.
Rotor winding short-circuited, open-circuited, or grounded.	Check, and replace defective coil or coils.
Stator winding short-circuited, open-circuited, or grounded.	Check, and replace defective coil or coils.
Bearings	Check for worn, loose, dry, or overlubricated bearings. Replace worn or loose bearings, lubricate dry bearings, relieve overlubrication.

16. No Output Voltage

Probable cause	Remedy
Stator coils open- or short-circuited	Check, and replace defective coil or coils.
Rotor coils open- or short-circuited	Check, and replace defective coil or coils.
Shorted sliprings	Disconnect field coils and check ring-insulation resistance with megger. Repair.
Internal moisture	Check with megger and dry windings.
No dc voltage at the slipring brushes. (No dc exciter voltage.)	Check for defective switch or blown fuse in exciter feeder lines. Repair switch or replace fuses. Check feeder cables for opens or shorts. Repair connections or replace cables. Refer to FAILURE TO BUILD UP VOLTAGE (par. 1).
Voltmeter defective	Check with a voltmeter known to be working properly. Replace.
Ammeter shunt open	Replace ammeter and shunt.

17. Output Voltage Unsteady

Probable cause	Remedy
Poor commutation at sliprings	Clean sliprings and brushes. Reseat brushes.
Loose terminal connections	Clean and tighten all connections and contacts.
Maladjusted voltage regulator and speed governor	Readjust speed governor and voltage regulator.

18. Output Voltage too High

Probable cause	Remedy
Overspeeding	Adjust speed-governing device.
Overexcited	Adjust voltage regulator.
Delta-connected stator open on one leg	Remake connection, repair or replace defective coil or coils.

19. Frequency Incorrect or Fluctuating

Probable cause	Remedy
Speed incorrect or fluctuating	Adjust speed-governing device.
Dc excitation fluctuating	Adjust belt tension of exciter generator.

20. Voltage Hunting

Probable cause	Remedy
External field resistance in total out position	Readjust resistance.
Voltage regulator contacts dirty	Clean and reset contact points.

21. Stator Overheats in Spots

Probable cause	Remedy
Short-circuited phase winding	Check and replace defective coils.
Rotor off center. (Improper air gap.)	Check for bent shaft, loose or worn bearings. Straighten and realine shaft. Replace bearings.
Unbalanced winding circuits	Balance winding circuits.
Loose winding connections	Tighten winding connections.
Wrong phase polarity connections	Correct connections for proper phase polarity.

22. Field Overheating

Probable cause	Remedy
Shorted field coil or coils	Check and replace defective coil or coils.
Dc excitation current too high	Reduce exciter current by adjusting dc voltage regulator.
Clogged air passages (poor ventilation)	Clean equipment. Remove obstructions.

23. Alternator Produces Shock when Touched

Probable cause	Remedy
Reversed stator field coil	Check polarity. Make correction to connections.
Static charges or grounded stator field coil	Check generator frame-ground connection or connections, clean and tighten. Repair or replace stator field coil.

Section IV. AC INDUCTION MOTORS

24. Failure to Start

Probable cause	Remedy
Circuit breaker or fuse open	Check for grounds. Close breaker or replace fuse.
Overload relay open	Wait until motor cools and relay closes.
Low supply voltage	Apply correct voltage.
Stator or rotor windings open or shorted	Check and replace shorted coil or coils.
Winding grounded	Check and replace grounded coil or coils.
Overload	Check meter readings against nameplate ratings. Reduce or install larger motor.

25. Noisy Operation

Probable cause	Remedy
Unbalanced load or coupling misalinement	Balance load and check alinement.
Air gap not uniform	Center rotor by replacing bearing.
Lamination loose	Tighten bolts. Dip in varnish and bake (chapter 4, par. 70). Repeat several times.
Coupling loose	Tighten.

26. Overheating

Probable cause	Remedy
Overloaded	Check meter readings against nameplate ratings. Reduce load.
Electrical unbalance	Balance supply voltage.
Open fuse	Replace line fuse.
Restricted ventilation	Clean. Remove obstructions.
Rotor winding shorted, open, or grounded	Check and replace defective coil or coils.
Stator winding shorted, open, or grounded	Check and replace defective coil or coils.
Bearings	Check for worn, loose, dry, or overlubricated bearings. Replace worn or loose bearings, lubricate dry bearings, relieve overlubrication.

Section V. AC WOUND ROTOR MOTORS

27. Runs Slow with External Resistance Cutout

Probable cause	Remedy
Cables to control box have insufficient current-carrying capacity.	Replace with larger cables.
Open circuits in rotor, cables, or controls	Clean, remake connections, and repair.
Excessive brush sparking	Clean sliprings and reseat brushes.

Section VI. AC SYNCHRONOUS MOTORS

28. Failure to Start

Probable cause	Remedy
Open fuse	Replace fuse.
Faulty starter	Check and repair or replace faulty contacts or contactor coils.
Low supply voltage	Apply correct voltage.
Bearings	Check for bent shaft or worn, loose, dry, or overlubricated bearings. Replace and realine bent shaft. Replace worn and loose bearings, lubricate dry bearings, relieve overlubrication.
Overloaded	Check meter readings against nameplate ratings. Reduce load or install larger motor.
Stator coil open or shorted	Repair or replace coil or coils.
Field exciter current is being applied	Make sure that field contactors are open, and that field-discharge resistors are connected.

29. Runs Slow

Probable cause	Remedy
Overloaded	Check meter readings against nameplate. Reduce load or install larger motor.
Low supply voltage	Apply correct voltage.
Field excited too soon	Adjust time-delay relay so that exciter current will not be applied until rotor reaches synchronous speed.

30. Failure to Pull into Step

Probable cause	Remedy
No field excitation. Open rotor coils. Exciter inoperative. Faulty field contactor.	Tighten or solder open or loose connections. Repair or replace defective rotor coils. Be sure field contactor is operating properly.
Overloaded	Check meter readings against nameplate ratings. Reduce load or install larger motor.

31. No Field Excitation

Probable cause	Remedy
Grounded or open rotor coil	Repair or replace rotor coil or coils.
Grounded or short sliprings	Check and reinsulate.
No output from exciter	See dc generator (par. 1).

32. Pulls out of Step, or Trips Breakers

Probable causes	Remedy
Low exciter voltage	Readjust voltage regulator on exciter to increase voltage.
Intermittently open or shorted cables	Check, and replace defective cables.
Reversed field coil	Check polarity. Change coil leads.
Low supply voltage	Increase voltage if possible. Raise excitation voltage.

33. Hunting

Probable causes	Remedy
Fluctuating load	Increase or decrease size of flywheel on load or loads. Increase or decrease excitation current.
Uneven commutator	Recondition commutator.

34. Stator Overheats in Spots

Probable causes	Remedy
Open phase coil	Check and repair or replace faulty coil or coils.
Rotor not centered	Check for bent shaft, loose or worn bearings. Straighten and realine shaft. Replace bearings.
Unbalanced circuits	Repair loose connections, or correct wrong internal connections.
Shorted coil	Check and replace faulty coil or coils.

35. Field Overheats

Probable causes	Remedy
Shorted field coil	Check and replace faulty coil or coils.
Excitation current too high	Reduce exciter current by adjusting dc voltage regulator.

36. Overheating

Probable causes	Remedy
Overloaded	Check meter readings against nameplate ratings. Reduce load or install larger motor.
Underexcited rotor	Adjust to rated excitation.
Improper ventilation	Remove obstructions and clean air ducts.
Improper supply voltage	Adjust to rated voltage.
Reverse field coil	Check polarity. Change coil leads.

Section VII. AC REPULSION-INDUCTION MOTORS

37. Failure to Start

Probable causes	Remedy
Open fuse	Replace fuse.
Overloaded	Check meter readings against nameplate ratings. Reduce load or install larger motor.
Low supply voltage. Lead wires insufficient current capacity.	Apply correct voltage. Install larger lead wires.
Stator coil open	Check and replace open coil or coils.
Stator coil shorted	Check and replace shorted coil or coils.
Stator coil grounded	Check and replace defective coil or coils.
Centrifugal mechanism not operating properly	Disassemble, clean, inspect, adjust, repair or replace.
Incorrect brush setting	Locate neutral plane by shifting brushes until there is no rotation when current is applied. Shift brushes in the direction of the desired rotation, 1⅓ bars from neutral on 4-pole motors of ½ hp and smaller, and 1¾ bars on larger 4-pole motors. On 2-pole motors, set ⅓ bar farther than setting given above.
Bearings	Check for bent shaft or worn, loose, dry, or overlubricated bearing. Straighten and realine bent shaft. Replace worn and loose bearings, lubricate dry bearings, relieve overlubrication.

38. Runs Slow

Probable cause	Remedy
Overloaded	Check meter readings against nameplate rating.
Centrifugal mechanism not operating properly	Disassemble and clean.
Bearings binding	Clean and lubricate bearings.

39. Overheating

Probable cause	Remedy
Overloaded	Check meter readings against nameplate ratings. Reduce load or install larger motor.
Incorrect supply voltage	Apply correct voltage.
Centrifugal mechanism not operating properly	Disassemble, clean, inspect. Repair, adjust, or replace.
Bearings	Check for bent shaft, or worn, loose, dry, or overlubricated bearings. Straighten and realine bent shaft. Replace worn or loose bearings, lubricate dry bearings, relieve overlubrication.

40. Noisy Operation

Probable cause	Remedy
Bearings	Check for bent shaft, or worn, loose, dry, or overlubricated bearings. Straighten and realine bent shaft. Replace worn or loose bearings, lubricate dry bearings, relieve overlubrication.
Excessive end play	Adjust end-play takeup screw, or add thrust washers to shaft.
Motor not alined properly with driven machine	Realine.
Loose motor mounting and accessories	Tighten all loose components.

41. Motor Produces Shock when Touched

Probable cause	Remedy
Grounded stator coil	Replace defective coil or coils. Check motor-frame connection or connections to ground. Clean and tighten.
Static charge	Check motor-frame connection or connections to ground. Clean and tighten.

Section VIII. AC SPLIT-PHASE, CAPACITOR-START, AND TRANSFORMER-CAPACITOR MOTORS

42. Failure to Start

Probable cause	Remedy
Open fuse	Replace fuse.
Low supply voltage	Apply correct voltage.
Stator coil open	Replace open coil or coils.
Centrifugal mechanism not operating properly	Disassemble, clean, inspect. Adjust, repair, or replace.
Defective capacitor	Replace capacitor.
Stator coil grounded	Check and replace grounded coil or coils.
Bearings	Check for bent shaft, or worn, loose, dry, or overlubricated bearings. Straighten and realine bent shaft. Replace worn or loose bearings, relieve overlubrication.
Overloaded	Check meter readings against nameplate ratings. Reduce load or install larger motor.

43. Overheating

Probable cause	Remedy
Shorted coil	Replace shorted coil or coils.
Centrifugal mechanism not operating properly	Disassemble, clean, inspect. Adjust, repair, or replace.
Incorrect voltage	Apply correct voltage.
Overloaded	Check meter readings against nameplate ratings. Reduce load or install larger motor.
Bearings	Check for bent shaft, or worn, loose, dry, or overlubricated bearings. Straighten and realine bent shaft, replace worn or loose bearings, lubricate dry bearings, relieve overlubrication.

44. Noisy Operation

Probable cause	Remedy
Worn bearings	Replace. Realine.
Shaft bent	Straighten shaft. Realine or replace rotor.
Excessive end play	Adjust screw of end-play takeup device, or put shim washers on shaft between end bells and rotor.
Loose motor mounts or accessories	Tighten all loose components.

11. TROUBLESHOOTING DATA FOR DC AND AC CONTROLLERS

Section I. DC CONTROLLERS

45. Failure to Close

Probable cause	*Remedy*
No power	Check power source. Replace faulty fuses.
Low voltage	Check power-supply voltage. Apply correct voltage.
Inadequate lead wires	Install lead wires of proper size.
Loose connections	Tighten all connections.
Open connections and broken wiring	Locate and repair or replace. Remove dirt from controller contacts.
Contacts affected by long idleness or high operating temperature.	Clean and adjust.
Contacts affected by chemical fumes or salty atmosphere.	Replace with oil-immersed contacts.
Inadequate contact pressure	Replace contacts and adjust spring tension.
Open circuit breaker	Check circuit wiring for possible fault.
Defective coil	Replace with new coil.
Overload-relay contact latched open	Operate hand- or electric-reset.

46. Failure to Open

Probable cause	*Remedy*
Interlock does not open circuit	Check control-circuit wiring for possible fault. Test and repair.
Holding circuit grounded	Test and repair or replace grounded parts.
Misalinement of parts; contacts apparently held together by residual magnetism.	Realine and test for free movement by hand. Magnetic sticking rarely occurs unless caused by excessive mechanical friction or misalinement of moving parts.
Contacts welded together	See paragraph 50, below.

47. Sluggish Operation

Probable cause	*Remedy*
Spring tension too strong	Adjust for proper spring tension.
Low voltage	Check power-supply voltage. Apply correct voltage.
Operating in wrong position	Remount in correct operating position.
Excessive friction	Realine and test for free movement by hand. Clean pivots.
Rusty parts due to long periods of idleness	Clean and renew rusty parts.
Sticky moving parts	Wipe off all accumulations of oil and dirt. Bearings do not need lubrication.
Misalinement of parts	Check for proper alinement. Realine to reduce friction, and test for free movement by hand.

48. Erratic Operation (Unwanted openings and closures, and failure of overload protection)

Probable cause	*Remedy*
Short circuits	Test and repair or replace defective parts.
Grounds	Test and repair or replace defective parts.

Probable cause	Remedy
Sneak currents	These are usually caused by intermittent grounds or short circuits in the machines or wiring circuit. Test and replace faulty parts or wiring.
Loose connections	Tighten all connections. Eliminate any vibrations or rapid temperature changes that may occur in close proximity to the controller.

49. Overheating of Coils

Probable cause	Remedy
Shorted coil	Replace coil.
High ambient temperature or poor ventilation	Relocate controller, use forced ventilation, or replace with suitable type controller.
High voltage	Check for shorted control resistor. Check power-supply voltage. Apply correct voltage.
High current	Check current rating of controller. Check for high voltage, above. If necessary, replace with suitable type controller.
Loose connections	Tighten all connections. Check for undue vibrations in vicinity.
Excessive collection of dirt and grime	Clean but do not reoil parts. If covers do not fit tightly, realine and adjust fasteners.
High humidity, extremely dirty atmosphere, excessive condensation, and rapid temperature changes.	Use oil-immersed controller or dusttight enclosures.

50. Contacts Welded Together

Probable cause	Remedy
Improper application	Check load conditions and replace with a suitable type controller.
Excessive temperature	Smooth off contact surface to remove concentrated hot spots.
Excessive binding of contact tip upon closing	Adjust spring pressure.
Contacts close without enough spring pressure	Replace worn contacts. Adjust or replace weak springs. Check armature overtravel.
Sluggish operation	See paragraph 47, above.
Rapid, momentary, touching of contacts without enough pressure.	Smooth contacts. Adjust weak springs. Where controller has "JOG" or "INCH" control button, operate this less rapidly.

51. Overheating of Contacts

Probable cause	Remedy
Inadequate spring pressure	Replace worn contacts. Adjust or replace weak springs.
Contacts overloaded	Check load data with controller rating. Replace with correct size contactor.
Dirty contacts	Clean and smooth contacts.
High humidity, extremely dirty atmosphere, excessive condensation, and rapid temperature changes.	See paragraph 49, above.
High ambient temperature or poor ventilation	See paragraph 49, above.
Chronic arcing	Adjust or replace arc chutes. If arcing persists, replace with a more suitable controller.
Rough contact surface	Clean and smooth contacts. Check alinement.
Continuous vibration when contacts are closed	Change or improve mounting of controller.
Oxidation of contacts	Keep clean, reduce excessive temperature, or use oil-immersed contacts.

52. Excessive Arcing of Contacts

Probable cause	Remedy
Arc not confined to proper path	Adjust or renew arc chutes. If arcing persists, replace with more suitable controller.
Inadequate spring pressure	Replace worn contacts. Adjust or replace weak springs.
Slow in opening	Remove excessive friction. Adjust spring tension. Renew weak springs. See paragraph 47, above.
Faulty blowout coil or connection	Check and replace coil. Tighten connection.
Excessive inductance in load circuit	Adjust load or replace with proper size controller.
Faulty capacitor	Replace with new capacitor.

53. Pitting or Corroding of Contacts

Probable cause	Remedy
Too little surface contact	Clean contacts and adjust springs.
Service too severe	Check load conditions and replace with correct size controller.
Corrosive atmosphere	Use airtight enclosure. In extreme cases, use oil-immersed contacts.
Continuous vibration when contacts are closed	Change, or improve, mounting of controller.
Oxidation of contacts	Keep clean, reduce excessive temperature, or use oil-immersed contacts.

Section II. AC CONTROLLERS

54. Failure to Close

Probable cause	Remedy
No power	Check power source. Replace faulty fuses.
Low voltage	Check power-supply voltage. Apply correct voltage. Check for low power factor.
Inadequate lead wires	Install lead wires of proper size.
Loose connections	Tighten all connections.
Open connections and broken wiring	Locate opens and repair or replace wiring. Remove dirt from controller contacts.
Contacts affected by long idleness or high operating temperature.	Clean and adjust.
Contacts affected by chemical fumes or salty atmosphere.	Replace with oil-immersed contacts.
Inadequate contact pressure	Replace contacts and adjust spring tension.
Open circuit breaker	Check circuit wiring for possible fault.
Defective coil	Replace with new coil.
Overload-relay contact latched open	Operate hand- or electric-reset.

55. Failure to Open

Probable cause	Remedy
Interlock does not open circuit	Check control-circuit wiring for possible fault. Test and repair.
Holding circuit grounded	Test and repair or replace grounded parts.
Misalinement of parts; contacts apparently held together by residual magnetism.	Realine and test for free movement by hand. Magnetic sticking rarely occurs unless caused by excessive mechanical friction or misalinement of moving parts. Wipe off pole faces to remove accumulation of oil.
Contacts welded together	See paragraph 59, below.

56. Sluggish Operation

Probable cause	Remedy
Spring tension too strong	Adjust for proper spring tension.
Low voltage	Check power-supply voltage. Apply correct voltage.
Operating in wrong position	Remount in correct operating position.
Excessive friction	Realine and test for free movement by hand. Clean pivots.
Rusty parts due to long periods of idleness	Clean or renew rusty parts.
Sticky moving parts	Wipe off all accumulations of oil and dirt. Bearings do not need lubrication.
Misalinement of parts	Check for proper alinement. Realine to reduce friction and test for free movement by hand.

57. Erratic Operation (Unwanted openings and closures and failure of overload protection)

Probable cause	Remedy
Short circuits	Test and repair or replace defective parts.
Grounds	Test and repair or replace defective parts.
Sneak currents	These are usually caused by intermittent grounds or short circuits in the machines or wiring circuit. Test and replace faulty parts or wiring.
Loose connections	Tighten all connections. Eliminate any vibrations or rapid temperature changes that may occur in close proximity to the controller.

58. Overheating of Coils

Probable cause	Remedy
Shorted coil	Replace coil.
High ambient temperature or poor ventilation	Relocate controller, use forced ventilation, or replace with suitable type controller.
High voltage	Check for shorted control resistor. Check power-supply voltage. Apply correct voltage.
High current	Check current rating of controller. Make check for high voltage, above. If necessary, replace with suitable type controller.
Loose connections	Tighten all connections. Check for undue vibrations in vicinity.
Excessive collection of dirt and grime	Clean but do not reoil parts. If covers do not fit tightly, realine and adjust fasteners.
High humidity, extremely dirty atmosphere, excessive condensation, and rapid temperature changes.	Use oil-immersed controller or dusttight enclosures.
Operating on wrong frequency	Replace with coil of proper frequency rating.
DC instead of ac coil	Replace with ac coil.
Too frequent operation	Adjust to apply larger control.
Open armature gap	Adjust spring tension. Eliminate excessive friction or remove any blocking in gap.

59. Contacts Welded Together

Probable cause	Remedy
Improper application	Check load conditions and replace with a more suitable type controller.
Excessive temperature	Smooth off contact surface to remove concentrated hot spots.
Excessive binding of contact tip upon closing	Adjust spring pressure.
Contacts close without enough spring pressure	Replace worn contacts. Adjust or replace weak springs. Check armature overtravel.
Sluggish operation	See paragraph 56, above.
Rapid, momentary, touching of contacts without enough pressure.	Smooth contacts. Adjust weak springs. Where controller has "JOG" or "INCH" control button, operate this less rapidly.

60. Overheating or Contacts

Probable cause	Remedy
Inadequate spring pressure	Replace worn contacts. Adjust or replace weak springs.
Contacts overloaded	Check load data with controller rating. Replace with correct size contactor.
Dirty contacts	Clean and smooth contacts.
High humidity, extremely dirty atmosphere, excessive condensation, and rapid temperature changes.	See paragraph 58, above.
High ambient temperature or poor ventilation	See paragraph 58, above.
Chronic arcing	Adjust or replace arc chutes. If arcing persists, replace with a more suitable controller.

Probable causes	Remedy
Rough contact surfaces	Clean and smooth contacts. Check alinement.
Continuous vibration when contacts are closed	Change or improve mounting of controller.
Oxidation of contacts	Keep clean, reduce excessive temperature, or use oil-immersed contacts.

61. Arcing at Contacts

Probable causes	Remedy
Arc not confined to proper path	Adjust or renew arc chutes. If arcing persists, replace with more suitable controller.
Inadequate spring pressure	Replace worn contacts. Adjust or replace weak springs.
Slow in opening	Remove excessive friction. Adjust spring tension. Renew weak springs. See paragraph 56, above.
Faulty blowout coil or connection	Check and replace coil. Tighten connection.
Excessive inductance in load circuit	Adjust load or replace with more suitable controller.

62. Pitting or Corroding of Contacts

Probable causes	Remedy
Too little surface contact	Clean contacts and adjust springs.
Service too severe	Check load conditions and replace with more suitable controller.
Corrosive atmosphere	Use airtight enclosure. In extreme cases, use oil-immersed contacts.
Continuous vibration when contacts are closed	Change or improve mounting of controller.
Oxidation of contacts	Keep clean, reduce excessive temperature, or use oil-immersed contacts.

63. Noisy Operation (Hum or Chatter)

Probable causes	Remedy
Poor fit at pole face	Realine and adjust pole faces.
Broken or defective shading coil	Replace coil.
Loose coil	Check coil. If correct size, shim coil until tight.
Worn parts	Replace with new parts.

64. Vibration After Repairs

Probable causes	Remedy
Misalinement of parts	Realine parts and test for free movement by hand.
Loose mounting	Tighten mounting bolts.
Incorrect coil	Replace with proper coil.
Too much play in moving parts	Shim parts for proper tightness and clearance.

ELECTRIC WIRING

TABLE OF CONTENTS

CABLE WIRING

		Page
I.	Armored Cable Wiring	1
II.	Non-metallic Sheathed Cable Wiring	5

CONDUIT WIRING

I.	Rigid Conduit Installation	8
II.	Thin-wall Conduit Wiring	15
III.	Flexible Conduits	17

MAINTENANCE

I.	Preventive Maintenance	18
II.	Wire Circuits	19
III.	Miscellaneous Equipment Maintenance	21

CABLE WIRING

Section I. ARMORED CABLE WIRING

78. Advantages and Uses

Armored cable wiring commonly called BX is permissible by code for all interior installations, except where it is exposed to moisture or acid fumes. In moist areas a lead covered cable is required. From an economic viewpoint the labor costs for armored cable installations compare favorably with the open or knob-and-tube wiring installation.

The material requirements for armored cable wiring are greater, and thus overall cost is generally higher. This increased cost is often warranted because an armored conductor has greater mechanical damage protection, and thus eliminates the need for porcelain insulators and loom, which are required in open wiring.

79. Materials

a. Cable. Armored cable construction is made up in 2 or 3 rubber- or thermoplastic-covered wire combinations encased in flexible steel armor. It is obtained from the manufacturer as Type AC without a lead sheath, and Type ACL with a lead sheath under the armor. One of the conductors of armored cable always has white insulation while the other is always black. The third conductor in three-wire cable is always red. Because of this color coding, the code allows a white wire in a switch installation (with armored cable and also nonmetallic sheathed cable) to be used as a hot wire and thereby allows its connection to a black wire. This is shown in the wiring of lampholder No. 3 and switch No. 4, figure 78.

b. Three-Wire Armored Cable.
   (1) *Service.* Three-wire armored cable is used to carry power from the service-entrance switch to the fuse panels or to local load centers if the voltage in a building is 3-wire 110 or 220 volts. The minimum size conductor recommended for this use is No. 10 AWG. In this type of service the neutral wire can be of the same gage as the 2 hot wires because its maximum current will be no greater than the maximum for either of the other 2 wires. Three-conductor cable cannot be used as a service carrier for any other distribution system. A 3-wire cable connection is shown at the load center, No. 1, in figure 78.

   (2) *Two-circuit.* Sometimes in laying out and circuiting armored cable installations several circuits feed out in the same general direction from the protection (fuse) panel. When the power distribution system uses 3-wire 110 to 220 volts, and the circuits are not fed from a common hot-line wire, it is

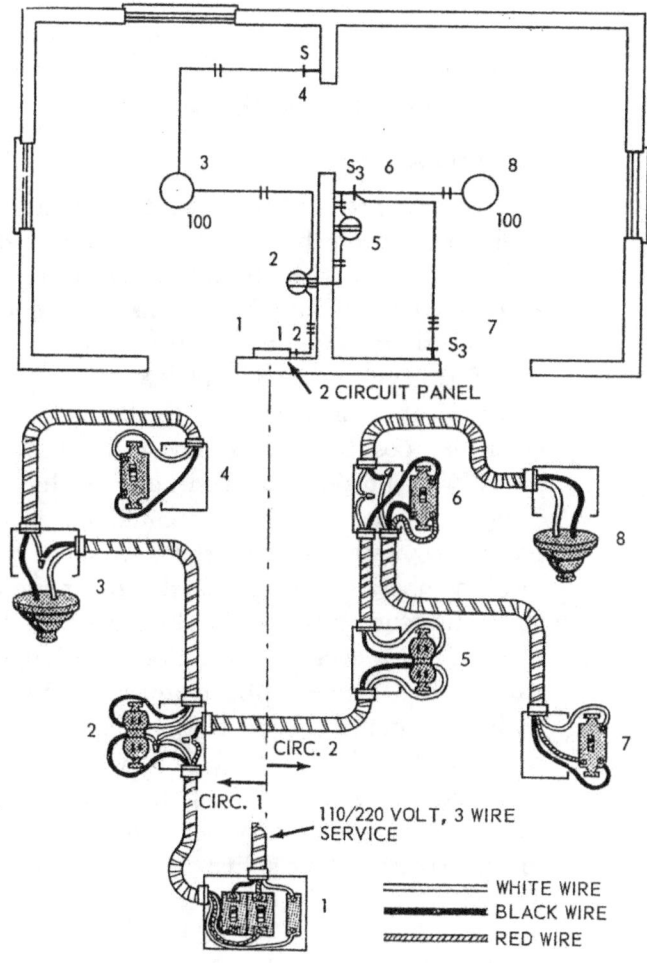

Figure 78. Typical armored cable connections.

149

advantageous, both from a voltage-drop and economic standpoint, to install 3-wire cable as a 2-circuit carrier as far as possible. An example of this use of 3-wire cable is shown in figure 78, between the 2-circuit and the circuit breaker panel, No. 1, and the receptacle box, No. 2. Similarly, many installations are made wherein a switch and an outlet receptacle are connected from wires originating in an overhead light which is to be switch controlled. Rather than use two 2-wire cables for circuiting these devices, a 3-wire installation from the light to the switch (fig. 79) is made.

c. Supports. Armored cable may be fastened to wooden building members with a 1- or 2-hole type mounting strap formed to fit the contour and size of the cable, or by staples made specifically for armored cable use. The cable is normally supported at the box entry by integral BX clamps built into the boxes or by BX connectors.

d. Boxes and Devices.

For quick installation, the electrical boxes with the integral cable clamps and attached mounting brackets are used.

80. Installation

a. Cable Support. Whenever possible an armored cable installation should be run through holes centrally drilled in the building structural members, and the holes should be at least one-eighth inch oversize to facilitate easy "pull through" of the BX. The flush type mounting of BX accomplished by notching the joists and studs should be avoided whenever possible. This type installation exposes the BX to possible short circuits by locating the cable in a position where it could be accidentally pierced by nails and materially weakens the structural member. When armored cable is run between joists and studs it should be supported by staples or straps at least every 4½ feet along the length of the cable run. These supports must also be installed within 12 inches of each box entry, unless the support interferes with installations which require extreme flexibility. This requirement assures the continuance of a satisfactory box connection by relieving the strain on the splices and connection within the outlet box. Cable runs installed across the bottom of ceiling joists and studding faces at least 7 feet above the floor must be supported on each joist or stud. If preferred they may also be installed on

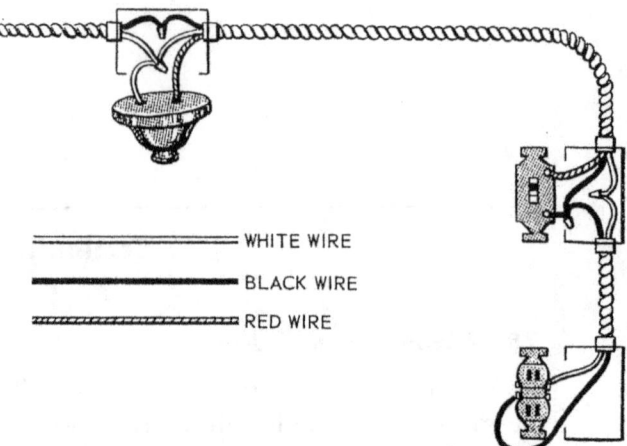

Figure 79. Three-wire cable, two-circuit use.

Figure 80. Typical armored cable wiring installation.

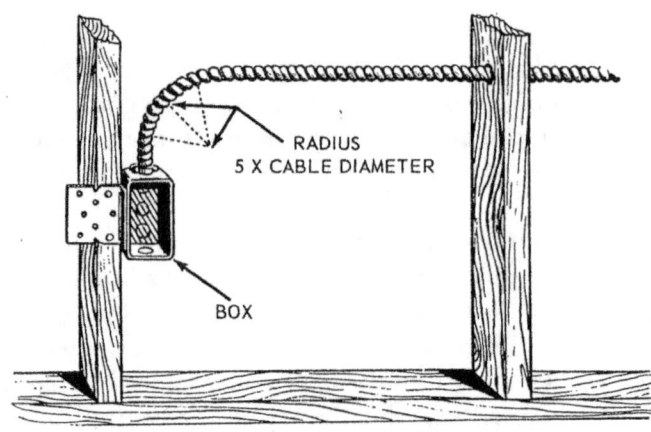

Figure 81. Armored cable bend.

running boards similar to those used in open wiring installations. Figure 80 illustrates a joist-and-running board installation for armored cable.

b. Damage Protection. When armored cable is installed on the top of floor joists or studding in accessible locations (attics and temporary buildings) at a distance less than 7 feet from the floor, guard strips at least as high as the cable must be installed.

c. Armored Cable Bending. When installing armored cable, care must be used to avoid bending or shaping the cable in a manner which damages the protective armor. This type of installation damage may occur in drilled holes for BX, in corner runs, or when locating boxes on studs and joists. To prevent this, the radius of the inner edge of any bend must not be less than 5 times the cable diameter. Figure 81 illustrates an acceptable armored cable bend at box entry.

    d. Box Connection.

        (1) *General.* Armored cable must only be spliced or connected to devices in standard boxes. All the cable used, therefore, must be cut long enough to run from box to box. To prevent cutting the cable too short, the BX should first be threaded through the mounting holes drilled in the joists or studs and attached to one box. The slack is taken out of the cable by using just enough force to maintain the proper bends. Keeping this tension the cable is cut from the roll and connected to the box. The procedure to be followed in preparing and attaching the cable to a box is shown in figure 82.

        (2) *Cable cutting.* Though armored cable can be cut with a BX cutter specifically designed for the job, the majority of electricians generally use a hacksaw. In making an outlet connection the cable should first be cut completely through about 8 inches longer on each end than required for the run. In removing the armored cable from the wire, the armor should be cut approximately 8 inches from the cable end so that ample wire will be inserted in the box for connecting to the outlet device. These lead lengths may be increased when the wire run terminates in a fuse or circuit breaker panel box and a longer cable is required. The cutting of cable armor is a simple operation but care must be taken to avoid damaging the wire insulation when making the cut. With the hacksaw in one hand and the cable end held firmly in the other, the cut should be made with the blade of the hacksaw placed at right angles to the lay of the armor strip. The hacksaw and cable should form 2 legs of a 60° triangle. When the blade has cut almost through the armor strip, the cable end should be bent back and forth several times until it breaks. The loose armor can then be stripped from the wire leads by a twisting and pulling action.

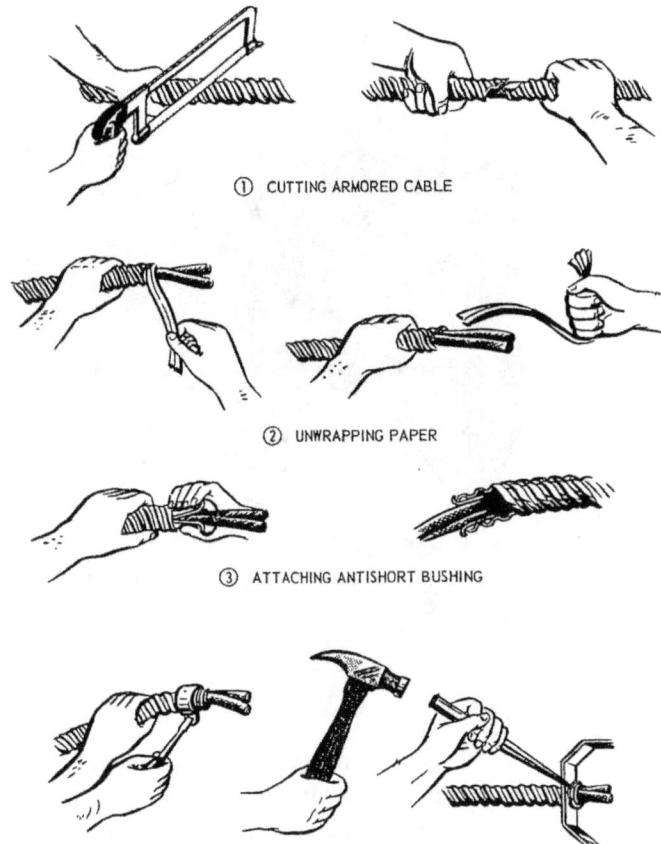

① CUTTING ARMORED CABLE

② UNWRAPPING PAPER

③ ATTACHING ANTISHORT BUSHING

④ ATTACHING CONNECTOR TO CABLE AND CABLE TO BOX

Figure 82. Procedure for preparing and attaching cable.

If one end of the cable has already been threaded and attached to a box, the cable should be pulled tight enough to assure a steady sawing surface. When cut from a coil, the armor is held firm by stepping on the coil cable end and pulling it tight. Rough or sharp ends of the cut are then smoothed with a file.

        (3) *Unwrapping paper.* The fiber paper which is twisted around the conductors before the metallic armor is attached must be removed to allow free wire movement. Normally two or three turns of the paper are removed from under the armor by tearing the loose paper away from the wire at the armor end by a jerking action. The free space between the armor and the wires facilitates mounting the antishort bushing.

        (4) *Attaching the antishort bushing.* When the ends of the cut armor are filed, only the outer burred edges are removed. The inner edges are always sharp and jagged at the cut end, and if not covered, would tend to puncture the wire insulation and cause short circuits and grounds. To prevent

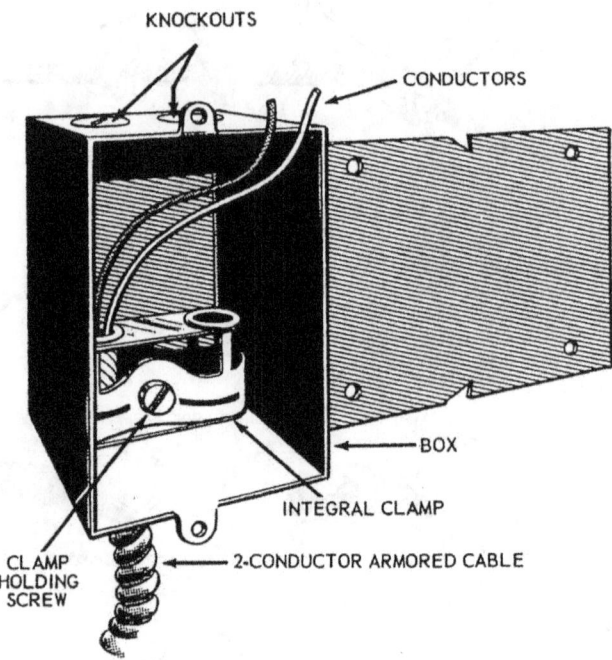

Figure 83. Cable connection to box with integral clamps.

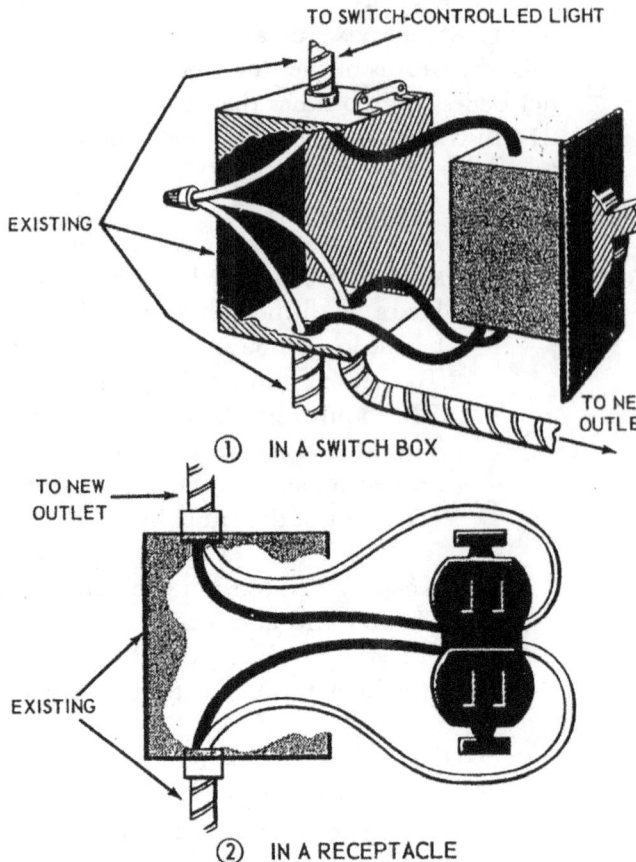

Figure 84. Additions to existing wiring.

this, a tough fiber bushing, commonly called an antishort, must be inserted between the armor and the wire to protect the wire against damage.

(5) *Attaching cable to box.*

(a) When the cable is used with a box having integral cable clamps, the knockout at point of entry must first be pried out. Next the clamp-holding screw is loosened and the cable is inserted through the knockout opening and the leads threaded through the clamps (fig. 83). The armor is then forced snugly against the clamp end and the clamp screw retightened, forcing the clamp into the ridges of the cable.

(b) When a BX connector is used in attaching the armored cable to a box, the cable is first inserted in the connector and the holding screw or screws are tightened against the armor, securely connecting the cable and connectors. The BX connector is then inserted through a box knockout opening and is secured to the box by a locknut threaded on the connectors from inside the box.

81. Additions to Existing Wiring

a. Circuiting. Additions to existing armored cable layouts require analysis to determine whether additional circuit capacity is needed to handle the new load. These considerations are the same as those required for other types of installations and outlined in paragraph 55.

b. Cable Connection. Armored cable additions must always originate and terminate in electrical boxes. The junction box used for the addition should be located close enough to the desired outlet so that the voltage drop to the new device is within allowable limits. The box from which the additional outlet or outlets are to originate must also have both a neutral and hot wire of the same circuit for the new load connection. This means that the conductors from an added outlet can be connected only to the conductors of an existing cable in an outlet box (white to white and black to black) if the existing conductors can be traced to the fuse or circuit breaker without interruption. Figure 84 illustrates two methods of connecting to existing conductors, one in a switch box and the other in a receptacle box.

c. Installation of Armored Cable Additions.

(1) *Exposed.* The installation of exposed armored cable additions to existing wiring must be patterned in accordance with the rules outlined for original installations. If

an armored cable installation is to be made into another type of wiring system the changeover must be made in a junction box specifically installed for the purpose or in an existing outlet box, provided its conductor capacity will allow the entry of additional wires.

(2) *Concealed.* Armored cable is preferred over all other types of wiring when additional outlets are required on completed buildings. The armor provides damage protection and adequate continuous ground to the metal outlet boxes. BX is also flexible enough to allow feeding it through small openings from attic or basement areas to boxes mounted on walls and ceilings. The cable is usually pulled in to the concealed box with a fish wire or drop chain. The fish wire is used when the cable is to be fed from below the box location, whereas the drop chain is used when the installation is to be made from above. In these cases the junction box in which the power tap is to be made should be in a clear, readily accessible area since the fishing and catching of a fish wire and drop chain becomes a tedious and time-consuming operation if the junction box is concealed. If it is difficult because of building construction to feed into the power tap box, the finished wall may have to be removed to allow entry. This will necessitate a replastering job after the addition has been installed.

Section II. NONMETALLIC SHEATHED CABLE WIRING

82. Advantages and Uses

Nonmetallic sheathed cable is approved for use in concealed or exposed dry indoor locations, and is recommended for use where a good system ground is not available. Since the cable is inexpensive light weight, and requires no special installation tools, it is generally used in farm or rural wiring systems. Because of its construction it is not approved for imbedded installation in masonry, concrete, fill, or plaster. It should not be installed in potentially dangerous areas where wire damage may occur, such as commercial garages, theaters, storage-battery rooms, and hoistways. It is not used in humid or wet areas such as ice plants or cold storage warehouses.

83. Materials

a. Cable. Nonmetallic sheathed cable consists of rubber- or thermoplastic-covered wires in 2- or 3-wire combinations. These are individually wrapped with a thick spiral paper tape for damage protection, and covered with a woven fabric braid which has been saturated with a moisture-resistant and flame-retardant compound. The entire assembly is then coated with wax. The local codes in some areas also require the addition of a bare uninsulated conductor in the nonmetallic sheathed cable. This bare wire provides the same type of equipment ground at the outlet boxes as the armor in armored cable installation. The bare wire is attached to the outlet box either by clamping it under the connector locknut at box entry or under one of the screws of the cable clamp.

b. Supports. Nonmetallic sheathed cable is generally mounted on wooden building members with 1- or 2-hole mounting straps formed to fit the contour of the cable. BX staples are not approved for this type of installation because of the danger of possible cable damage.

c. Boxes and Devices. The boxes and devices used in nonmetallic sheathed cable wiring or knob-and-tube wiring are similar. They are made of metal or nonmetallic materials such as porcelain or bakelite. They can be obtained with built-in clamps or knockout holes for the cable connectors. The knockouts in porcelain boxes however are designed for cable entry only. It is recommended that metal boxes with integral clamps be used whenever possible to assure a safe and efficient installation. Insulated switches, outlets, and lampholder devices may be used without boxes in exposed nonmetallic sheathed cable wiring. The cable-entry holes to these devices must clamp the cable securely and the device must fully enclose the section of the cable from which the outer sheathing has been removed. No splicing can be done in these devices. Consequently, since all wires must be connected to terminals, use of these devices is limited to installation in rural or other areas wherein only a small number of outlets and switches are required.

84. Installation

a. Cable Support. Nonmetallic sheathed cable installation should be supported in a manner similar to that outlined for armored cable. As shown in figure 85, the cable can be either installed on run-

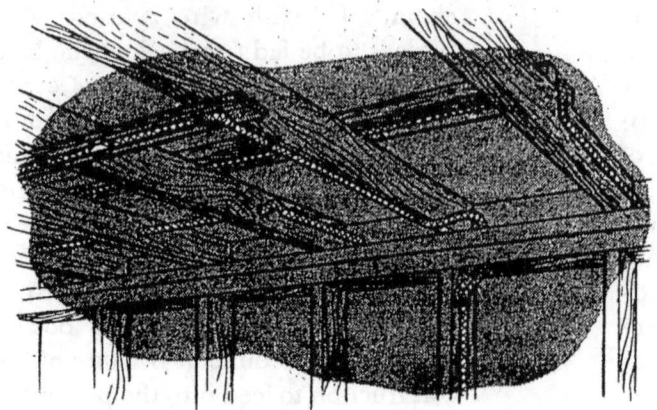

Figure 85. Nonmetallic sheathed cable installation.

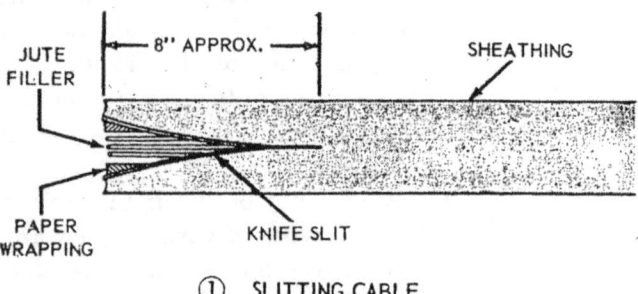

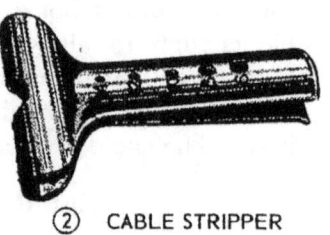

Figure 86. Removal of sheathing.

ning boards, in holes drilled in the center of the joists, or on the sides of joists and studs. When running boards or the sides of joists and studs are used, straps should support the cable, a cable strap should be attached within 6 inches of the box. When the cable run is to be made at an angle in an overhead installation and is supported on the edge of the joists, at least 2 No. 6 gage or 3 No. 8 gage wires must be used in the wire assembly. If smaller size wires are used, they must be installed through holes bored in the joists or mounted on running boards.

b. Damage Protection. If the cable is installed across the top of a floor or floor joists, it must be protected by guard strips at least as high as the cable. When the wire installation is made in a location not normally used, such as an attic or crawl space under a building, damage-protection devices such as guard strips are required only within 6 feet of the entrance. Concealed nonmetallic cable installations should not be installed near baseboards, door and window casings, or other possible locations of trim or equipment because of the possibility of damage from building nails. If thermal insulation is to be installed where nonmetallic sheathed cable is in place, only noncorrosive, noncombustible, nonconductive insulation should be used. During the installation of the insulation, care must be used to prevent adding additional strain on the cable, its supports, or its terminal connections. This is especially necessary if the NM installation includes porcelain outlet boxes.

c. Nonmetallic Sheathed Cable Bending. To prevent accidental damage to the sheathing on nonmetallic sheathed cable, the minimum allowable radius of bend is five times the cable diameter. Though this bend limit is similar to the armored cable requirement, nonmetallic sheathed cable can be bent in a smaller arc. This is true because the cable diameters are smaller for the same wire gage combinations.

d. Box Connection. Cable runs must be continuous from outlet to outlet because wire splices are only permitted inside a box. NM cable (NM is the code designation for nonmetallic sheathed cable) is prepared for box connection in the same manner as outlined for armored cable. In removing the protective sheathing from the conductors for connection, an electrician's knife rather than a hacksaw is used. In removing the covering a slit should be cut in the sheathing parallel to the wires without touching the individual wire insulation. A cut approximately 8 inches long for cable entry to ordinary boxes is satisfactory but can be increased to suit entry to panels. The knife is then used to remove the slitted sheathing. The moisture preventive paper should also be removed from the wires. Figure 86 ① illustrates the slitting of a cable end and figure 86 ② shows a special tool called a cable stripper which can be used instead of a knife to remove the sheathing from NM cable, lead covered cable, and portable cords. In operation, the stripper is inserted over the cable, squeezed together and then pulled off the conductor. This action rips off the outer braid quickly and efficiently. The use of a stripper instead of a knife for outer braid removal is recommended since it cannot damage the wire insulation.

85. Additions to Existing Wiring

a. Circuiting. The factors pertinent for additions to existing wiring systems outlined in paragraph 55 are the same as those which should be considered for NM wiring.

b. Cable Connection. Connection additions for nonmetallic sheathed cable are the same as the connection additions for armored cable outlined in paragraph 81.

c. Installation of Nonmetallic Sheathed Cable Additions.
  (1) *Exposed.* The installation of exposed NM cable additions to existing wiring must conform to the same requirements outlined for original installations. If a wiring system other than nonmetallic sheathed cable is to be extended with nonmetallic sheathed cable the systems must be coupled with a junction box. Existing boxes with available spare conductor capacity can be used.
  (2) *Concealed.* Additions to concealed nonmetallic sheathed cable are similar in method and procedure to those outlined in paragraph 81c(2) with the exception that insulated switches, outlets, and lampholders may be installed without boxes on the wall surfaces. In these installations the cable is fished through the wall and fed to the device at the point of entry.

CONDUIT WIRING

Section I. RIGID CONDUIT INSTALLATION

86. Uses and Advantages

Either black enameled or galvanized rigid metal conduit is approved for use under all conditions and locations. Though it is generally the most expensive type of wiring installation, its inherent strength permits installation without running boards and damage protection. Its conductor capacity facilitates carrying more conductors in one run than in any other system, and its rigidity permits installation with fewer supports than the other types of wiring systems. Moreover, the sizes of conduits used in the system's installation generally provide for the possible addition of several more conductors in the conduit when additional circuits and outlets are required in the run.

87. Materials

a. General. Though the materials used in rigid conduit wiring have been outlined in detail in chapter 4, *b* through *h* below will review the advantages of these standard materials as well as their limitations.

b. Rigid Conduit. Rigid conduit (fig. 87 ①) has the same size designations as water pipe. Under the code limitations no conduit smaller than ½ inch may be used except in finished buildings where extensions are to be made under plaster. In these installations ⁵⁄₁₆-inch conduit or tubing is permitted. The size of conduit is determined by the inside diameter. For example, ½-inch conduit has an inside diameter of approximately ½-inch (0.505). Standard conduit used in interior wiring is ½, ¾, 1, 1¼, 1½, 2 and 2½ inches. Larger sizes are available for special use, such as their required employment in certain commercial and factory installations. Though conduit is made in dimensions similar to water pipe it differs from water pipe in a number of ways. It is softer than water pipe and thus can be bent fairly easily. In addition, the inner surface is smooth to prevent damage to wires being pulled through it. Moreover, the finish is rust-resistant. Black enamel conduit is used for dry and indoor installations, and exterior galvanized conduit is used in outside installations to provide moisture protection for the conductors. For wiring installations in corrosive atmospheres, aluminum or Everdur alloy conduit is available.

c. Conductors. Rubber-covered insulated type R or RH wire is used with conduit in the majority of interior wiring installations though the thermoplastic insulation types T or TW are gaining favor because of their superior insulating characteristics. Underground or wet installations requires the insertion of lead-covered cables in rigid galvanized conduit for permanent protection.

d. Supports. The conduit strips illustrated and described in chapter 3 are preferred for use in mounting conduit in interior wiring systems. In accordance with code requirements, the conduit should be supported on spacings as shown in table XII.

e. Fittings (fig. 87 ②). There are two types of fittings. These are the standard ordinary size outlet box and the small junction or pull box. The standard outlet box fittings are classified as type F and are used normally in exposed installations to house receptacles or switches where high quality of installation is desired. The junction or pull box fittings are

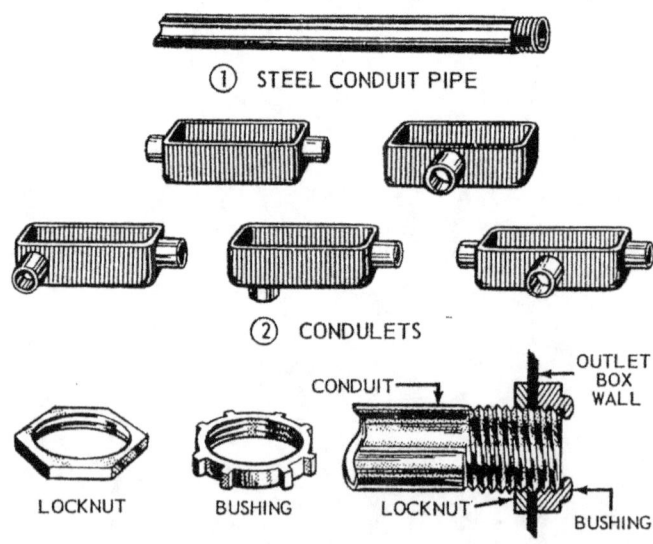

① STEEL CONDUIT PIPE

② CONDULETS

③ DEAD-END CONDUIT IN OUTLET BOX

Figure 87. Rigid conduit and fittings.

Table XII. Spacing of Supports for Conduit Runs

Size of conduit, inches	Maximum support spacing, feet		
	Horizontal runs		Vertical runs
	Flat ceilings	Where building construction causes support difficulties	
½	5	7	7
¾	5	7	7
1	6	10	8
1¼	6	10	8
1½	6	10	10
2	6	10	10
2½	6	10	10

used to either provide intermediate points in long conduit runs for pull through of wire or junctions for several conduit runs. Conduit fittings are not permitted in concealed installations where they will not be accessible. They are classified by the manufacturers as follows:

(1) Service entrance, type SE.
(2) Elbow or turn fittings, type L.
(3) Through fittings, type C.
(4) Through fittings with a 90° take off, type T.

f. Boxes and Connectors. Steel or cast iron outlet boxes are used in rigid conduit installations. Boxes normally used are supplied with knockouts which are removable for conduit insertion. Bushings and locknuts are provided for attachment of the conduit to the boxes as shown in figure 87 ③. Boxes to be used in wet or hazardous locations must have threaded hubs into which the conduit is screwed.

g. Devices. The devices used in conduit installations are all box mounted units and are covered in chapter 4.

h. Conduit Accessories.

(1) *Threaded couplings.* A threaded coupling (fig. 88 ①) is furnished with each length of rigid conduit.
(2) *Threadless couplings.* Rigid conduit may be installed using threadless couplings provided the couplings are installed tightly.
(3) *Elbows.* Standard conduit elbows (fig. 88 ②) are manufactured for use where 90° bends are required.
(4) *Conduit unions.* To permit the opening of a conduit at any point without sawing or breaking the conduit run, conduit unions (fig. 88 ③) are installed. By the use of unions, conduits may be started from two outlets and joined together at any convenient place in the run.

① CONDUIT COUPLING

② CONDUIT ELBOW

③ CONDUIT UNION

Figure 88. Rigid conduit accessories.

88. Installation

a. Bends. Bends of rigid conduit must be made without collapsing the conduit wall or reducing the internal diameter of the conduit at the bend.

(1) Most bends are made on the job by the electrician as an integral part of the installation procedure. These are called field bends. The radius of the curve of the inner edge of any field bend must be at least 6 times the internal diameter of the conduit for rubber-, braid-, or thermoplastic-covered conductors, and not less than 10 times the internal diameter of the conduit for lead-covered conductors. The maximum number of quarter bends for a conduit run between 2 openings is 4. Moreover, a 10-foot length of conduit should have no more than 3 quarter bends. Factory made bends may be used instead of bending conduit on the job. However, they are not generally used since they increase the wiring cost. This is because more conduit cutting and threading is required and additional couplings must be used.
(2) Conduit up to and including ¾ inch is usually bent with a hand conduit bender called a hickey as shown in figure 89 ①.

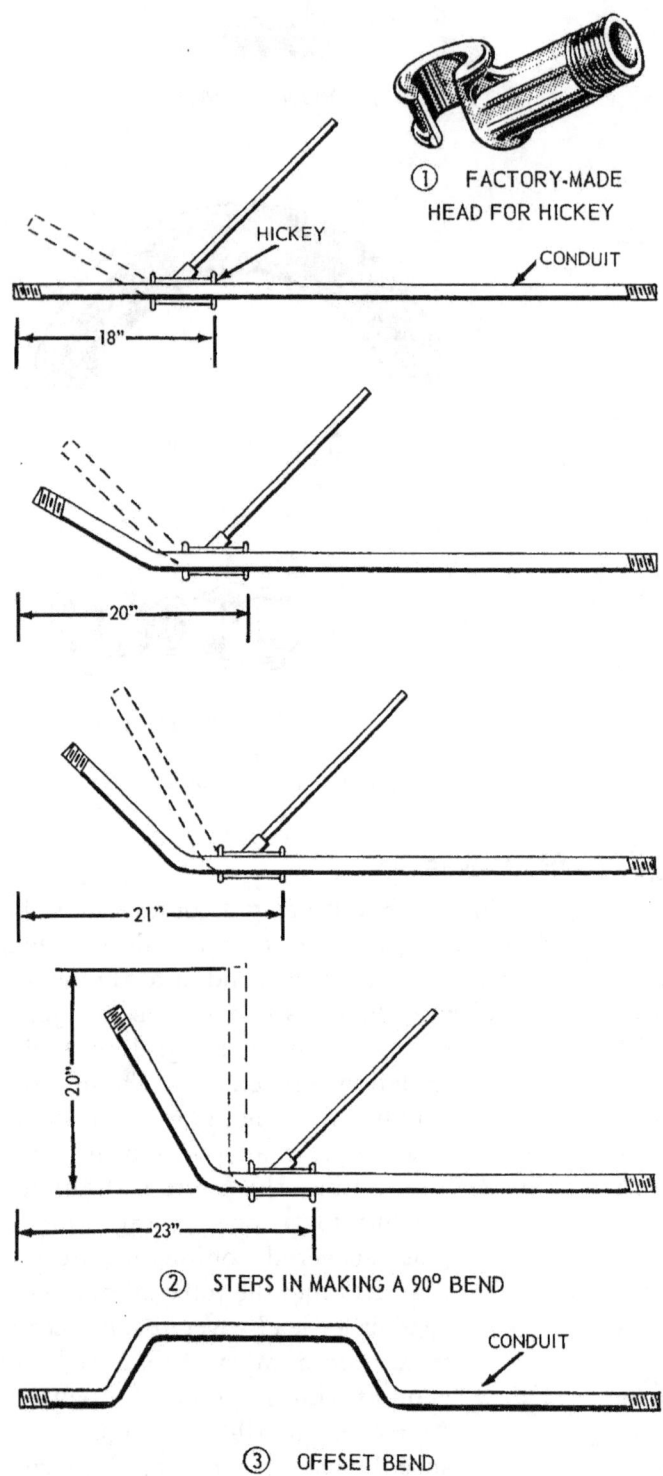

Figure 89. Bending rigid conduit.

This can be slipped over the conduit. Conduit bending forms are also available as built-in units of pipe-vise stands. If either of these tools are not available, bends can be made using the lever advantage between 2 fixed posts or building members.

(3) The procedure in (a) through (e) below, illustrated in figure 89 ② is recommended as one method of making a right angle bend in a length of ½-inch conduit. If a 90° bend is to be made in a length of conduit at a distance of 20 inches from one end the electrician must—

(a) Mark off 20 inches from the end of the conduit.
(b) Place the conduit hickey 2 inches in front of the 20-inch mark and bend the conduit about 25°.
(c) Move the bender to the 20-inch mark and bring the bend up to 45°.
(d) Move the bender about 1 inch behind the 20-inch mark and bring the conduit up to 70°.
(e) Move the hickey back about 2 inches behind the 20-inch mark and bring the bend up to 90°.

(4) Miscellaneous conduit bends (offset bends, figure 89 ③) can be made more accurately if the contour of the bend is drawn with chalk on the floor and the bend in the pipe is matched with the chalk diagram as the bend is formed.

b. Cutting Conduit. Conduit can be cut with either a hacksaw or standard pipe cutter. When a hand hacksaw is used, the conduit should be held in a vise and care should be taken that the cut is at right angles to the length of the pipe. If a large number of conduits are to be cut, a power hacksaw is recommended. Though pipe cutters may be used and are considered standard equipment, a hacksaw is recommended for electrical conduit cutting since considerable time is required to remove the burr left in the inside of a pipe by a pipe cutter. Cutting oil should always be used when cutting pipe.

c. Reaming Conduit. Irrespective of the cutting method used, a sharp edge always remains inside the conduit after cutting. Consequently, to avoid conductor damage, this edge must be removed before the conduit is installed. Pipe reamers or files are generally used for the reaming operation.

d. Cutting Threads. Since the outside and inside diameter of rigid conduit are the same as that used in gas, water, or steam pipes, the standard thread forms, and consequently similar threading tools and dies, are used. Normally the smaller sizes of pipe are threaded with dies that cut a thread for every turn of the die. For larger sizes (1½ inch and over) electricians generally use a ratchet type cutter. Motor driven pipe-threading machines are also available when large installations are made and when considerable conduit must be threaded. Good practice requires an electrician to examine, before installation, each piece of threaded conduit for—

(1) *Foreign matter inside the pipe.* This should be removed to prevent conductor damage.

(2) *Thread condition.* Mishandling, extraneous paint, or dirt may require the conduit to be rethreaded before installation. Cutting oil should always be used when threading conduit.

e. Conduit Installation. Conduit should be run as straight and direct as possible. When a number of conduits are to be installed parallel and adjacent to each other in exposed multiple-conduit runs, they should be erected simultaneously instead of installing one line before starting the others. Conduits installed on building surfaces can be supported by either pipe straps or pipe hangers. On wooden surfaces nails or wood screws can be used to secure the straps. On brick or concrete surfaces, holes must be drilled first with a star or carbide drill and expansion anchors installed. The strap is then secured to the surface with machine screws. On tile or other hollow material, the straps are secured with toggle bolts. If the installation is made on a metal surface, holes for the straps or hangers can be drilled and tapped into the metal, and the supports secured by machine screws to the metal surface. An adequate number of supports should be provided in accordance with table XII. The conduit run, as the conduit between boxes is called, must be cut to proper length, threaded, reamed, and then bent to suit the building contours. The conduit-run ends are then attached to the boxes. Figure 90 illustrates a typical rigid conduit exposed installation. In a concealed installation the building members may be notched sufficiently to allow placing the conduit behind the wall surface. Care must be taken to avoid undue weakening of the structure.

f. Box Connection.

(1) When the boxes are of threaded-hub construction, the conduit ends are screwed into the box hubs and the conduit runs are connected at some midpoint by a coupling.

(2) If the boxes are of knockout type construction, they should be loosely located in the required position on studs and joists. A bowed locknut having teeth on one side should then be screwed onto the threads at the run ends of the conduit with the teeth of the locknut adjacent to the box. The conduit ends should next be inserted into the knockout openings. Bushings, which

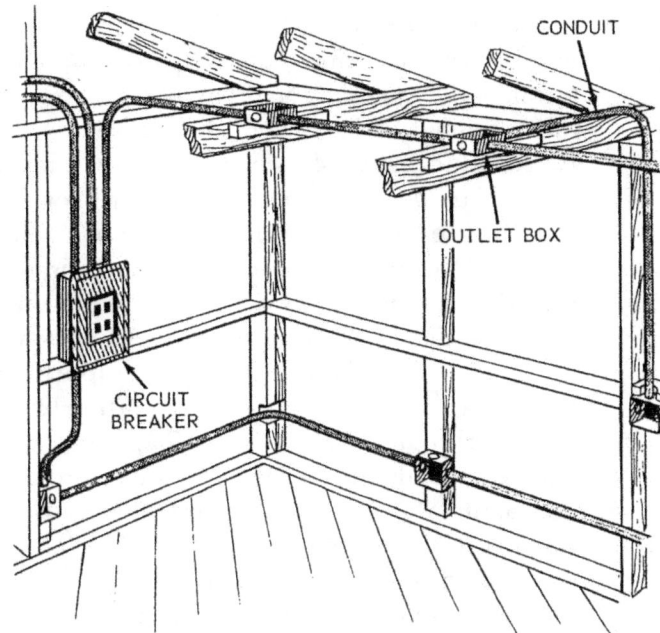

Figure 90. Typical installation of conduit wiring.

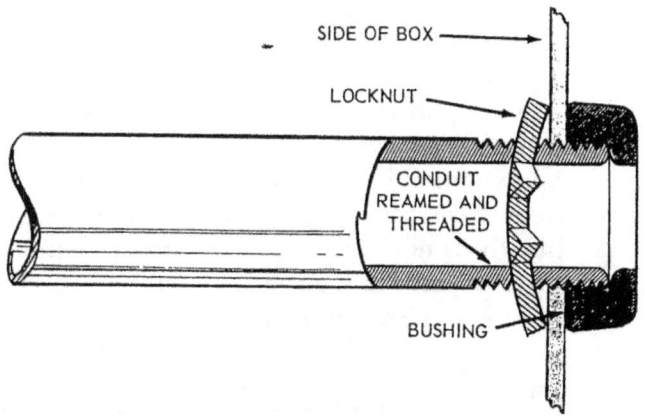

Figure 91. Conduit and box connection.

have smooth surfaces on their inside diameter to insure damage-free conductor installation, should then be screwed tightly onto the conduit ends in the boxes. Finally the locknuts should be tightened against the boxes so that the teeth will dig into the metal sides of the box. This operation can be accomplished by driving a screwdriver tip against one of the locknut lugs and forcing the locknut to move on the threaded conduit against the box. Figure 91 shows a standard box connection for conduit using locknuts and bushings. After this connection and all other box connections have been made, the box can be fastened securely to the building.

g. Wire Pulling. Upon installation of the boxes and conduit runs the conductor wires should be pulled into the conduit. For short runs with few wires, the conductors can be paired and pushed through the conduit run from box to box. When the conduit run has several bends and more than two conductors, a fish wire must be used in pulling wire. For normal runs the fish wire (or tape) is pushed through the conduit run from one end to the other. Occasionally, on long conduit runs, separate fish wires are used from either end of the conduit as shown in figure 92 ①. After the conductor ends are bared of insulation, they are wrapped around the fish-wire (fig. 92 ②) and taped (fig. 92 ③) for pulling through the conduit. Taping of the fish-wire and conductor junction is required to preclude damaging the conduit interior and existing conductors in the conduit. In taping, the joint is also compacted and strengthened, thus insuring easier pulling. For efficient and safe operation wire pulling is generally a 2-man operation. One electrician is required to pull the conductors through the conduit while the other feeds the conductors into the conduit. In this operation care must be used in feeding and pulling the wires so they maintain their same relative position in the conduit throughout the run length, thus avoiding insulation injury. For ease of operation, a wire lubricant such as powdered soapstone may be rubbed on the conductors or blown into the conduit. In intricate runs, wire pulling may be performed in sections between boxes. This procedure requires a large amount of additional splicing to be made in the boxes and requires that more time be taken in wiring. The preferred practice in wire pulling is to pull the conductors from the source through to the last box in the conductor run. Loops which extend about 8 inches from the box openings are made for each conductor which is to be tapped or connected to a device in the box. Conductors which are not to be tapped are pulled directly through the box to their connection.

h. Splices. Wire splices in conduit installations are not under tension and a simple pigtail splice, carefully made to obtain a good electrical joint, can be used. No wire splices which will be concealed in the conduit runs are to be made. This requirement is necessary because splices would reduce the pulling area in a conduit and would easily be a source of electrical failure.

89. Circuiting

a. Layout. The layout and circuiting of devices in a conduit installation should be made in accordance with the directions and procedures in chapter 5. The availability of different sizes of conduit along with their varying conductor capacities makes the wiring installation for conduit somewhat different from that of the open or cable types. For example, where cable installation requires several runs in a particular location, a conduit installation would use a single conduit with multiple conductors. Consequently, conduit layouts and runs should be planned to use the minimum amount of conduit possible and also keep the conductor runs to each outlet short enough to maintain a low voltage drop. Figure 93 shows a typical wiring layout in conduit.

b. Conductor Connection. No exceptions to the standard color coding of wires as outlined in the other systems are permitted in conduit wiring. All devices in a grounded neutral system must be connected to both a white and a black, or substitute color, wire. The white wire is always the grounded neutral wire. Black wires are the hot leads which are fused and which are switched when controlling power to a lampholder or outlet. Red-, blue-, and orange-colored insulation wire can be used as substitutes for black wire when wire combinations are combined in a conduit or circuit. The white wire must never be connected to a black or substitute color wire. The white wire must not be fused and must never be switched. A green-colored insulated conductor denotes a wire used to provide an auxiliary equipment ground. As an expedient measure, the ends of the wire insulation may be painted to obtain proper color coding when the colored insulation is

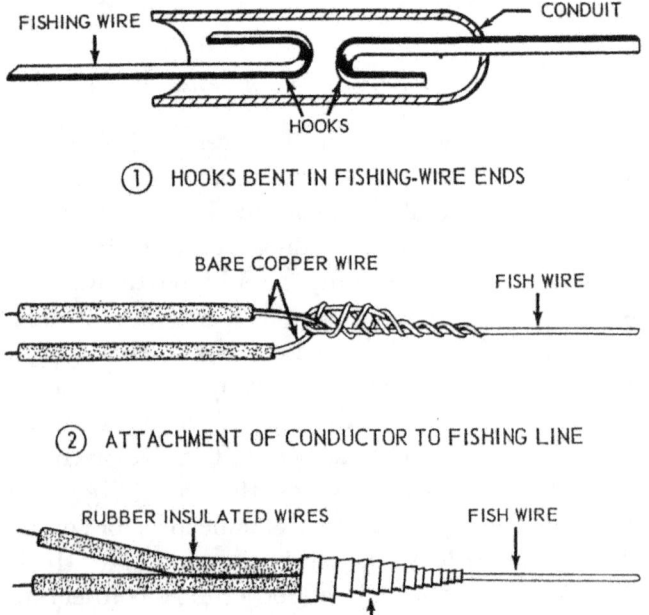

Figure 92. Fish-wire pulling.

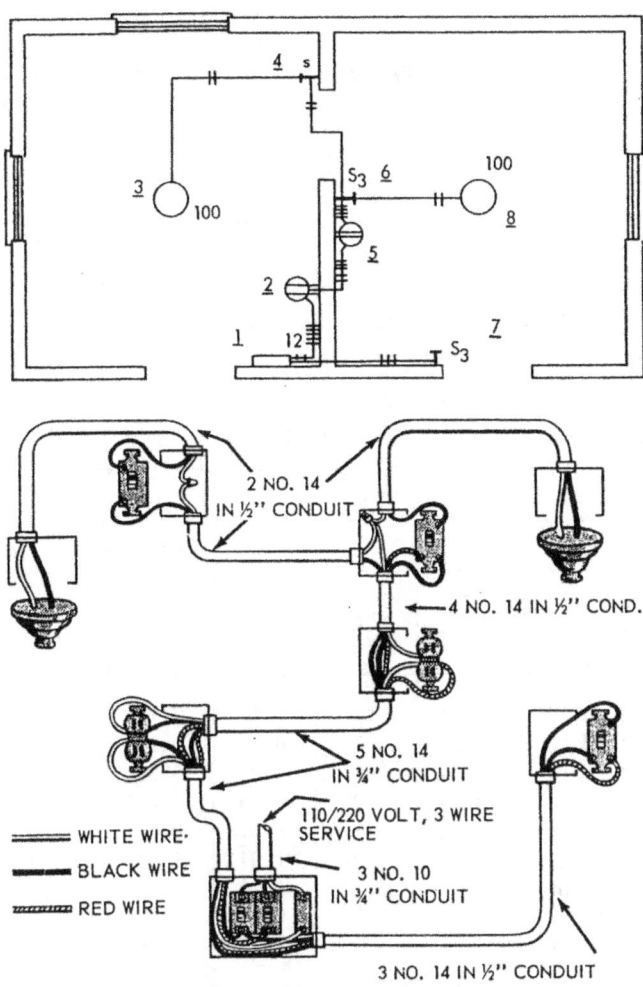

Figure 93. Typical wiring layout in conduit.

not available. They may also be identified by the use of wire code markers, paragraph 27.

c. Conduit Capacity. Cable wiring described in chapter 7 was normally limited to 2 or 3 standard combinations of wire sizes. Conduit, however, has the capacity to accommodate many more conductors than 2 or 3 in 1 run. Table XIII lists the maximum number of conductors of a certain gage which can be inserted in the various size conduits used in interior wiring. For example, the table shows that 6 No. 14 gage wires would require the installation of a ¾-inch conduit run. In many installations it is necessary to use more than 1 size wire in a conduit run. In such cases the conductors can not have a combined or cross sectional area equal to more than the allowable percent of cross sectional area of conduit as shown in table XIV. Table XV lists, for each size conduit, the percent of conduit cross sectional area in square inches available for conductor use. For example, if 3 No. 10 gage type R and 4 No. 8 gage type R conductors are to be inserted in a conduit, their combined cross sectional area, obtained from table XVI is $3 \times 0.0460 + 4 \times 0.0760$ or 0.4420 square inches. The proper size conduit for this installation is 1¼ inches using table XV. This is found by first looking for the total area under the headings "not lead covered" and "4 cond. and over." It is seen that 0.4420 lies between 0.34 square inches (for 1-inch conduit) and 0.60 square inches (for 1¼-inch conduit). Consequently, as the 1-inch conduit is too small, the 1¼-inch size is selected.

Table XIII. Minimum Size (inches) of Conduit of Electrical Metallic Tubing to Contain a Given Number of 600-Volt Conductors

Wire size gage No.	Number of conductors—types R, RW, RH, RU, RUW, TF, T, and TW								
	1	2	3	4	5	6	7	8	9
18	½	½	½	½	½	½	½	¾	¾
16	½	½	½	½	½	½	¾	¾	¾
14	½	½	½	½	¾	¾	1	1	1
12	½	½	½	¾	¾	1	1	1	1¼
10	½	¾	¾	¾	1	1	1	1¼	1¼
8	½	¾	¾	1	1¼	1¼	1¼	1½	1½
6	½	1	1	1¼	1½	1½	2	2	2
4	½	1¼	1¼	1½	1½	2	2	2	2½
3	¾	1¼	1¼	1½	2	2	2	2½	2½
2	¾	1¼	1¼	2	2	2	2½	2½	2½
1	¾	1½	1½	2	2½	2½	2½	3	3
0	1	1½	2	2	2½	2½	3	3	3
00	1	2	2	2½	2½	3	3	3	3½
000	1	2	2	2½	3	3	3	3½	3½
0000	1¼	2	2½	3	3	3	3½	3½	4

Table XIV. Size Conduit of Electrical Metallic Tubing for Combinations of Conductors. Percentage of Cross Sectional Area of Conduit or Tubing

Conductors	Number of conductors				
	1	2	3	4	4 and over
Not lead covered...................................	53	31	43	40	40
Lead covered.......................................	55	30	40	38	35
For rewiring existing conduits.......................	60	40	40	50	50

Table XV. Dimensions and Percent of Area of Conduit and Tubing for Combinations

Conduit size	Internal diameter in.	Area, square in.									
		Total 100%	Not lead covered				Lead covered				
			1 cond. 53%	2 cond. 31%	3 cond. 43%	4 cond. and over 40%	1 cond. 55%	2 cond. 30%	3 cond. 40%	4 cond. 38%	Over 4 cond. 35%
½	0.622	0.30	0.16	0.09	0.13	0.12	0.17	0.09	0.12	0.11	0.11
¾	0.824	0.53	0.28	0.16	0.23	0.21	0.29	0.16	0.21	0.20	0.19
1	1.049	0.86	0.46	0.27	0.37	0.34	0.47	0.26	0.34	0.33	0.30
1¼	1.380	1.50	0.80	0.47	0.65	0.60	0.83	0.65	0.60	0.57	0.53
1½	1.610	2.04	1.08	0.63	0.88	0.82	1.112	0.61	0.82	0.78	0.71
2	2.067	3.36	1.78	1.04	1.44	1.34	1.85	1.01	1.34	1.28	1.18
2½	2.469	4.79	2.54	1.48	2.06	1.92	2.63	1.44	1.92	1.82	1.68
3	3.068	7.38	3.91	2.29	3.17	2.95	4.06	2.21	2.95	2.80	2.58
3½	3.548	9.90	5.25	3.07	4.26	3.96	5.44	2.97	3.96	3.76	3.47

Table XVI. Dimensions of Rubber-covered and Thermoplastic-covered Conductors

Size, gage No.	Types R, RH, RW		Types T, TW, TF, RU	
	Approximate diameter in.	Approximate area sq. in.	Approximate diameter in.	Approximate area sq. in.
18	0.146	0.0167	0.106	0.0088
16	0.158	0.0196	0.118	0.0109
14	0.171	0.0230	0.131	0.0135
12	0.188	0.0278	0.148	0.0172
10	0.242	0.0460	0.169	0.0224
8	0.311	0.0760	0.228	0.0408
6	0.397	0.1238	0.323	0.0819
4	0.452	0.1605	0.372	0.1087
3	0.481	0.1817	0.401	0.1263
2	0.513	0.2067	0.433	0.1473
1	0.588	0.2715	0.508	0.2027
0	0.629	0.3107	0.549	0.2367
00	0.675	0.3578	0.595	0.2781
000	0.727	0.4151	0.647	0.3288
000	0.785	0.4840	0.705	0.3904

d. Circuit Wiring. A fundamental law of electricity generation can be restated for wiring purposes as follows: When a conductor carrying current changes position or the current reverses direction in the conductor, it induces a current in the conduit carrying the conductor. Consequently, if this conductor were isolated in a conduit, the conduit would be heated by the reversing alternating current, resulting in considerable power loss. In an alternating current system, both wires of a circuit are encased in a single conduit thereby causing the induced current of each to balance and cancel each other. To eliminate any possibility of induced heating of the conduit, both the wires of a circuit must travel in the same conduit. If the conductors in the circuit (fig. 94) are run separately in these conduits, induced current (indicated by arrows) will flow through the conduits.

90. Additions to Existing Wiring

a. Increase of Circuit Amperage. A standard conduit installation has enough flexibility to accommodate a

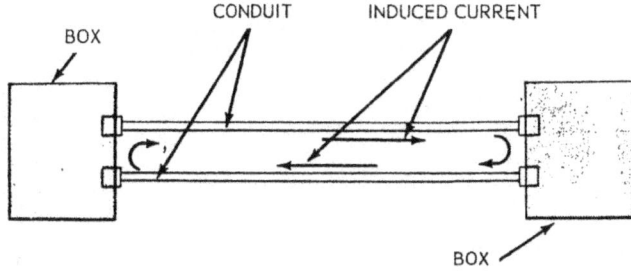

Figure 94. Circulating current in conduits, showing induced-current flow.

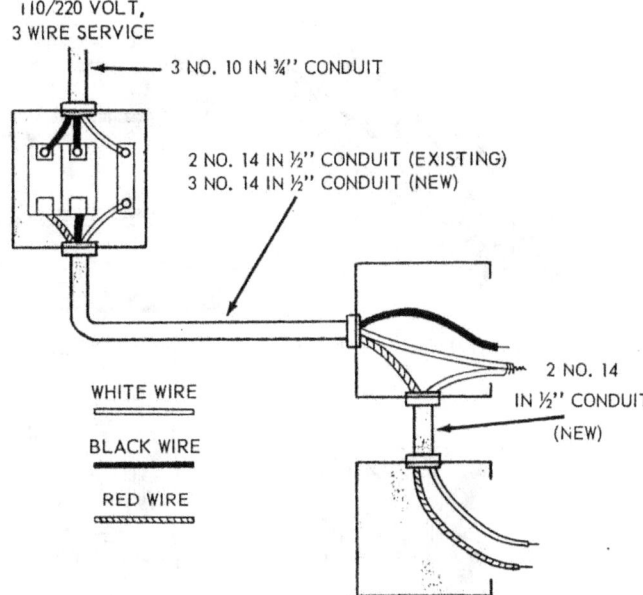

Figure 95. Circuit addition in existing conduit.

normal increase in circuit load even if an increase in circuit amperage is required. For example, a ½-inch conduit in a standard conduit-wiring installation generally carries 2 No. 14 gage conductors which have a 15-ampere capacity. From table XIII it is evident that the ½-inch conduit can also accommodate 2 No. 12 gage conductors having a 20-ampere capacity. Consequently, if the load in an existing circuit must be increased, the No. 14 gage wire can be replaced by 2 No. 12 gage wires. Hence, when all the wires in the circuit are replaced, the amperage for the fuse or circuit breaker in the central fuse panel for the circuit can be safely increased from 15 to 20 amperes to accommodate the additional load.

b. Addition of New Circuit. When adding a new load to an existing building with conduit wiring, and the circuit analysis indicates the need for a new circuit, the existing conduit in many cases can be used to carry the new circuit most of its distance. Figure 95 illustrates this principle. The new circuit is installed by pulling in an additional wire (red) from the circuit breaker panel to the existing outlet, and then adding the required outlet box beyond this location. The new load is connected to the additional circuit. Table XIII was used to determine whether the existing conduit could accommodate an additional wire. The installation of the additional outlet box and conduit should conform to the rules and practices outlined in paragraph 82. In this type of installation a common ground wire is used.

Section II. THIN-WALL CONDUIT WIRING

91. Uses and Advantages

Thin-wall conduit is a metallic tubing which can be used for either exposed or concealed electrical installations. Its use should be confined to dry interior locations. This is necessary because it has a very thin plating which does not protect it from rusting when exposed to the elements or humid conditions. It is less expensive than rigid conduit and much easier to install. The process of bending requires less effort and the ends are not required to be threaded. In comparison with the other systems of wiring, it ranks behind rigid conduit, but ahead of the other types of wiring when considering the quality and durability of the installation. For this reason, and because of the decreased cost in materials and labor, it is most generally specified for home-building construction. It is installed in the same manner as rigid conduit except that pressure type couplings and connectors are used instead of threaded units.

92. Materials

a. Thin-Wall Conduits and Fittings. Electrical metallic tubing (EMT) commonly called "thin-wall conduit" is more easily installed than rigid conduit. This conduit, as its name implies, has a thinner wall than rigid conduit but has the same interior diameter and cross sectional area as the rigid conduit type. EMT is available in sizes from ⅜ to 2 inches. The ⅜-inch size is used only for underplaster extensions. The inside surface is enameled to protect the wire insulation and minimize the friction in wire pulling. All couplings and connections to boxes are threadless and are of either the clamp or compression type. Figure 96 illustrates thin-wall conduit and the fittings commonly used. Some fittings are

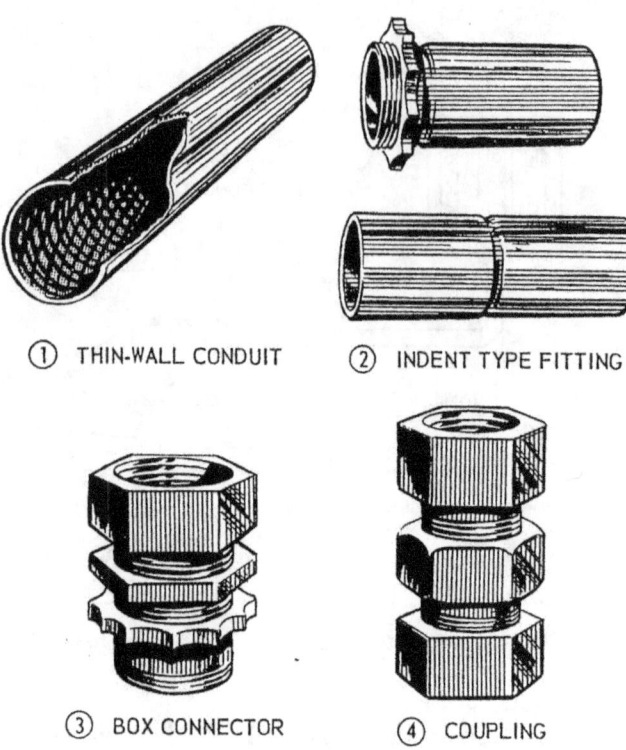

Figure 96. Thin-wall conduit and fittings.

Table XVII. Minimum Radii for Field Bends When Braid-covered Cable is Used

Tubing size (in.) nominal inside diameter	Minimum radius (in.)
⅜	3
½	3¾
¾	5
1	6¼
1¼	8¼
1½	9¾
2	12½

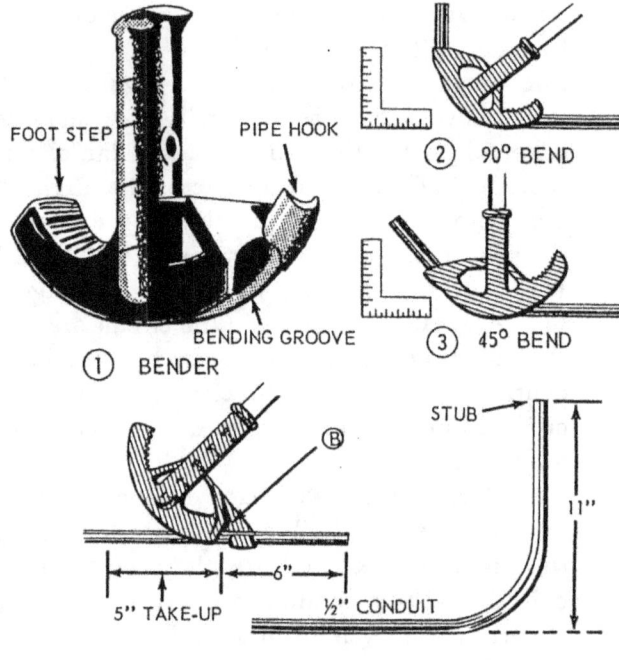

Figure 97. Bending thin-wall conduit.

similar to sleeves and are secured to the conduit by an indenter tool (fig. 17) which pinches circular indentations in the fitting. This holds it firmly against the conduit. Others have threaded bushings which, when tightened, force a tapered sleeve firmly against the tubing. Figures 96 ③ and ④ show a box connector and coupling fitting of this type. An adapter for joining rigid conduit to thin-wall conduit is also shown.

b. *Wire Conductors.* The same type, capacity, and maximum number of conductors per size of conduit previously given in tables XIII through XVI for rigid conduit also apply to thin-wall installations. The maximum size wire or cable which can be installed in thin-wall conduit is No. 0 gage.

93. Bending

a. *General.* Extreme care must be used when bending metallic tubing to avoid kinking the pipe or reducing its inside area. The radius of the curve of the inner edge of any field bend must not be less than 6 times the internal diameter of the tubing when braid-covered conductors are used, and not less than 10 times the interior diameter of the tubing when lead-covered conductors are used. Table XVII shows the minimum radii for field bends when braid-covered cable is used.

b. *Construction.* The thin-wall conduit bender (fig. 97 ①) has a cast steel head which is attached to a steel-pipe handle approximately 4 feet long. It is used in the field to form thin-wall conduit into standard and offset bends. Benders are made for each size of conduit and must be used only on those sizes for which they are designed. Each size bends the conduit to the recommended safe radius. The projection on the head of the bender, sometimes called a "foot step," is used to steady the bender in operation, and reduces the pressure required on the handle for bending. The numbers cast on the bender shaft are inch measurements and are used to check the depths of offset bends.

c. *Operation.* In operating the bender, first place the conduit on a level surface and hook the end of the proper size tube bender under the conduit's stub end. Then, with the bending groove over the conduit and using a steady and continuous force, while firmly holding the conduit and bender with the body, push down on the handle and step on the foot step, bending the conduit to the desired angle. To make a 45° bend in this manner (fig. 97 ③) move the bending tool until the handle is vertical. For accurately bending conduit stubs the bender must be placed at a predetermined distance from the end of the conduit. This distance is equal to the required stub dimension minus an amount commonly called a takeup height. This takeup height is based on a constant allowance determined by the bending radii for various size conduits. The takeup height is 5 inches for ½-inch conduit, 6 inches for ¾-inch conduit and 8 inches for 1-inch conduit. In the bending of an 11-inch stub in a ½-inch conduit, for example, (fig. 97 ④) the takeup height of 5 inches is first subtracted from the 11-inch dimension of the stub. The mark "B" on the bender is then set at the resultant value of 6 inches and the bends made.

94. Installation

Thin-wall conduit may be cut with either a hacksaw or with a special thin-wall cutter, similar to rigid conduit, the sharp edge in thin-wall tubing should also be reamed after cutting to prevent premature wire damage. Exposed thin-wall conduit is supported in a similar manner and with the same type of supports as used with rigid conduit. Since there is no positive link between the couplings, box connectors, and thin-wall conduit, care must be taken during the installation to make sure each conduit joint is electrically and mechanically secure. All conduit ends must be inserted into the fittings until they touch the inner limiting edges. The fittings should then be tightened firmly, securely gripping the conduit walls. Care is also necessary to prevent the loosening of the conduit from the fittings which could cause a loose connection, short circuit, or electrical fire at the point of wire and conduit contact. A mechanically loose conduit joint will not maintain the ground continuity required in an electrical wiring installation. This could also create an operating hazard for Army personnel.

Section III. FLEXIBLE CONDUITS

95. Materials

Flexible metal conduit is generally called "Greenfield." It resembles armored cable in appearance but it is more adaptable than cable since various sizes and numbers of wires can be pulled into it after it is installed. Plastic-covered Greenfield may be used where the internal conductors are subject to oil, gasoline, or other materials which have a deteriorative effect on the wire insulation. This metal conduit has a thermoplastic outer-sheath covering similar to that used on type T-wire, the characteristics and uses of which are detailed in table I. The standard dimensions for flexible conduit are shown in table XVIII. Figure 98 shows Greenfield conduit and the various fittings available.

96. Installation

Flexible conduit installation is similar to that covered in paragraph 94 for thin-wall conduit except that Greenfield must be supported more frequently, as an armored cable. Its prohibitive cost limits its use to connections between rigid wiring systems and movable or vibrating equipment such as motors or fans. It may also be installed where the construction requires a conduit bend which is either difficult or impossible to make.

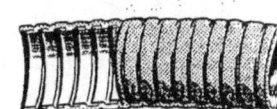

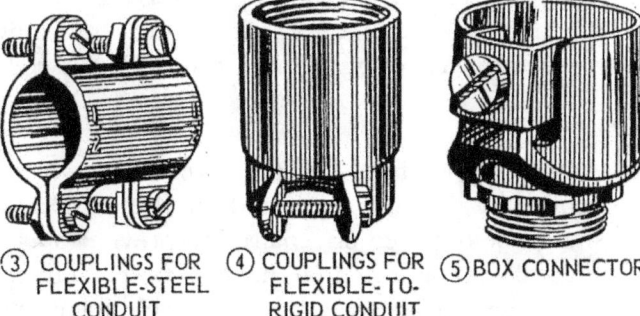

Figure 98. Greenfield flexible conduit and fittings.

Table XVIII. *Standard Dimensions for Flexible Conduit*

Inside diameter (inches)	Outside diameter (inches)
5/16	0.470
3/8	0.617
½	0.910
¾	1.090
1	1.400
1¼	1.665
1½	1.975
2	2.440
2½	3.000
3	3.350

MAINTENANCE

Section I. PREVENTIVE MAINTENANCE

106. General

The rules and routines outlined for a maintenance program for any electrical wiring system are primarily determined by the selection, location, and installation of the original equipment installed. In a well-planned system, maintenance is merely a system of routines designed to keep the equipment in satisfactory operating condition through periodic inspections, cleaning, testing, tightening, adjusting, and lubricating. These basic maintenance operations should be set down in the above listed order and the various duties delegated to specific electrical personnel to prevent operating breakdowns. This chapter reviews and outlines the various procedures and recommended practices necessary to perform the maintenance operation duties efficiently.

107. Insulation

a. The insulation materials designed to shield or protect the conductors from accidental contact with other conducting substances are built into the conductor during manufacture, or may be installed in the field as part of the system's installation. Since it is important to maintain these protective coatings or shields on the wire conductors, preventive maintenance should include periodic tests and checks to expose potential trouble locations where the wire insulation has become frayed or protective devices have been damaged. These wire areas and locations should either be taped, repaired, or replaced as required.

b. Conductor shielding installed in the field such as loom, antishort bushings, and damage protection should always be maintained and when dislodged or damaged should be replaced.

c. Conductor or conductor-inclosure supports should also be periodically inspected and maintained to insure a trouble-free operation system. In case of damage, they should be replaced.

108. Loose Fittings

To avoid the possibility of short circuits the maintenance organization responsible for power distribution in an electrical system should periodically spot check the electrical fittings. These fittings include such items as conduit couplings, connectors, and box-entry devices. The fittings should be checked for looseness or separation, and should be tightened or the conduit reclamped when necessary.

109. Conductor Connection

The conductor connections made to electrical devices or other conductors should also be included in the periodic maintenance checks to determine the condition of solder splices, wire taps, or terminal connections. Loose, partly contacting, or partly broken connections at the screw terminals or splices of an electrical device can cause short circuits or arcing. This facilitates the rapid oxidation of the connecting materials. This may also result in a dangerous short circuit if the free wire contacts other metallic components which are grounded. Moreover, the increased resistance resulting from a loose or poor connection increases the voltage drop in the circuit, causing inefficient operation of the power load on the system. If this increased resistance in the wire or terminal connections is high enough, the heat resulting from the resistance in an electrical connection may reach a temperature which will ignite the surrounding materials and cause a fire. Consequently, all electrical connections should be repaired as required.

110. Devices

The importance of periodically inspecting all operating devices for defects as a preventive maintenance function to forestall more serious difficulties must be stressed for all of the wiring systems discussed.

Any devices which fail these tests, or which are broken or loosely supported in their mountings, should be replaced or repaired to prevent operation breakdown or potential hazard to personnel. If breakage repeatedly occurs in specific locations the electrical devices should be replaced with items able to withstand the use intended, or the outlets or switches relocated.

Section II. WIRE CIRCUITS

111. Open Circuits

a. An open circuit occurs in a wiring system when one or more conductors in the circuit is broken, burned out, or otherwise separated. During operation, an open circuit is determined by the nonoperation of a part or all of an electrical circuit even though the fuses are not blown. The maintenance procedure for locating the source of the trouble is given in *b* through *d* below.

b. Initially a visual check should be made for a broken or loose connection at the first "dead" (nonoperating) outlet in the circuit. If a defective connection is found, the connection should be tightened or repaired. If necessary a new wire may be spliced into the circuit at this point.

c. If the trouble or "open" is not found by a visual check, a test lamp should be used to determine whether the circuit is "alive" (operating) up to the point of the outlet. For this operation two 115-volt lamps connected in series or one 230-volt lamp can be used.

d. When the circuit is open between the outlet and the fuse block in the power panel, a test lamp can be used to determine which wire is open. If the test prods are placed between a phase or hot wire and the conduit, cable sheathing, or ground connection and the lamp does not glow, the phase or hot wire is open. If the phase or hot wire is alive up to the outlet, the neutral or ground lead may be open. If the neutral wire is believed to be open, a similar test cannot be made between the neutral wire and the conduit, cable sheathing, or ground since they are at the same potential, and the test lamp would never light. In this case if the neutral wire is in a 2-wire circuit and is insulated, the leads of the phase and neutral wire can be temporarily interchanged at the fuse block and the test outlined above for an open in the hot wire circuit is applicable. If this method is used care must be exercised to make sure the neutral lead is returned to its former position in the fuse panel as soon as the test is over.

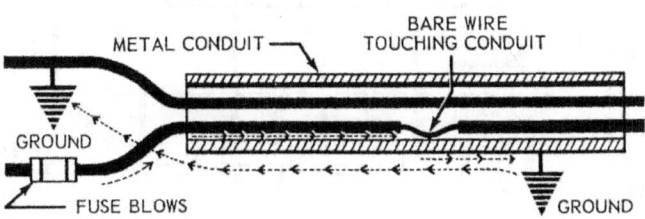

Figure 99. Short circuit or ground.

112. Short Circuit or Ground

a. General. A short circuit results when 2 bare conductors of different potential come in contact with each other. If a conductor inadvertently contacts a metallic part of a wiring system such as a motor frame or conduit as illustrated in figure 99, the system is sometimes said to be grounded instead of having a short circuit. Grounds or short circuits can be solid, partial, or floating.

   (1) *Solid.* A solid ground or short circuit is one in which a full voltage test is obtained across the terminals of a blown fuse when the load is disconnected from the circuit. The circuit resistance in this case is very low and the current very high so that fuse operation is incurred and the fuse "blows."

   (2) *Partial.* A partial ground or short is one in which the resistance between each of the phase wires or between the phase wire and the ground is partially lowered, but still remains high enough to prevent enough current flow to blow the fuse. Grounds of this type are generally more difficult to locate than solid grounds.

   (3) *Floating.* A floating ground is a condition in which the resistance of the defect in the system varies from time to time. Grounds of this type may be present in an electrical system for some time before their existence becomes known. A floating ground is indicated when fuses are blown on the phase side of a circuit a number of times, and a circuit test shows no defects in the system. In grounds of this type, fuse trouble may not occur for several days. Then the ground reappears and the fuses are blown again.

b. Troubleshooting. To determine the cause and location of short circuits or grounds in a building-wiring circuit, the procedure in (1) through (6) below is recommended.

   (1) Remove the blown fuse and screw a 25-watt light bulb (no larger) into the fuse receptacle on the phase or hot side of the circuit. If the lamp burns brightly with the neutral lead open, the circuit is grounded. If the test lamp in the fuse socket burns with the neutral closed, and an ammeter test indicates the circuit is not overloaded, there is probably a short circuit in the system. This is positively determined if the

test lamp goes out when the neutral is opened.

(2) If there is a short circuit in the system, the lamp should be removed from the fuse socket and a 250-watt resistor connected in series with the wiring circuit to prevent the flow of excessive current in the system.

(3) If the short circuit is not located by a cursory check of all the devices and connections in the system, it must be isolated step by step. This isolation process is accomplished by progressively disconnecting the plugs of all portable equipment on the circuit and turning off all switches controlling the ceiling or wall lights and outlets. If the short circuit is cleared during this progressive isolation process, the remaining lamps or equipment loaded in the circuit will receive enough current to burn or operate, and the short circuit is isolated.

(4) If all the load is disconnected and the short circuit still has not been located, a test lamp is connected to the nearest outlet in the circuit being tested. If the lamp burns when the test leads are placed in the outlet, the circuit is clear. If it does not burn, the short circuit is in the wiring, switches, sockets, or convenience outlets of the circuit which has been operated.

(5) In many cases, the circuit will be cleared after the wall switches are turned off and the portable equipment has been disconnected. If the short circuit was undetected during the test described in (4) above, the circuit may be rechecked as follows:
  (a) With the wall switches still in the off position and the test lamp still connected in the nearest outlet, the portable equipment is reconnected. As each piece of equipment is connected the test lamp should be checked. The lamp will dim or go out when the defective equipment is reconnected.
  (b) If the portable equipment is not at fault, the wall switches should be checked. This is done in a similar manner to that outlined above. As each fixture is turned on, a check of the lamp or lamps in the fixture should be made to determine if they light while in series with the resistor. If they do, this part of the circuit is clear and they can be disconnected from the circuit. The test procedure is then repeated with the remaining fixtures in the circuit until the defect is located.

(6) An alternate method of checking a wiring circuit if several fixtures are connected to a circuit and not controlled by remote switches is as follows:
  (a) Remove all portable equipment as outlined in $b(3)$ above. To reduce the time required to locate the short circuit, primary consideration should be given to the kind of equipment connected. Approximately 90 percent of the short circuits on an interior wiring system occur in motors or the flexible cord feeding the fixtures or electrical devices. When troubleshooting the circuit where more than 1 outlet or fixture is connected, this type of equipment should be visually inspected and isolated first.
  (b) After this equipment has been isolated and if a short circuit still exists, the wiring must be checked. To reduce the time required to locate the short circuit in the main or fixture wiring a method of troubleshooting called sectioning is used. For example, assume that 6 fixtures (fig. 100) using a 150-volt lamp are on a circuit where the short circuit has not been located. These fixtures are switched on and off by individual pull switches installed on each fixture. To determine the location of the short circuit, an electrician should first remove the lamps and all other energy consuming equipment from the sockets. Next, he should drop the canopies of the fixtures and open the circuit by unsplicing the connections on the energized or hot side of the main line

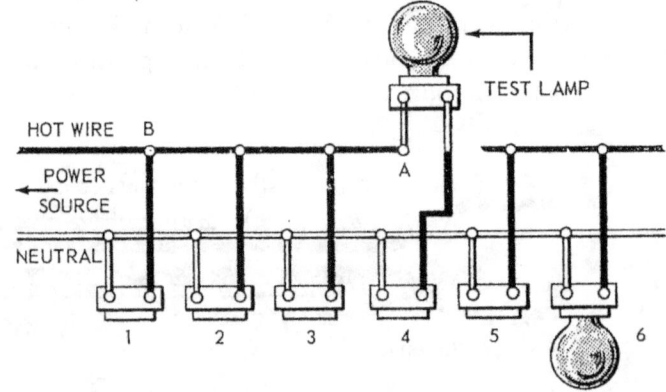

Figure 100. Testing for short circuit.

as shown at A. This should be done as close as possible to the center of the circuit being tested, since this procedure minimizes the amount of testing required. In this example this is done between the third and fourth fixture.

(c) Connect the test lamp in series as shown at the unspliced connection. At this point the test lamp completes the connection between the energized and neutral side of the circuit to which approximately one-half the load is connected. If the test lamp does not burn the disconnected branch or section is assumed to be clear.

(d) Remove the test-lamp leads at A, resplice the connection, and repeat the test at B. Connect the test lamp at this point in the same manner. If the test lamp now burns with full brilliancy, the short has been isolated to the fixtures or connections ② or ③ (fig. 100). The splice at B is remade and this procedure repeated at fixtures ② and ③. When the test lamp does not light at one of these fixtures the fault, or short circuit, is isolated and can be repaired.

(e) After the faulty wiring has been replaced or the short circuit removed from the fixture, all connections should be resoldered and retaped, completing the circuit installation.

Section III. MISCELLANEOUS EQUIPMENT MAINTENANCE

113. Housekeeping

a. Rotating Equipment. All electrical rotating equipment is manufactured to operate at a particular temperature rated in degrees above ambient temperature. This term limits the maximum operating temperature of the equipment which is derived by adding this rating to the atmospheric temperature of the operating location. For example, if a motor was rated at 30° F. above ambient, and the temperature of the surrounding area was 80° F. the maximum operating temperature of the motor would be 110° F. To help maintain the operating temperatures of the rotating equipment below a danger point it is necessary to keep the equipment clean and dry. An excessive amount of dust or moisture on the equipment surfaces acts as an insulator preventing the temperatures from being dissipated to the atmosphere through the housings of the equipment. Poor housekeeping conditions in a wiring area or wiring installation increase the possibility of short circuits.

b. Lighting. The efficiency of a lighting installation is also reduced when poor housekeeping conditions prevail. When dirt collects on the reflectors, lamps, walls, or ceilings the initial or designed footcandle power of the installation drops. Though original installations are usually planned with an expected drop of 10 to 15 percent in candle power, sporadic or unplanned cleaning may drop the lighting output as much as 50 percent. For proper maintenance in normal Army installations all fixtures and lamps should be cleaned at least every 3 months. This period is shortened when necessary.

114. Lubrication

All rotating equipment such as motors and fans rotate in their housings on either ball, roller, or sleeve bearings. To insure maximum operating performance of this equipment, maintenance routines should include definite periodic lubrications in accordance with the lubrication orders for the equipment. The data relative to the type of lubricant and lubricating period, as well as the points of lubrication on the equipment, is often attached to the equipment as an extra data plate. Though it is important to lubricate the equipment at regular intervals, it is of equal importance not to overlubricate by using too much oil or grease, or to shorten the lubrication intervals. This can cause as much malfunctioning in the equipment as not lubricating at all. For instance, when oil or grease comes in contact with insulated conductors it hastens their deterioration. Overlubrication also results in overheating and grease leakage. In addition, equipment surfaces which are oily or greasy collect the dust and abrasive materials in the air, and, if not cleaned promptly, can cause wear on the bearing ends and eventual breakdown of the equipment.

www.ingramcontent.com/pod-product-compliance
Lightning Source LLC
Chambersburg PA
CBHW082042300426
44117CB00015B/2581